Coaching & Mentoring

2nd Edition

by Leo MacLeod and Marty Brounstein

A Wiley Brand

Coaching & Mentoring For Dummies®, 2nd Edition

Published by: **John Wiley & Sons, Inc.**, 111 River Street, Hoboken, NJ 07030-5774, www.wiley.com

Copyright © 2023 by John Wiley & Sons, Inc., Hoboken, New Jersey

Published simultaneously in Canada

For general information on our other products and services, please contact our Customer Care Department within the U.S. at 877-762-2974, outside the U.S. at 317-572-3993, or fax 317-572-4002. For technical support, please visit https://hub.wiley.com/community/support/dummies.

Wiley publishes in a variety of print and electronic formats and by print-on-demand. Some material included with standard print versions of this book may not be included in e-books or in print-on-demand. For more information about Wiley products, visit www.wiley.com.

Library of Congress Control Number: 2023938924

ISBN: 978-1-394-18117-9 (pbk); ISBN: 978-1-394-18118-6 (ebk); ISBN: 978-1-394-18119-3 (ebk)

SKY10048642_060223

Contents at a Glance

Table of Contents

Introduction

Welcome to the newest edition of *Coaching & Mentoring For Dummies*. This book can help you grow from a doer manager to a coach and mentor who motivates employees to find purpose in their work and grow as independent problem solvers — without micromanaging them.

A lot has happened in the world and in the workplace since the first edition of this book was published more than 20 years ago. Organizations are struggling to find and keep good people. Workers are exercising their options to pursue new career opportunities, switch jobs, start their own businesses, and retire altogether from working. The rules have changed in which employers compete for talent and employees hold more of the power. With the increasing labor shortage, no organization can afford to lose people, especially good people. Coaching and mentoring employees to support them in work/life balance, fitting in with the culture, and doing their best work has never been more important than it is today.

This book not only helps you understand what it means to be a coach and mentor. It also helps you to adapt and meet the challenges of the changing workplace by altering your role and having a lasting impact in people's lives. Invest in changing yourself and you'll grow as a leader and person.

About This Book

Over my (Leo) 20 years of coaching, training, and consulting managers, I've heard clients often joke: *My job would be easy if I didn't have to manage people.* People-performance issues are complicated and often messy. My clients came to me because they've actively avoided dealing with their staff or else they're too hard and demanding of them. Neither is a good recipe for keeping and retaining people. This book helps you unlock a different way to work and guide people you supervise. You can find out how to

>> Gain or improve the coaching skills that drive employee performance and commitment in diverse workforces

>> Encourage colleagues to deliver results and guide employees to think for themselves

>> Motivate teams both in person and virtually

>> Navigate intergenerational issues

>> Be a sounding board for others and get the best out of your teams

>> Foster mentoring relationships that help employees grow and stay engaged in their careers

The fundamentals of coaching and mentoring haven't changed: Respect people, take the time to get to know them, ask questions rather than tell, be clear, and take a genuine interest in their growth and success.

Here's what's new to this edition:

>> Rapid changes in technology and society mean today's managers need to be accept that nothing stays the same and learn to adapt to continual changes in the workplace. The traditional office environment is increasingly becoming more digital, as more work is done anywhere that has Wi-Fi. Managing teams remotely and creating a cohesive culture continues to present challenges.

>> Recruiting and retaining talent continues to be a top priority for organizations. This edition dedicates an entire chapter on emotional intelligence (EQ), which has emerged as a critical skill for leading diverse teams and creating an attractive company culture in which people can do their best work. EQ can help you understand the role of emotions, behaviors, and attitudes in working effectively with people.

>> Changing demographics and social and political initiatives have made diversity, equity and inclusion (DEI) a front-burner issue for many companies. You'll gain clarity on common DEI terms and find a practical, grounded way to coach and mentor every employee so they feel like they can be themselves and contribute fully.

>> Employees aren't as motivated to help the organization be successful as they are in how the organization can help them achieve their personal and professional goals. Through coaching and mentoring, you'll find ways to give more meaning and balance to employees.

>> Mentorship has evolved beyond the traditional pairing of senior leader with junior staff. Learning from other people takes many forms. A new chapter explores the importance of encouraging employees to develop a diverse support team to help develop in their careers and life.

You have the opportunity to play a much larger role in your organization by helping others by following the principles and strategies in this book. You'll discover that when employees are given the opportunity and supported to do their best work, everyone wins. The journey in becoming a successful coach and mentor starts here.

Foolish Assumptions

When revising this edition, I (Leo) make the following assumptions:

» You have a basic understanding of what the job of being manager entails. You have the responsibilities for business functions and for the performance of people, not just yourself.

» Managing and evaluating staff performance is a major part of your job, or you're someone who aspires to take on such responsibilities in your career one day.

» Your manager told you need to *coach* employees, though you're not sure what that means. Or your employees keep asking how they wish they had managers who could *mentor* them. And you don't want to give them an excuse to go to another company.

Icons Used in This Book

Throughout this book, you may notice small graphics in the margins, called *icons*, which grab your attention. Here are the ones in this book:

This icon symbolizes practical tips, ideas, and strategies to make your coaching efforts work.

The example icon signals a real or made-up story that illustrates a point being discussed or highlights a manager's experience with a coaching effort.

This icon is a reminder of good ideas or points of information to use when you put coaching into practice.

This icon points out areas to watch out for and avoid.

Beyond This Book

There's more than enough to keep you busy with the strategies, tips, templates, and checklists in this book. However, you can find more helpful info online:

>> **Cheat Sheet:** Go to www.dummies.com and type "Coaching & Mentoring For Dummies Cheat Sheet" in the search box to access information you can refer to again and again.

>> **My website (www.leomacleod.com):** You can access free resources and tools for help with managing priorities, delegating, mentoring, and having hard conversations. You can also learn about my online courses, which feature short videos and exercises.

>> **My book:** *From the Ground Up: Stories and Lessons from Architects and Engineers Who Learned to Be Leaders* (Pie House Publishing) is useful to any new leader who struggles with transitioning from doer to leader and still wants work/life balance.

If you have any questions or feedback on the book or want more information on coaching training or speaking, contact me directly at leo@leomacleod.com.

Where to Go from Here

This book isn't linear, so you can glance at the Table of Contents and jump into any chapter that interests you. To get a good foundation, start with Chapter 2, which illustrates the differences between a doer manager and a coach manager. Chapter 4 lays out the fundamentals of what it takes to build commitment in employees. Chapter 5 dives into how to build your emotional intelligence skills, which I can't stress the importance of enough in coaching and mentoring.

Like any book, the information sits on a page until it's put into practice. My suggestion is to carve out specific blocks of time — 15 to 30 minutes — to focus on a chapter. Take notes, use a highlighter, or use sticky notes. Try to apply the strategies in the book and journal (if you like journaling) about your observations and progress.

I also encourage you to find colleagues to discuss what you've learned, the challenges you both face, and what's worked and what hasn't. Buy copies of this book for your management team and host a book discussion group.

Lastly, tons of other Dummies books go into greater depth into areas I touch on in the book. I can recommend two, including *Diversity, Equity, & Inclusion For Dummies* by Dr. Shirley Davis and *Managing Millennials For Dummies* by Hannah L. Ubl, Lisa X. Walden, and Debra Arbit (both by John Wiley & Sons, Inc.).

1

Getting Started with Coaching and Mentoring

Explain what coaching in the business world is, particularly how coaching can help you improve the performance of your team, keep them engaged and motivated, and give you some time in your schedule.

Distinguish between a doer manager and a coach manager in your role with employees, how you interact, and how you spend your time.

Help you value your time differently and provide specific time-management strategies to give you time to build commitments and boost performance by staying connected with your staff.

Lay a foundation for building trust, engagement, and commitment from your employees by understanding how to set the right tone and introducing a model for building commitment.

Leverage the power of knowing yourself and others by developing your emotional intelligence (EQ).

Understand how to build strong collaborative relationships that help grow you as a manager and also helps your employee grow.

Chapter **1**

Understanding Coaching and Mentoring: Just the Basics

You're a manager, possibly a first-level supervisor, middle manager, or executive. Whether you came upon the role recently or have many years of experience, you know that the job of being a manager isn't getting any easier. You carry a great deal of responsibility, and with the pace of change these days, more may be coming your way before you know it.

At the same time, you're expected to lead your group(s) and make them productive. And while you're at it, you have to keep your employees motivated and committed — you can't afford turnover problems.

Trying to do it all yourself isn't working as well as you would like it. Maybe your manager has strongly suggested that you change your approach. "Stop telling people what to do. Start coaching them." You've heard that coaching is a better way to lead people, but you're not sure what that means or where to start.

This chapter lays the conceptual foundation for the book. It introduces what coaching in the business world is all about and delves into its benefits, particularly how coaching can help you improve the performance of your team, keep them engaged and motivated, and give you some time in your schedule for important things that seem to fall by the wayside — like lunch!

Getting the Lowdown on Business Coaching

The business of coaching has grown dramatically in the past 20 years. These days it seems everyone wants to be a coach. But what kind of coach? There are life coaches, relationship coaches, career coaches, and spiritual coaches. All coaching, however, shares a basic orientation to guide people and support people to find their own path.

Coaching, as defined in this book, has two aspects to it:

>> It's an approach to how someone functions in the role of being a manager. In the approach of managing as a coach, the manager operates as the leader, developer, and guide of the team and its individuals.

>> It's a set of management skills aimed at getting the most productivity out of employee performance. These skills or tools require hard work and often, a change in old habits, but they work.

Together, these two aspects of coaching give managers the best tools to deliver results and positively influence employee commitment.

Being a coach means that you see and approach the role of manager as a leader: one who challenges and develops your employees' skills and abilities to achieve the best performance results. In other words, if you manage as a coach, your staff members learn, grow, and work hard, too. Coaching is the pathway for multiplying your effectiveness through others, for getting the best out of people's performance. Managers who have discovered how to do this not only have stronger, more functional teams, but they also sleep better and have more time for more important things in their lives.

The work of developing as an effective coach and mentor starts by understanding how most managers approach managing people and what kind of changes need to happen to make the transition (see Chapter 2 for more on the skills needed for coaching and mentoring).

MY PATH TO EXECUTIVE COACHING

I (Leo) started my career in marketing and advertising. When I was laid off, I fell into consulting, mostly writing, PR, and client surveys. Clients started to see that I had the ability to relate to their employees and make them feel comfortable discussing their problems. This led to beginning to coach people, though I wasn't sure what that meant. I learned from experience, reading, and taking courses to build my skills. Everything I know, however, is from directly helping people with problems: delegating, having hard conversations, managing their crushing workload, motivating teams, listening, learning to communicate clearly and persuasively, and focusing on the best use of their time.

I developed courses with templates and checklists to give people these tools to use. Along the way, I've seen and learned from managers who didn't lead people effectively and others who had figured it out. I made mistakes and learned what sticks and what doesn't and what changes behavior and what you need to be successful as a coach. I've taken my years of hard-earned experience of coaching specific skills and put them into this book. What you have is the effective tools and strategies I've used in my successful business that you, as a manager, can use in managing teams.

The following sections gives you an orientation to all the ways coaching can help you engage and motivate employees.

Sneaking a quick look at the tools of coaching

Understanding and putting coaching tools into practice is a critical step in becoming a coach. Here's a quick look at various coaching tools, all of which I cover throughout this book:

>> Setting goals and performance plans (see Chapter 15)

>> Giving constructive performance feedback (see Chapter 14)

>> Conducting periodic performance reviews (see Chapter 16)

>> Guiding development through mentoring and tutoring (see Chapter 18)

>> Coaching with questions (see Chapter 11)

>> Taking employees under your wing

>> Motivating employee performance

>> Delegating to empower and increase productivity (see Chapter 13)

» Training for skill development

» Stimulating and supporting career development (see Chapter 17)

» Intervening to build improvement in performance

The focus of these 11 coaching skills is on performance, which is the emphasis of coaching — getting the best out of people's performance and helping people grow in their careers.

Coaching applies to any personality type, and although it does involve building working relationships, the nature of those relationships varies by individual. Some employees need pushing and firmness; others need little direction and a light touch. Sometimes you need to give direction and other times support. That is, the use of the coaching skills or tools is tailored to fit individual skill levels and needs.

You carry out these coaching skills through conversation and collaboration. These skills involve working with an employee in order for that person to go back to their job and perform successfully. Dedicating focused time to coach people is the key (refer to Chapter 3).

Getting on board with coaching

Do any one of the following challenges and pressures affect you in your job as a manager?

» Do more with fewer resources.

» Get employees to adapt to change.

» Find ways to increase efficiency and productivity.

» Create an environment to retain employees.

» Meet greater customer expectations.

» Deliver results.

Thought so. In today's increasingly fast-paced, ever-changing, and highly competitive environments, demands such as these are affecting many organizations — especially their managers. Demands and pressures cut across all types of businesses — private and public sectors, for-profit and nonprofit enterprises — and across all levels of management, from the top executive to a newly promoted first-level manager.

Yet what hasn't always kept pace with all these changes and expectations is the way that managers manage. Far too many managers still operate in a task-focused or a must-maintain-control fashion. If I just do more hands-on myself and tell everybody to do more, and everyone will get along just fine, right? Or I can toss in a few buzzwords or phrases to help: "All right everyone, you've been empowered. Now work smarter, not harder." The problem is, managing this way just doesn't work.

TIP

Because today's challenges aren't going away, managing as a coach is a necessity not only for your success, but also for your survival. Coaching is about helping others become more effective, developing employees to perform to their best ability and to function as self-sufficiently as possible, and challenging employees to take on responsibility instead of waiting to be told what to do. It also means supporting and involving your employees in the process.

REMEMBER

Coaching influences employee adaptability, productivity, and retention. It helps you make better use of your time. But many new and different efforts are needed. The road to success starts by making the shift from managing as a doer to managing as a coach. Read Chapter 2 to understand the differences.

Differentiating between Coaching and Mentoring

In the business world, the terms *coaching* and *mentoring* are often used synonymously. Here's how this book distinguishes the two:

» **Coaching:** Coaching is a set of skills to interact and empower employees to be more self-sufficient problem solvers. Unlike other forms of coaching, the focus here is on job performance — what's needed and expected in this position. A coaching approach can be used in mentoring employees by asking questions and engaging them, but the primary focus here is helping them do their job.

» **Mentoring:** Mentoring is more focused on supporting the employee in their own development as a professional. It's often driven by the employee's needs rather than the demands of the job. It can include learning from a more senior person to fill in gaps in knowledge. But mentoring often goes beyond teaching someone by taking them under your wing. Mentors often advise and support people on their career and life. The focus isn't just on performance but on the needs of the employee.

Coaching and mentoring often work together, and the lines aren't always clear. Here are some examples to help you see how the roles play out:

EXAMPLE

Judith was a new hire at a marketing agency. Her role was to support the client managers with administration of social media campaigns. Judith's experience was limited to doing some case studies in college. She didn't understand what to do. Her manager, Samantha, sat down with her to explain what was expected and how to be successful at the agency. She asked Judith questions to understand her experience and career goals.

Samantha could see that Judith was feeling overwhelmed. She suggested that for the first week that Judith just observe more experienced people doing the tasks. She bonded with Jack, who was also fairly new. Jack and Judith went out to lunch, and Jack played an important role in helping her feel comfortable.

Samantha played more of a coaching role in guiding and engaging Judith. Her meetings were intentional; they were goal oriented toward getting her up to speed. She used a lot of questions to learn about Judith and took time to spell out the expectations. Samantha also suggested a course of action that would help Judith learn gradually.

Jack, on the other hand, played more of a mentor for Judith. He taught her his approach by letting her observe. He waited for her to ask questions. It was relaxed and friendly and gave Judith someone she could start to confide in. The relationship was more balanced. Jack was there for her, but he didn't have an agenda other than to help her with whatever she needed.

As this example illustrates, coaching and mentoring are both valuable tools. And like any tool, it all depends on the specific need. A wrench and pliers are similar, but one is better in certain applications. Flip to Chapter 2 to look more closely at the role and approach that coaches take. For more information on mentoring, check out Chapters 18 and 19. Coaching and mentoring share the same end goal: to help and support the employee's growth.

Chapter **2**

Switching from Doer to Coach

This chapter explains why the switch from doer to leader is important but often difficult. It helps you distinguish between a doer and a coach in everyday practice and how you can begin to make the switch. You may want to return to this chapter to see how you're doing in making the transition. Pace yourself. It's natural and too easy to slip back into the doer role.

Managing as a Coach versus as a Doer

Coaching is an approach to management: how you function in the position of a manager. Although different leadership or management styles exist, how managers approach their roles tends to be one of two ways — as a coach or as a doer. The following are descriptions of how the two approaches generally function:

» **Coach approach:** Managers work to achieve the best operational performance results by developing and maximizing the talents and abilities of employees to their fullest.

Those who manage as a coach still perform tasks; in fact, many work alongside their staffs doing some of the same duties. Yet those who approach management as a coach recognize they also need to lead and develop others to top performance, because that is how the tasks best get done. Such managers live by the principle of *and*; that is, they approach their jobs as a balance of managing both task issues *and* people issues. They see the two as connected. They see managing people as part of managing the work the people do.

>> **Doer approach:** In this approach, managers tend to focus more on task issues of the job (and also the technical issues of their work), as well as on the group's performance. Their attention tends to go first to the things they themselves have to do and to the areas of greatest comfort — task and technical issues. Doers, as a result, tend to function as senior individual contributors.

While the style of doers varies from controlling to very hands-off to a combination of the two, the doer approach to management tends to live by the principle of *or*. They have task issues to handle *or* people issues to handle. These issues are often viewed as separate sides of the manager's role rather than interrelated ones. So doers tend to put much less emphasis on how people are performing, which is usually less comfortable to deal with, than on getting things done.

REMEMBER

A common feature of both management approaches is that managers have their own tasks to perform. Few ever focus solely on managing others. The key difference in the two approaches, however, is on where a manager focuses their attention.

Table 2-1 gives you a quick preview of the tendencies that coach and doer managers exhibit when handling six of the most common management functions. To help you see this difference in greater detail, the following sections illustrate how managers using the two approaches would handle various functions. (As you check out the general tendencies of each approach, keep in mind that general tendencies mean just that; things don't work exactly the same way all the time.)

TABLE 2-1   **Coaches versus Doers: Approaches to Management Functions**

Management Function	Coach	Doer
Planning	Invests time in doing it.	Has little time for planning ahead.
	Often involves others in shaping plans.	Tends to operate on a day-to-day or short-term basis.
	Is future-focused.	Often crisis-driven and fire-fighting.
Goal setting	Works with others to develop goals and plans to achieve them.	If operates with goals, tends to give staff their goals — little employee involvement.
	Ensures that goals are written and expectations are clear, and then manages by them.	Often tends to be activity- and task-oriented as opposed to results- and goal-driven.
Giving performance feedback	Does so on an ongoing basis. Feedback is tied to what employees are doing.	Seldom, unless something goes wrong, or gives occasional, vague praise.
	Provides both positive and negative feedback so staff knows where they stand.	May do so at annual review time.
Dealing with performance issues	Addresses issues in a timely way with solutions-oriented approach.	Many avoid dealing with these issues. Is outside of comfort zone.
	Works with employees to map out plans for improvement.	May seek punitive measures as the first action to deal with problems.
Delegating	Does so as much as possible to maximize resources and increase productivity.	Finds letting go of responsibility to others hard to do and thus delegates little beyond simple tasks.
	Provides necessary support, lets people handle the job, and holds them accountable.	If willing to delegate, dumps assignments — gives little guidance and support.
Mentoring and developing staff	Takes an active interest and involvement in employee learning and growth.	Tends not to put much attention in this area.
	Supports training and encourages opportunities to expand employee capabilities.	Takes a learn-on-your-own approach to employee development.

Planning

Planning is a critical management function that entails looking to the future and setting a course of action to get there. Here's how the coach and doer deal differently with planning:

>> **Coach approach to planning:** The manager as coach takes time to plan — after all, you don't get ahead unless you plan ahead. The coach realizes this and doesn't just focus on what's happening now, but constantly looks to the future and often involves others in shaping plans to reach future goals. This future-focus is often part of the conversation that a coaching manager has with their staff.

>> **Doer approach to planning:** The doer manager tends not to spend much time planning — too much to deal with now to worry about that later-on stuff. Doers tend to have a day-to-day focus, reacting to the problems at hand and incurring frequent interruptions. In other words, their days are often full of other people interrupting them with one problem after another. Crisis management and fire-fighting is the norm. "I don't have the time to plan" is a common complaint of doer managers.

The coach manager can sometimes fall into this reactive mode. However, when a coaching manager senses that people are getting caught too much into fire-fighting, they'll coach them on fire prevention.

Goal setting

Goal setting is defining what needs to be accomplished in performance to achieve desired results. Here's how the two approaches differ:

>> **Coach approach to goal setting:** The coach manager often involves group members in shaping the group's goals and most definitely works with individual team members so that they know what their individual goals are. When you work for someone who manages as a coach, you know what your priorities are and what's expected of you. In fact, goals and plans are usually written so that no one has to rely on memory.

>> **Doer approach to goal setting:** If goals exist, the doer approach tends to give people their goals. Less time is spent discussing and working together to shape goals and plans.

In many cases, no set or articulated goals exist. Doer managers tend to be more task-oriented than goal-focused. They know what needs to get done now and maybe in the near future. But goals are the bigger-picture stuff — a series of tasks that together accomplish an end result. Goals are about achieving significant results. The major improvements to be made and the targets to be hit aren't often on the doer's radar screen, or if goals exist, they're rarely part of conversations between managers and employees. As a result, the doer manager's staff tends to be absorbed with activities and being busy (or at least looking that way) instead of being focused on important results to achieve.

Giving performance feedback

Performance feedback is letting others know what you've observed in their efforts and performance. It's acknowledging what people have done and how they've performed. Coach managers and doer managers sharply differ on how they regard performance feedback:

>> **Coach approach to giving performance feedback:** The coaching manager provides ongoing, timely feedback to their employees so they know where they stand in terms of their performance. When something is done well, coaches provide performance feedback; when something needs to be done better, coaches provides performance feedback.

The coach works to give the feedback, both positive and negative, with specifics and timeliness — as near as possible to the time the performance occurred. The coach provides feedback about both the individuals' work and behaviors. Whatever issues of performance are involved, when something is worth acknowledging, the coach avoids sitting back and saying nothing. These managers verbalize their observations.

Coaches understand that providing performance feedback as a regular practice reinforces behaviors that align with company values and create a culture where employees can do their best work. (For more on giving constructive feedback, see Chapter 14.)

EXAMPLE

Here is what it might sound like to give positive feedback: "Bob, I really like how flexible you are when working with challenging customers. You have a great way of deescalating emotions and working toward sound solutions. Thank you."

Similarly, managers know how to criticize but often don't know how to give specific reinforcing performance feedback either. For instance, "Susan, I've noticed you've been spending time each month sharing your expertise with junior staff. You're modeling of how to collaborate and develop the skills of others is impressive, and I appreciate your initiative to do so."

>> **Doer approach to giving performance feedback:** The doer manager tends to give feedback less frequently and with less specifics. Employees tend to hear from them only when something goes wrong or during their annual

review time. Otherwise, no news usually means good news, or so employees hope. Little recognition takes place, and areas for improvement are often glossed over. Similarly, providing vague and useless positive feedback like "good job" or "keep up the good work" isn't useful. Vague performance feedback like "you need to do a better job collaborating with others" or "I need you to be at work on time." What do "better" and "on time" mean?

Employees working for a doer often aren't sure where they stand in their performance, or some may think their performance is better than it really is. In the latter case, no news means distorted views. When doer managers spend all their time focused on work, they miss the opportunity to provide feedback that can reinforce company values. As a consequence, people don't understand how they're doing unless it's during a formal review process. But the opportunity to consistently build culture from regularly providing performance feedback is lost.

Dealing with performance issues

Sometimes, employees aren't performing to the level you need. Such situations are one of the biggest challenges for managers. Coaches and doers have fundamentally different ways of handing performance issues:

>> **Coach approach to dealing with performance issues:** When someone isn't performing as well as needed, the coach approach is to work *with* the person first. The emphasis is on coaching to improve, clarifying expectations, developing plans of action that target improvement, and providing support to help make improvement happen.

The coach doesn't wait for performance issues to turn into big problems, either. They respond with early intervention using a positive, solutions-oriented, firm touch.

>> **Doer approach to dealing with performance issues:** The doer manager quite often follows the *management-by-osmosis* path in dealing with performance problems — avoiding them and hoping for the best. The idea is that employees will read your mind and figure out that better performance is needed.

You don't have to be an experienced manager to figure out what happens when performance issues aren't dealt with — they get worse. But for many doers, dealing with a performance issue is as far from the comfort zone as you can go, so they practice big-time avoidance.

For some doers, often after avoiding the problem for a while, the mode of operation is to get tough, if not down-right punitive: threatening the employee with their employment, putting the poor performer on written warning, or outright firing them. These punitive-type efforts, especially when done without two-way communication and an attempt to coach the employee, can ripple through the company. People may wonder if they're next. Motivation and engagement suffers when employees are consumed with fear and anxiety about their positions and how they're doing.

Throw a group of doer managers a technical problem and what do they do? They go into problem-solving mode. Throw them a personnel-related problem, and they either run from it or want to eliminate it as soon as possible.

Delegating

Delegating is entrusting others with assignments and responsibilities. The coach and doer contrast greatly in how they handle this function. Here's a more detailed explanation:

» **Coach approach to delegating:** The coach delegates as much as possible for one simple reason — you can't do everything yourself. The coach looks to maximize the resources at hand and increase productivity.

The coach delegates meaningful responsibilities and projects, not just busywork, and provides the necessary support, resources, and accountability that employees need to do their jobs well. They understand that people will fail as they grow, just as they themselves did. They're patient and understand- ing and mentor employees as they develop the skills and confidence. Effective coaches rely on delegation to free themselves to focus on important matters that are often ignored or left alone, such as planning, networking, professional development, and mentoring.

» **Doer approach to delegating:** Take a guess at the doer approach to delegat- ing. For many a doer manager, delegating meaningful responsibilities and assignments to staff isn't a frequent practice. How come? For many, delegating beyond assigning simple tasks feels like a loss of control. In addition, the doer lives by the adage that if you want to get a job done right, you do it yourself.

Doers who do believe they're delegating are more often dumping tasks without taking the time to coach and support the employee. "Here, you do it (because I don't want to), and don't screw the job up or bother me with it." Not surprisingly, such assignments often end up making the employee look bad and reinforces the doer's belief that they're the only ones who can really do good work. Some leaders may be perfectionists who feel it's easier to do everything themselves or believe that their work is better than others. Sometimes referred to as a *self-enhancement bias,* the practice of holding on to work and not delegating is counterproductive to building and growing employees, as well as the productivity of the organization.

Mentoring and developing staff

Mentoring and developing involves making the effort and showing interest in helping your staff grow in their skills and capabilities. It involves teaching, encouraging, and challenging them to do their best. As you may suspect, coaches place far more emphasis on employee development than doers. Here are some of the differences:

REMEMBER

>> **Coach approach to mentoring and developing staff:** Such managers thrive on working with their employees and helping them develop their skills and capabilities. They ask questions more than they give answers, they give their staff challenging opportunities, and they share their insights and stories. They regularly take an interest in employees' careers and job situations and encourage training and other learning experiences.

  From the coach perspective, the more capable your employees, the more productive and self-sufficient they are. Developing strong people resources is a source of pride, not a source of insecurity. It's also important to the business because it creates the next generation of leaders, computer programmers, surgeons, and so on, and ensures a steady talent pipeline for continuity of business.

>> **Doer approach to mentoring and developing staff:** Quite often, the doer is too busy to spend time mentoring and stimulating employee development — the comfort to do this is lacking. If employees are particularly observant, they can still learn from the doer because many doers are knowledgeable and skilled in their work. But employees tend not to learn *with* the doer. (And if employees watch carefully, sometimes they may learn what not to do.) Beyond good, old-fashioned on-the-job training (OJT) in which you learn on your own, any organized or focused efforts on employee development are infrequent occurrences. The lack of development or development opportunities is one of the top reasons people leave their jobs.

De-coding the Doer Culture

Many doer managers are hard workers and high achievers and are sometimes even technically brilliant. But in terms of effectiveness in a management role and the ability to develop others to deliver high levels of performance, doers tend to fall short in comparison to managers who are coaches.

Yet in my (Marty) experience as an employee, a manager, and as a consultant working for a number of years with managers at all levels in a wide variety of organizations, the vast majority of managers tend to function more as doers than as coaches. In fact, when I discuss this point with most managers, from first-level supervisors to top executives, they agree with me and are often insightful at answering the question, "How come?"

The next section explores the reasons why doer managers are more the norm.

Identifying why more managers are doers

So, why do more managers function as doers? Take a look at the following.

REMEMBER

If you see yourself as one of the millions who tend to manage more like a doer than a coach, should you be worried? Yes, if you care about being a leader who brings the best out of people.

Who gets promoted?

How do people usually get started in management roles? They're promoted from the ranks of the individual contributors. And the ones who earn the promotions are generally good doers — that is, those who are technically competent. Few people who are technically incompetent are made managers.

The high-performing salesperson is promoted to sales manager. The top engineer becomes the engineering manager, the hard-working accountant is promoted to accounting supervisor, and so on. The logical career path for good performers is to move into management. But the preparation for the role and the demonstration of leadership abilities required for the role are seldom seen. And after they're promoted from the ranks, organized training and mentoring efforts on how to become an effective manager generally don't occur on a regular basis, beyond the one-day shot at an external or internal seminar.

Many doers continue to earn promotions and work their way to higher levels of management because they're high achievers and show technical competence, if not brilliance. If they have strong personalities, they have an added advantage. A track record of coaching and developing others and functioning as a real leader (rather than as a senior individual contributor) aren't usually major prerequisites for advancement.

Who are your role models?

Because most managers are doers, having been promoted because of their worker-bee mentality, most managerial role models are doers. And although you may admire their technical expertise, you may have less admiration for their leadership and coaching skills. Because little training or mentoring is done to guide them in different ways of managing, they follow in the path that's familiar to them.

In addition, the recognition and rewards that managers get often has little to do with their abilities to coach and develop others. Certainly, they're rewarded when they're effective coaches, but more often, the recognition and rewards come because managers show that they're strong performers and high achievers in their areas of expertise (sales, finance, engineering, operations, and so on). A vice president or department head, for example, often has years of management experience. But experience tells only how long someone performed, not how well they performed.

What do managers work to develop?

The final reason for an abundance of doer managers relates to the background and the expertise of most managers: A vast majority of managers have their educational degrees in a field related to their career work — engineering, business, marketing, public administration, finance, and so on, and not in management. Although some managers may have degrees unrelated to their current managerial functions or no college degree at all, you seldom find that they have a degree or related training in management with an emphasis on coaching.

So, what they lack in education related to their current position, they make up for in what they have learned through experience in their jobs, right? More often than not, managers tend to focus their own educational development (through seminars, conferences, reading material, and so on) on their technical fields of expertise. Ongoing concentrated learning efforts in leadership and coaching aren't the norm for many people in management roles. Do a comparison for yourself. How many hours have you devoted to management development versus technical development during the past year or two?

Many managers and executives overlook the fact that management is a discipline itself — a field of study. Mastery is never achieved. Being effective requires continuous learning, because managing people and helping them achieve their best performance is no small feat. You don't have to be remarkable to know how to coach. You just have to be open to learning and willing to work hard at it.

Doing the work to make the switch

Switching from doer to coach takes time and commitment. Keep these in mind:

>> Doers aren't bad people — they just need to focus on coaching.

>> You're part of a very big club.

>> Coaches are doers, too. They carry out tasks, but also focus on leading, developing, and maximizing the resources they have to get the best performance results.

>> Technical competence is important for coaching effectively. You certainly have to understand the functions that people work at in order to help develop them to better perform in these functions.

MOVING FROM DOER TO COACH — EMBRACE THE *AND*

EXAMPLE

Consider this example with a story: Joy, an engineering manager, was given two main responsibilities: Take a production group that now reports to her out of a restructuring situation and build them into a productive team *and* lend her technical expertise to a cross-functional engineering project.

Joy had been in management a few years, but the job at hand was a new experience. To help her work effectively with this new group, Joy's manager made training and consulting resources available, but it was up to Joy to make use of the resources. What did she do?

After some initial efforts to start meetings with the production group and after facilitating a few hours of team training for them, Joy became engrossed with the responsibilities of the engineering project. Within a short time, 90 percent of her time went to the project, the rest to the group she was supposed to manage.

What happened to the group? Not hard to guess: They floundered. Chaos reigned and morale suffered. The training and cross-training that was available hardly occurred, and plans for building the team were never set.

What approach did Joy take? That of classic doer. She got caught in the tunnel vision of *or*. She approached her job with an all-or-nothing mindset, giving her attention to either one major responsibility or the other.

She quickly gravitated to the area of greatest comfort, her technical side. Little coaching and leadership took place. Joy wasn't able to balance her responsibilities and see that both tasks — her new group to manage and her project to complete — were equally important. In her previous position, she had managed a few engineers who worked fairly independently, so her doer tendencies had never gotten in the way. With her new group, however, coaching skills were in great demand, but she responded as a doer.

The key, then, is to work at making the shift from doer to coach. You begin the shift by grasping the concept of approaching your management role as a coach. This concept involves understanding that your people and task-management responsibilities go hand-in-hand; they're not separate entities. This is the view of *and* (balancing task issues *and* people issues) versus the tunnel vision of *or* (handling task issues *or* people issues).

REMEMBER

The view of *and* (balancing task issues *and* people issues) is critical for making the shift from doer to coach (as the nearby sidebar explains). You, as a manager, have many priorities, some related to the work activities within the group or groups you manage and others related to matters that take your time and attention outside your group. These priorities may range from working on your own projects to spending time with your boss to interacting with customers. The view of *and* says you have to see all of your priorities and coach your employees so that they will function as productively and self-sufficiently as possible.

Appreciating Your New Role as a Coach and not a Doer

When *Forbes* magazine compiled the top 50 attributes of leadership, the one skill that stands above others is influence. The most effective leaders understand and appreciate their unique role in getting more work done by engaging staff to bring their best thinking and hardest effort to projects — not by single-handedly producing work and billing more hours.

Liz Wiseman, in her book *Multipliers*, identified two types of managers:

>> **Multipliers:** They use coaching and mentoring to get the most of out of employees. Their impact is measured not by what they produce by themselves, but how they can multiply their efforts by generating more work from others. Multipliers have a much greater impact on firms by understanding they don't need to be responsible for the final work product but instead can tap the collective wisdom and energy of the team. The less they're involved, the more that gets done and the more people grow into independent problem-solvers and leaders. The art of leadership is understanding how to affect what the organization provides to clients and customers with minimal control of how it's done.

>> **Diminishers:** They control, criticize, alienate, and unempower employees. Their efforts diminish the total output of the team. Managers who come from a doer role often struggle with the switch from doer to coach. They hold on to control too tightly, they stifle creativity and ownership, and they direct and chastise employees for not doing it their way. As a result, they can easily fall into the diminisher camp, often without realizing it.

Rather than to judge doer/managers too harshly, the following sections look at why they often struggle with letting go of the doer role.

Calculating the cost of letting go

Imagine waking up one day to realize that your entire approach to work had to change for you to advance in your career. That's what it can be like for doers to transition into being team leaders. Why is it hard? These sections identify some challenges to switching from a doer to a coach.

Solving problems is natural

Great doers are really good problem-solvers. They take pride in analyzing and coming up with a solution that's unique and effective. It's ingrained in how they approach work and what gives them joy and personal satisfaction. As a coach, you have to learn to not problem-solve, but coach others to do the solving. It often takes time to appreciate coaching others versus doing it yourself.

Letting people down

When your identity is wrapped up in delivering a quality solution that customers come to expect, letting go of your way of doing a project doesn't feel good. As a coach, you're being encouraged to let others take ownership and be accountable for their work. And when that work doesn't meet the standards you've set with clients and yourself, you can feel like you're letting people down. After all, they've come to expect your results, not those of someone who is learning and has their own style and approach.

Missing the work

You came into your field — whether it's being a hospital administrator, safety inspector, or real estate salesperson — because you love the work. You've invested time into learning it and mastering it. And now the reward for being on top of your game is to do less of it. After all, missing the work as you transition from doer to coach is only natural.

Going back to the beginning

Learning how to be a coach and mentor is a new skill. You'll be challenged and humbled by how many times you get it wrong. Say the wrong thing. Do the wrong thing. You'll yearn for the days when you're on top of your game and not a beginner in a new game.

Recognizing that what got you here won't get you there

If you want to transition from doer to coach/mentor, reflect on what you may have to give up. Become more aware of the difference between doing versus coaching/mentoring.

Simon Sinek, author of many leadership books, says that the role of a leader isn't to come up with all the great ideas. The role of a leader is to create an environment in which great ideas can happen. The challenge before you is letting go of just being a doer and switching to a coach/mentor. On one side is doing it the way you're accustomed to. On the other side is having a greater impact in the company and growing as a leader.

REMEMBER

The reality is *what got you here won't get you there*. The skills and mindset of a doer are different than a coach. To get there — the place where you are respected as a professional — influence others to do their best work. To do so, you need to adopt a new sense of your role beyond being a doer — to be acutely aware of how you're spending your time, what you're focusing on at any one time during the day, and how you're interacting with people.

TIP

You're not the first one and won't be the last one to go through the transition from doer to coach. Find someone you respect and admire who has gone through it. Take them out to lunch and interview them on how they managed the transition. Did they find it difficult to let go? How did they learn to let go? Is it really worth it? You may have found a lifelong mentor who can help you along the way. And what better way to encourage mentorship in your organization than getting one yourself and modeling that it's okay to ask for help.

Chapter 3

Finding the Time to Stay Connected

C oaches recognize the importance of staying connected and involved with employees. Staying connected is what builds the working relationship and the personal influence that affect employee performance. Successful coaches make spending time with employees a priority.

Spending time with employees means stopping what you're doing and having a live conversation focused on tasks, challenges, and concerns. Coaching is a collaborative effort and requires a two-way conversation. Listening and asking questions drives coaching conversations.

Doer managers tend to be more directive and don't take the time needed for collaboration. Without collaboration, you're just telling someone what to do. When you operate from a position of authority instead of a personal influence, you don't get commitment. You get compliance.

This chapter uncovers the blocks that doer managers often face when trying to make the switch to coach. Here I help you shift how you value your time and give you specific time management strategies to give you time to build commitments and boost performance by staying connected with your staff.

Using Your Time — Coaches versus Doers

As you move up in your organization, time becomes one of your most valued assets. In my (Leo) experience, no manager has enough time to do everything they need to do be successful and meet commitments for clients, staff, management — not to mention themselves. As a manager, you have to constantly prioritize what's important and make hard decisions of what you aren't going to do. You have to weigh what's the most critical to focus on, and what to ignore, delay, or delegate.

To make the best decisions on how to manage time and what to prioritize in transitioning from doer to coach, the first step is understanding how doers and coaches each view and use time. Take this opportunity to evaluate how you currently manage your time and if there are ways you can better maximize your impact by coaching and mentoring employees rather than doing work.

Time and the doer

Doer managers often find themselves in *crisis mode*. Because they seldom delegate key decisions or responsibilities or develop others to the point that they can help tackle day-to-day problems, doers get stuck in a fire-fighting mode of dealing with one problem after another. Employees can walk into their offices with a problem ("the monkey") and walk out of the offices relieved that the monkey is off their backs. Where did it go? To the manager, of course, who takes on all problems and tries to solve them by themselves.

Because doer managers often are in crisis mode, their focus tends to be short-term — what's hot for today, maybe next week. Don't ask them where their groups will be in a year or even in six months. Don't ask them what issues they need to start working on in order to meet the future demands of their business. They have too many fires to fight today to worry or even think about the future. Who has time to do that anyway?

Doer managers may appear to be productive, but their focus is too often on projects. They're focused on the immediate, short-range tasks and busy work. Coaching managers, by contrast, take a longer view of how they spend time and understand taking time for people is a better investment for the organization and everyone involved. Doer managers often fall into the three particular groups.

Interruption-driven manager

These managers let themselves be interrupted by anything or anyone who wants a response right away. Let me tell you a story to see if it resonates.

One day, I (Leo) arrived for a coaching session with a project manager. The receptionist said the project manager was wrapping up a call and would be out soon. From my seat, I could see across the office to where my client was immersed in her call. As she hung up, she glanced at her computer screen and dove into, I assume, responding to an email. And then someone came up to her desk to ask her a question while she was typing. After 15 minutes of observing her, I decided to approach and remind her of our appointment. She literally jumped out of her chair. "Oh, my gosh, I forgot about you. I mean, I didn't. I had our meeting in my calendar until a client called, and then I tried to answer somebody's question. I got distracted!"

Sound familiar? Microsoft conducted a study and found that every interruption costs employees about 15 minutes of productivity — whether they're being interrupted or breaking from a task. Part of that loss is due to the time it takes to recover and refocus on the task. But the study also found that a new distraction, in the form of a new email, text, call, or a person with a question, keeps employees from refocusing on their original task. Employees often spend as much time managing interruptions as they do completing work.

The only criteria that interruption-driven managers use is urgency — not importance — by responding immediately to anything and everything that comes their way. Coaching staff almost never falls into an immediate emergency that requires attention. Coaching conversations aren't rushed; they're deliberate, intentional, and thoughtful. Interruption managers are too easily distracted and pulled away from coaching conversations.

The multitasking manager

Because time is finite, these managers try to cram as much in as possible by multitasking — thinking and doing many things at the same time. Job descriptions often ask for candidates who can multitask, but according to neuroscience, multitasking is a myth. What is commonly referred to as multitasking is better described as *task-switching.*

The brain isn't capable of intently focusing on two serious tasks at the same time. The human brain doesn't perform tasks simultaneously. It performs them in sequence, one after another. When you're multitasking, you're switching back and forth between the things you're doing. Trying to multitask introduces several problems, such as the following:

>> Working quickly and incompletely in any one area makes it easy to make mistakes.

>> The switching breaks your thought patterns in any one task, often compromising the connection of ideas and momentum of building on ideas.

>> Pulling away from one task — a conversation for instance — to focus on another — a text message — shortchanges both tasks. Someone can easily rush through tasks or conversations and not be totally present.

>> You can easily lose your place when you don't finish one task before doing another. A person can risk with half-done work or have to spend time backtracking to find their place again.

>> Your pile of work gets larger as new tasks go on top of the pile of half-finished tasks.

>> Multitasking all day is exhausting. Minds are muscles that can get overworked by all that switching during the day.

Multitasking managers are rarely good coaches, because they're too accustomed to splitting their attention on many things instead of focusing on one person and one issue at a time. They aren't particularly good listeners and aren't patient communicators because their minds are on other things they should be doing.

Isolated manager

The isolated manager simply doesn't make the time for anything other than work. They see their primary value as doing work, which is quantifiable, important, and can always be rationalized as the most important priority. Businesses like attorneys, consultants, and architects make money by billing their time. A coaching conversation doesn't qualify as billable time that they can charge a client. It's time that's unbillable and unprofitable.

As a result, they isolate themselves in doing tasks rather than on coaching or mentoring staff. In addition, they may feel uncomfortable socially interacting or teaching staff. Maybe they don't like it because they're not good at it. It's just too much work and easier to not be available by hiding behind work.

Time and the coach

Coaching managers view their time like money; it's an investment to use wisely. They view spending time with people and issues as the way to get a return on their investment. So, like money, time isn't to be wasted. For example, if spending time with an employee — perhaps to help them get a better handle on doing an assignment — will yield more self-sufficiency for that employee, a coaching manager invests the time now and receives a payoff later.

If, on the other hand, your employees frequently interrupt you with questions, constantly giving them answers isn't the best use of your time. So a coach manager will teach employees how to find their own answers so that they can become more self-sufficient.

The theme here is helping people do a better job themselves. Coaching is about getting the best performance out of people so that they can do for themselves. Because coaches see that people have an effect on the tasks to be done, they know that investing time in people in order to increase their abilities to perform well is an investment well worth making. Your reward for doing so is increased productivity. And you actually save time: Instead of going from one interruption to another, your time and attention can be spent on the critical issues, which is what managers are really being paid to do.

Because coaching managers realize that they don't have a quantity of time to give to their employees, they know that the time they spend must be *quality* time. Quite simply, they make the time count, making it productive time rather than inefficient time.

Here are some concrete examples of how coaching managers decide to use time differently than doer managers:

>> Instead of being interrupted 60 times by one employee in the course of a week, a coach spends one hour with the employee preparing them to handle the challenges of the daily job. That's quality time.

>> Instead of watching employees become frustrated and stuck over a problem, and instead of falling into the trap of telling them how to solve every problem they encounter (so that they can't think for themselves), a coach spends time helping them map out a plan to solve problems. That's quality time.

>> Instead of chasing after an employee three times a day to see whether they're completing tasks (the dreaded *micromanagers,* as employees call them), a coach takes a half-hour with that employee once a week to do a status review on the project. That's quality time.

>> Instead of wasting time redoing an employee's sloppy work, losing sleep on whether to replace the employee, and complaining to colleagues for hours, a coach sits down with the same employee to explain the importance of accuracy and engages the employee to solve the problem together. That's quality time.

Even though the doer manager is just on the go, a coach manager makes their time count. To make your time count, structure and organize your time by asking the following questions:

>> What's the best use of my time?

>> What are my current commitments before I take on anything new?

>> Does this task require my attention or should someone else do it?

A coaching manager's approach is to make these questions part of the planning process so that they're more intentional and purposeful about how they use time.

Recognizing What's Important and Urgent

There's no shortage of tasks and distractions that fill each day. *Urgent* tasks demand your immediate attention. *Important* tasks have greater significance. Many people often get the two things mixed up. There's a common expectation for immediate feedback. When people want to know something, they search online and get the information immediately. They want to know if their partner can pick up eggs from the store, so they quickly text. They even get frustrated if the internet speed is slow and the page takes a few seconds to load or someone doesn't text them back right away. In many ways, people are addicted to a sense of urgency, driven by the speed of technology. They want it now, no matter how unimportant that thing is. They expect immediate responses from everyone. They want answers now. When they don't get a response from an email right away, they send a text.

EXAMPLE

Maria is walking to her desk and sees Floyd getting up from his chair to corner her about work she gave him. Meanwhile, a text comes in from her partner that the gas company needs access to their furnace in the basement. Maria sees a sticky note from her supervisor on the back of her chair to come see her as soon as possible. She does need to talk to Floyd so he can complete the project on time. After sitting down, she quickly glances at her email inbox and sees 200 unread messages. She starts to read and answer the most recent email, so she can feel like she's getting something done, when she gets another text from her partner and Floyd shows up at her desk.

Maria needs help! She needs a way to first distinguish between tasks that require her immediate attention and those tasks that can wait. And she needs a way to prioritize and focus on the important tasks.

REMEMBER

Not everything that's urgent is important. Ask yourself these questions throughout the day to help you identify what is really important:

>> What am I currently doing?

>> Is it the best use of my time?

>> Am I just reacting or this email, text, interruption really important?

>> Do I need to pay attention to this task right away or can it wait?

>> How much time will it take?

>> How can I stay focused on important tasks and not distract myself or be distracted?

You can easily focus on things that drain your time that could be spent coaching employees, such as the following:

>> Attending long meetings you don't need to really need to, but you just said yes anyway, without thinking

>> Responding to every email that comes into your inbox, right away

>> Spending your time doing busy work on tasks that don't add value (reformatting documents, getting lost on LinkedIn, watching endless YouTube videos, mindlessly scrolling through TikTok)

>> Reading and responding to group emails about a project or policy that doesn't affect you

>> Drafting an overly detailed email telling you what you already discussed with someone

>> Allowing employees who just want to complain or gossip to interrupt

Delegate, Ignore, Shrink (DIS)

You may feel like you don't have options: race to keep up with the constant demands on your time and ignore employees or spend time coaching and mentoring employees and let the work pile up. The good news: You can use strategies to stay on top of important issues and spend time coaching and mentoring employees.

REMEMBER

To stay focused on important tasks, like coaching and mentoring, you can strategize and discover how to manage all the other demands on your time so you have the time to spare. I (Leo) have developed a handy tool to help managers called DIS: Delegate, Ignore, Shrink. Here it is in a nutshell:

>> **Delegate what you can.** It not only moves tasks off your plate, but it builds your team. (Chapter 13 discusses how you can delegate.)

>> **Ignore the unimportant.** Not everything demands your full attention, either immediately or in many cases at all. Your days as a manager are filled with distractions that pull for your attention and keep you from getting important things done.

>> **Shrink to what works.** You can complete most things in a shorter amount of time. Work more in triage mode, assessing what's important to do and then working in smaller blocks of time to get the most important elements done. Refer to the section, "Breaking it down in four blocks," later in this chapter.

EXAMPLE

One Friday afternoon, when I arrived for an hour coaching session, my client, Amy, came out of her office, looking sheepish. Just 20 minutes before, she had learned that the corporate office told her a major report needed to be done by the end of the day. So much for trying to prioritize and ensure she had to time to develop herself as a manager. Amy asked me if I could reschedule, and instead I asked her if there was another solution she could try to do the work and keep her coaching appointment. She paused and thought about it. "Give me 30 minutes, and we can at least meet for 30 minutes." She delegated much of the task to someone else, ignored the urgency of the client to get it all done today, and shrunk the deliverable to a first draft the corporate office could use right away. In reality, it only took her 15 minutes to write that first draft, giving her 45 minutes to focus on our coaching session and her mountain. Amy told the senior manager the full report could be delivered by Tuesday, after reviewing her calendar and other commitments. She had employed DIS. Today, Amy owns her own firm with two other principals and has learned the value of boundaries and not simply saying yes to everything and everyone.

To find out more about DIS and other time management strategies, check out my leadership manual, *From the Ground Up: Stories and Lessons from Architects and Engineers Who Learned to Be Leaders* (https://leomacleod.com/from-the-ground-up/).

REMEMBER

Keep in mind that although some matters may not be urgent, they may be important. Coaching recognizes this fact and the need to sometimes make time for the important matters.

Scheduling in Blocks and Sticking to Your Calendar

The single most important thing you can do to improve your time management is create a schedule and live by it. When your time isn't scheduled, it's open to any interruption. When your time is scheduled on a calendar, it's filled with appointments and time blocks for you to focus on important tasks. You can plan your day, protect against people wanting to hijack it for their own purposes, and ensure you're making time for staff. Here I delve into dividing your calendar into manageable pieces.

Breaking it down in four blocks

Your calendar should reflect how you spend your time down to the minute. To be the most efficient, use time blocking to group like-minded or similar tasks together. Working in blocks allows your mind to stay focused on similar activities so you can make the connections, follow the threads, catch the details, and find what some call the *flow of work*. When you choose to work in blocks of time, you gather tasks that are connected so your attention and mindset are concentrated in one mode.

Here are four types of time that can help you be more productive, meet commitments, and conserve energy:

>> **Focus:** During this type of time, you need to be fully engaged and focused on content and details. You're engaged in the things that make you money or get essential tasks done — like applying your critical skills to a problem for a client, facilitating a staff meeting, or coaching an employee.

>> **Buffer:** This is all that time that impinges on focus time, which often doesn't get accounted for: preparing for a meeting, traveling, checking email, and fielding questions from staff. When calendars are packed end to end with focus time, like meetings, there isn't any buffer time for the things that naturally happen. Factor in buffer time to maintain quality focus time.

>> **Reflection:** This is time to step back and see how you're doing, where you're going, and what you need to work on. You're reviewing your vision, planning the next quarter's goals, envisioning steps for the next week, considering the strengths and challenges of your team, and considering how best to support them.

EXAMPLE

The most successful business leaders regularly schedule important-but-not-urgent time. Starbucks' founder Howard Schultz and media mogul Oprah Winfrey follow the practice to reflect daily on what's going right and what they want to achieve. George Shultz, who at one time held the positions of Secretary of State, Secretary of the Treasury, Director of Management and Budget, and Secretary of Labor, in addition to serving as an executive at engineering giant Bechtel Group, understood the value of time. He also understood he had to deliberately set aside time to get out from under the grind of work in order to expand his vision from what was right before him to what might be possible. Shultz regularly chose an hour in his day when the only people who could disturb him was his wife and the president. He found a quiet space and closed the door. The only thing he had was a notepad, pen, and his imagination.

>> **Free:** This is downtime to recharge. Free time is just that. Time for you not to do work and to give yourself a mental break and tune in to what you need: a walk, a nap, lunch, playing cards with your partner, catching up with an old friend, playing soccer with your kid in the backyard. Use free time to bring balance into your life to keep up your energy level.

Kaylee, a project assistant at a civil engineering firm, felt bad bugging her manager each time she had a question. She began a practice of writing down her questions on a legal pad and then scheduling a convenient time with the manager to review all her questions in one block of time. This approach had several benefits:

- She resolved some questions because she did the work on her own.

- She had more time to think about the questions and come up with her own solutions.

- She found other ways and people who could provide answers.

- When she did meet with her manager, the meeting was more efficient because he was focused on addressing her questions rather than distracted and not present.

Kaylee was being more intentional and conscious about her communication. She also impressed her manager, which only built more support for her as an emerging leader.

Guarding your calendar in six steps

Many managers find that their time and attention is pulled in several directions, often away from the people they should be coaching. It's common for this problem to only get worse as managers rise within the company and become more focused on strategic and organizational issues.

To guard against it, take these steps:

1. **Make coaching and mentoring a priority.**

Just because you have more things to pay attention to, protect your time with your employees. It's still the best use of your time.

2. **Delegate, ignore, and shrink tasks that aren't important.**

Refer to the section, "Delegate, Ignore, Shrink (DIS)," earlier in this chapter for more details.

3. **Schedule your time.**

Live by your calendar. Schedule important tasks and meetings and let people know that's how you work.

4. **Work in blocks.**

   Check out the previous section.

5. **Protect your calendar from hijacking.**

   You've heard the expression, "A lack of planning on your part doesn't constitute an emergency on my part." It's become common for people to disregard schedules and calendars and insist you break your commitments. Be polite but firm when people try to hijack your plans.

6. **Recap, redirect, and reschedule interruptions.**

   If a colleague who has a question or issue interrupts your scheduled work, try recapping what they're saying and either redirect them to someone else who can help them or reschedule to find a mutual time when you can revisit the conversation.

Focusing on One-on-One Meetings

One of the most effective strategies for structuring your time and staying connected with your employees is the one-on-one meeting. This is a set meeting in which you and your employee come together to work on issues collaboratively.

For many doers, meetings with their individual staff members take place in hallways or on a hit-and-run basis. "Bill, come into my office right away!" Or their involvement in a project is cursory, often because they don't have the time to really talk about it. "I don't like it." "Just do it this way." "That's not going to work." They don't make time for a real one-on-one conversation to listen to the employee, ask questions, and offer mentorship.

These rushed meetings can just as easily be initiated by your employees, like the ones I describe in the "Time and the doer" section earlier in this chapter, in which employees come running into your office asking for solutions to their work problems. If you keep telling them what to do (so that they don't think to do for themselves), what happens? They keep interrupting you and you keep telling them what to do, and the vicious cycle continues. As a result, you have no handle on your time. (And here's another common scenario: You're the manager at an off-site special meeting or seminar; your phone goes off throughout the day because your employees have this terrible dependency on you for every answer and decision. Sound familiar?)

These sections explain what a one-on-one meeting is and ways you can organize your own with a few examples.

Understanding the basics of a one-on-one

The one-on-one meeting can either be scheduled or occur spontaneously — as long as you can both take the time and not be distracted by other issues. If your employees are close at hand, when you or one of them has a need, you just set a time and get together. For other managers whose time and availability are limited, having regularly scheduled one-on-one meetings works best. In either case, the time is structured rather than haphazard, and the one-on-one meeting is a regular practice rather than an unusual occurrence. Avoid cancelling or moving these meetings — unless it's a true emergency. You don't want to give the employee the impression that this time with them isn't important.

REMEMBER

One-on-one meetings as a regular practice occur anywhere from once a week to once every few weeks, usually from 30 minutes to one hour, and longer for special situations. They don't preclude an informal touching-base or "Hi-how-are-you?" communications. Instead, one-on-one meetings provide a forum for focusing attention on issues and for in-depth communication.

Organizing a one-on-one meeting

Although not every one-on-one meeting with your employees is a coaching session (you may just be getting to know your employees), every coaching session takes place in a one-on-one meeting. *Coaching sessions* are the times that you work together with a staff member to check to see how they're doing, give feedback, delegate an assignment, set goals, develop plans, mentor to solve a problem, and whatever issue needs to be addressed. To maximize the time and productivity of both parties, the meeting works best when it's organized and has an agenda you both agree on.

TIP

Having a working agenda is wise, but you also want to remain flexible to what might come up. Manage the expectations by checking the clock and checking in with the employee, so any change in the agenda is agreeable to both of you. How many times has this happened to you? You plan to talk to your employee about their progress in the long-term career goals and you end up talking about an issue on a current project. Manage the expectations of the time you have by mutually agreeing on any changes in the agenda.

So with that understanding, here's a list of questions to address as you plan and organize effective coaching meetings:

>> **What's the objective for this meeting?** What are you trying to accomplish in this meeting with your staff member? You need to know this goal before going in, and you need to communicate the goal in advance so that your employee can be focused on that goal. You may give your employee a

heads-up, so they can mentally prepare: "I want to review your progress on delegating to your team."

» **What positive outcome are you seeking?** This question is tied to the first question. It serves as a reminder, especially with tough issues, that you need to aim toward a positive result. Sometimes, you can get caught in the emotions of an issue, and as a result, lose sight of the positive goal you're seeking. For example, if you're dealing with a problem, the positive outcome you're seeking with the employee is a solution. Or if you're dealing with a situation in which confusion exists, the positive outcome is a plan that provides clear direction (much better than seeking confessions or finding blame). Going into the session, you don't need to know what the exact solution or plan will be; you just need to know the positive outcome that you're aiming for.

» **What do you need to be prepared to do at the meeting?** You may need to give feedback about the employee's performance; you may have stimulating questions to ask, information to provide, or something to teach; or you may need to give direction or spell out expectations. Sometimes, you may need to prepare by reminding yourself to listen and be patient. Whatever the case, come ready.

» **What do you want your employee to come prepared to do?** Unless you want to waste your employee's time and give the individual a dose of frustration, let the staff person know how to come prepared for this meeting. Can the employee report on information, provide project status, share ideas, review plans, and so on? If you come ready and the employee comes ready, the one-on-one will actually be a very productive meeting.

» **What particular plan or agenda for this session will encourage employee participation?** When you figure out what you're trying to accomplish at this coaching session, what steps do you have to take to get there? Think these steps through so that you increase the likelihood of accomplishing something useful. As part of this effort, remember that coaching takes place through two-way conversation. If you dominate the conversation, you'll probably be able to get your employees to nod and smile (that's when you're in real trouble), but you won't get them thinking and learning how to do things for themselves. See the next section for a few sample meeting plans.

» **How can this meeting help the employee perform better or more self-sufficiently for the future?** This question is related to the previous one and is a reminder of what you want to do in a coaching session. Your overall goal in every coaching session is to ensure that your employee's performance benefits from the time you invest in the session.

» **What follow-up should be set?** If action items come out of the meeting or if an employee is going to work on implementing an idea you discussed, should a progress review be set? In most cases, the conclusion of the coaching meeting has the employee going forward to put something into action. As the meeting closes, set a follow-up time to check progress. Doing so allows you to stay connected, builds in accountability for the employee, and shows that you care about what happens. And setting the follow-up time at the close of your meeting helps prevent you from forgetting or chasing after the employee to see whether the action item is being handled. Make it the employee's responsibility to follow up with you.

REMEMBER

Ultimately, you want your employees to drive these one-on-one meetings. You want them to bring to the meeting the issues and ideas to discuss. In essence, the meeting is a two-way street. The employee's role is to take responsibility; yours is to provide support and add value that helps the employee perform well.

Looking at some examples

Using the questions in the previous section as a guide, use the three following sample one-on-one meeting plans as you prepare for your upcoming meetings.

Sample #1

>> **Objective:** Have the employee correct some mistakes in performance that you noticed occurring yesterday.

>> **Positive outcome:** Focus on solutions. The point of the meeting isn't to dwell on mistakes, it's to fix them.

>> **Plan or flow of the meeting:**

- Provide feedback about your observations of the mistakes made.

- Encourage two-way discussion. Let the employee comment on your feedback. Then solicit the person's ideas for correction and contribute ideas as needed.

- Close by recapping the solution worked out during the session (have the employee recap, as well), and set a follow-up meeting to review progress.

>> **Come prepared:** Be ready to give the feedback and ask the questions so that the employee develops ideas for correction.

Sample #2

>> **Objective:** To review progress on hitting a project milestone and set next steps for keeping the project on track.

>> **Positive outcome:** A chance to recognize accomplishments, set future direction, and maintain accountability.

>> **Plan or flow of the meeting:**

- Employee reports on deliverables produced to meet the project milestone. Your feedback is added as needed, especially to recognize good work.

- If problems are identified, engage in joint problem-solving to address them.

- With employee, set the deliverables for the next milestone to be hit in the project.

- Close by setting another status-review meeting around the next milestone.

>> **Come prepared:** Both parties should have a list of the deliverables for which the employee is to report progress. If the employee has any issues or problems, they are to come prepared to explain them and recommend ideas for solutions.

Sample #3

>> **Objective:** To evaluate how a customer meeting (a call and presentation) was handled by the employee. To be done as a debriefing after the customer meeting.

>> **Positive outcome:** A chance to recognize what was done well and to determine what can be improved upon for future efforts.

>> **Plan or flow of the meeting:**

- Employee evaluates their own efforts on what was done well in the presentation and customer meeting — and on what didn't go as well.

- You provide your specific feedback on these two points.

- On the areas for which improvement is needed, ask for the employee's ideas of what they can do the next time and provide suggestions as needed.

- Close the meeting by reinforcing the efforts that were done well and by setting action items for improvements with the employee.

>> **Come prepared:** Let the employee know that you want to conduct a debriefing after the customer meeting and that you want them to be ready to self-evaluate how the call went. Then let them handle the call while you stay in a support role.

Does the checklist and the plan for the coaching meeting need to be written out? If it helps you stay focused, then, yes. If it's not necessary, don't worry about it. Keep in mind that coaching is informal by nature.

The more you use these examples as your guide for coaching meetings, the more you'll know what notes to prepare and what you don't need to write down. You'll go into meetings with a positive mental road map that maximizes your time and your employees' time — and that keeps you well connected with how your employees are performing.

Building Connections — The How-To

Staying connected requires that you understand who your employees are and what's going on with each person's performance. Staying connected, therefore, improves the relationships that stimulate high levels of performance and build commitment. Many of the effective strategies for building relationships, staying connected with your employees, and maximizing your time are informal. These strategies fit well with coaching because coaching is informal by nature.

Management by walking around

MBWA, which stands for *management by walking around*, is about managers being visible and getting to know their staff members as people, not just as employees. This strategy involves showing an interest in each staff member as a person and being able to converse at times on nonbusiness issues. You carry out MBWA strategy by leaving your office periodically and going to your employees' offices or work areas just to engage in friendly conversation. This works great when people are actually in the office. But what if people are working remotely?

Working remotely

The biggest recent change in the workplace is the shift to working remotely. In a matter of months of the Covid-19 pandemic, strict regulations dictated that people quarantine at home. People adapted, setting up offices in their living rooms and converting their garages to workspaces. Zoom and Microsoft Teams became the ways employees engaged and worked. Many predicted that productivity would suffer when people weren't at work. How can you exercise MBWA if people weren't there? Are they working or goofing off? What about the quality of work?

What has surprised many is that working remotely does work for a number of reasons:

>> Allows flexibility in juggling caregiving and illness and meeting the demands of work and life, particularly for women.

>> Lets people work more effectively without being interrupted or distracted by other people in the office.

>> Saves employees money by not having to pay for dry cleaning, eating out, and getting to and from work.

>> Cuts down on commute time, which for some people can be two hours or more a day.

>> Helps organizations save money by contracting the office space they need in response to fewer people working in the office.

My (Leo) own informal poll of clients revealed that the *hybrid work environment* (in office and remote) is mixed. On one hand, many organizations say that productivity and profitability haven't suffered. They're making money and delivering on time. One recruiter I talked to mentioned that "flexible schedule" is the buzzword for getting top talent.

Working remotely can have a downside. I've worked for clients who had employees working remotely all over the world. Managing and communicating through videoconferencing and phone isn't the same. People often benefit from working together in the same space by building a sense of community and collaboration. Opportunities for mentoring are less frequent when people aren't working in the same space. Some companies have no issue with working remotely. Others are working to adapt and blend live and remote work. Employee policies regarding how much work can be done remotely is unique to every company and will most likely continue to evolve.

Coaching remotely

I coached people through the pandemic remotely with good success. I prefer eye to eye occasionally, but it works better for most people to coach remotely. Here are some tips for coaching employees remotely:

>> **Make sure people are in an environment where they won't be disturbed.** Focusing on coaching conversations when the TV is going in the background, their partner is a few feet away working, or kids are banging the door to get into the room is difficult.

>> **Start slowly with a warm-up question.** Don't be in a rush to get into work. Allow people to make the transition and open up.

>> **Focus on sound and lighting.** Use a headset for good audio. Eliminate any distractions like poor sound for distracting you. Make sure you have enough light on you so you're not in the dark or overexposed.

>> **Allow time for people to answer.** A strange gap can happen when talking with people when videoconferencing. Conversations take time to become natural. People aren't used to being on camera and are uncomfortable with making eye contact.

>> **Use visuals like screen sharing to increase engagement and attention.** Videoconferencing apps allow you to share your screen with participants, which can help illustrate what you're saying and keep people engaged by using their vision.

>> **Don't multitask by doing email.** Make sure you've both closed it.

>> **Start by stating the purpose of the meeting and the amount of time you have.** That's true for all one-on-one meetings, even if it's a short meeting.

>> **Fit coaching naturally rather than just doing one-on-ones.** Videoconferencing can make people less comfortable.

>> **Use the phone instead of video conferencing if you have several one-on-ones in a row.** Videoconferencing can cause fatigue if you're in back-to-back meetings. The other option is to turn off your camera.

Mixing it up — both live and remote

If you can schedule both live one-on-ones at work and remote ones, do it. What I'm finding is that the managers who are more intentional with their time and follow good time management skills are making hybrid work arrangements work. Here are some examples:

>> Schedule time with employees when you're both in the office.

>> Don't let others hijack your time together.

>> Stay focused on your agenda so you're hitting the important items.

>> Hold off on checking with each other prior to your meeting.

>> Vary how you meet by doing a walking meeting or go out to lunch.

>> Continue to use videoconferencing, email, text, and phone in addition to scheduled check-ins.

>> Send information ahead of time for people to read and digest to speed things up and make it more engaging.

>> Consider doing videos for technical processes, so people can learn another way.

REMEMBER

Many employees in today's workforce have grown up with video communication, Instant Messenger, FaceTime, and other forms of remote communication. They're generationally more comfortable with technology. Conversely, they aren't always equally as comfortable face-to-face. When in doubt, ask your employee how they want to structure your communications. After all, coaching is collaborative.

Staying in touch

Whatever mode of checking in and communicating you do with employees, be consistent and present. Don't be the isolated manager who disappears beneath work. Working remotely has made it easier for people to hide. The purpose of having regular coaching conversations is to build rapport and trust. If you stop by to have a friendly conversation with your staff members only once every few months and are otherwise seldom visible or sociable, your staff may wonder what you're doing hanging around and may think that something is wrong.

No set number exists as to how frequently you need to stay in touch. Many in today's workforce value social connection and are more informal. They like to have fun at work, whereas other employees may be more focused on getting work done. Remember not to make your connections all about work. Here are some questions to help lighten it up:

>> How was your weekend?

>> What are you doing for fun these days?

>> Got any travel plans?

Informal communication makes it more likely that your employees will come to you when they have issues; it also increases the probability that they'll be less defensive when you call them into your office because you have a concern to discuss with them.

In addition, you come to understand your employee on a more personal basis, which builds trust and a sense of belonging. As you find out more about your employees as people, including an understanding of what makes them tick, you have a better idea of how to work with them to motivate and stimulate their performance.

Being friendly versus being a friend

Although you may be able to see that building connections helps you, as a manager, develop relationships that make coaching work, perhaps you think that this stuff is getting just a tad too personal with your employees. Is it friendships that you're after?

The relationships that you're building are effective working relationships — relationships in which manager and employee know and trust each other. To pretend that your employees don't have personal lives hinders the rapport and trust needed to work together effectively. After all, you're spending a lot of time with each other at the same workplace.

REMEMBER

There's a big difference between being a manager who can be friendly and who cares about employees and being a manager who's trying to be everyone's caring friend. I'm talking the former and staying away from the latter. Difficulties often result when managers and their employees develop close personal relationships. Managers who become too close to their employees often have a hard time being objective and making tough decisions — or not becoming frustrated and baffled when their friends, also known as employees, seem to be taking advantage of their good nature.

You don't have to be someone's friend to build rapport. You don't have to be friends to take an interest in what is important in someone else's life. But you do need to know who your employees are and have some concern about them in order to be a manager that they can work with. Regularly staying in touch and being interested in your employees help you stay connected with your staff and build the foundation for a strong coaching relationship.

Chapter **4**

Laying a Foundation That Builds Commitment

Would you rather have a team of people do the work they're assigned dutifully, without enthusiasm, pride, or creativity or would you rather have a team of employees with high levels of commitment, doing their best work, enjoying what they do?

Employees with high levels of commitment are the ones most dedicated to the job and the organization. They're the ones who show drive and initiative, who work hard, and who aren't satisfied until they deliver top results. They're also the ones most likely to stick around and not leave the company. They're the ones who give you more time to focus on other important tasks. They're the ones who make you look good and don't give you problems.

Achieving this commitment is no small feat. This chapter shows you how.

Distinguishing between Personal versus Positional Influence

Influence, as defined here, means to have an effect on other people and on outcomes. From a negative perspective, influence can mean the use of manipulation, coercion, intimidation, and threats. It can create a toxic workplace where people live in fear and mistrust — not the conditions to grow committed employees.

However influence isn't all bad. Influence can use positive role models (walking your talk), aspirational messages (treating others as you want to be treated), and a boost to people's self-worth (seeing the best in people). Consider Gandhi, Jesus, Mother Theresa, Martin Luther King Jr., Brené Brown, Abraham Lincoln, and Mister Rogers.

If you're reading this book, I assume that you aim to be a manager who would rather have a positive influence on people rather than a negative influence. You want to discover how to be aspirational and positive rather than a bully who people don't want to work for.

REMEMBER

Managers influence just by the nature of their position of power. As manager, you have power over the terms of an employee's contract. Their livelihood and future are in your hands. Employees are acutely aware of this power deferential. You can rely on your positional power to influence behavior or you can develop your personal influence. With positional power, you get employees who are dependent on you. They fear making mistakes and aren't motivated to exert any ideas of their own. They may be obedient, but they're limited in how they could contribute. With personal influence, you're building a foundation of employee commitment. You are encouraging them to be independent from you, to grow, learn and bring all their energy and talent to the job.

The first step is to understand what kind of influence you can have:

» **Positional power:** Derives from holding and using power over employees

» **Personal influence:** Comes from being more intentional and doing the right things to build commitment

Spoiler alert: Personal influence is more effective.

These sections help you see in what ways you assert your influence. They look at how these two styles of influence usually work.

Managing by positional power

Management roles are positions of authority in organizations. Managers who wield *positional power* view their titles as important and expect employees to respect their authority. For managers who use positional power, having authority — and pushing it as needed — is how results are best achieved. Managers who exert their positional power also seek the following:

>> **Maintain the chain of command.** Private and public organizations historically have been patterned around hierarchy — the many levels of positions from the nonmanagement ranks through the management ranks. In military terms, the hierarchy represents a chain of command to be followed and never circumvented. Positional power managers generally follow this thinking. For them, the flow of communication and decision-making needs to adhere to this chain of command. The hierarchy of management is to be abided by and respected, starting with the authority of their own position.

>> **Gain control.** Traditional management was focused on four objectives: To plan, lead, organize, and control. Managers who exert positional power tend to really like that control part. Things are working right when everything is under their control and running the way they want it. In the groups they manage, they grant the approval for most decisions and give the solutions for most problems.

Control isn't necessarily a negative factor. Managers certainly need to monitor progress, know that everything is working and under control, and work with their employees to make modifications as needed. Most employees want this kind of organization or control. They tend not to respond well to chaos, but they tend not to respond well to stifling or controlling managers either. You have positional control already; exercise it sparingly and in those situations where it's called for.

>> **Promote compliance.** The result of this management influence is often employee compliance — people do what they're told and work does get done, and sometimes, quality performance does occur.

Managing by personal influence

Managers who exhibit *personal influence* strive to earn respect from others rather than expecting it automatically because of their titles. They do so by demonstrating traits and behaviors such as honesty, respect for others, and doing what's best for people. By exerting personal influence, they seek the following:

>> **Build working relationships.** Personal-influence managers attempt to establish positive working relationships with their employees instead of worrying about who has what authority in the organization. They do so by

getting to know their employees professionally and personally so that the qualities that make both the manager and their employees good people and good workers can come out. Ongoing two-way communication is the norm in these relationships.

REMEMBER

Incoming generations of the workforce expect to have personal relationships with their managers. They like to socialize and share stories and experiences. They seek a more collegial, team-oriented workplace. Managers with personal influence know that understanding both the professional and personal facets of an individual is helpful in working with that person. These managers are the ones who can be friendly with their staff members without trying to become friends with their employees. A friendly manager is far different than a boss who is trying to be your friend.

>> **Seek employee ownership and involvement.** Managers who exert personal influence encourage employees to take ownership in their jobs — that is, they delegate responsibility, provide support and guidance as needed, and expect results to be delivered. Employee involvement and initiative are invited. Control for these managers doesn't come from telling employees how to do their jobs; it comes by having people follow through on the responsibilities they're given. You're helping to build a culture of accountability. If the employee doesn't take accountability themselves for challenges or mistakes, you can remind them that you're trying not to use your power but giving them the opportunity to take responsibility for themselves.

>> **Develop commitment.** Managers who demonstrate positive personal qualities, build constructive working relationships and drive employee autonomy with accountability increase the likelihood of getting commitment in return. Management of this kind creates situations in which employees respect their managers. Employees like working for someone who knows and cares for who they are and, at the same time, provides challenges and opportunities to grow. The roots of employee commitment come from this kind of environment.

Seeking Commitment versus Compliance in Today's Workforce

Positional power and personal influence have radically different effects on employees and their performance. When employees are respected and have a good working relationship with their manager, they're more engaged with work. When they're more engaged, their commitment yields greater productivity and employee retention than compliance does — especially in today's work world in which employees feel like they have more options than just this job. As I explore in Part 2, the workplace continues to evolve and the traditional rules of enforcing compliance over commitment are outdated.

If the job situation isn't quite right, today's highly skilled workers are likely to look and go elsewhere for employment — often to your competitor! The competition for talent is fierce. Many employees, especially good ones, are often assessing which organization they want to work for. There was a time when employers held that ground and had their choice of who to pick. Now the roles are reversed. Employers are the buyers and employees are sellers.

The average person has 12 jobs in their lifetime, with an average tenure of three years, according to the Bureau of Labor Statistics. The employers' concerns about so-called unstable *job-hoppers* (individuals who have held many jobs, with short life spans at those jobs) are shifting to the reality that people will move around, so you can't assume they'll spend their careers with one company.

Are these employees prepared to follow orders and revere authority? It's more likely, "Don't tell me what to do." The more managers attempt to push compliance and their positional influence, the more employees push back with various forms of resistance.

When compliance is mandated, you find employees doing the minimum, taking little initiative, blaming you — the manager — for everything that goes wrong, and sitting back, taking little responsibility on their own. These employees still do what they're told, but their efforts are likely to be minimal and fall short of achieving the quality results you need and want. They don't care. Some call this *quiet quitting*, but passively doing the bare minimum isn't a new phenomenon. At its worst, disgruntled and disengaged employee go out of their way to undermine the team's or manager's success.

A wave of employees who are disengaged and uncommitted with work are taking it one step further, resigning from the workforce in record numbers. In 2021, according to the U.S. Bureau of Labor Statistics, more than 47 million Americans voluntarily quit their jobs — an unprecedented mass exit from the workforce. Chapter 6 goes deeper into the changing workplace, but the fact remains that investing in coaching and mentoring to create a better work environment is not just a nice thing to do. It's essential to your survival and success as an organization. Without good people working at your organization, success and growth are unlikely.

Cultivating more personal influence is a step in the right direction of attracting and retaining talent.

TIP

Despite the changes in the workforce, one thing remains constant: An employee's relationship with their manager is still the biggest factor in whether people stay in a position or leave. If they feel respected and valued by their manager, they'll tend to be loyal and stay. But if the relationship is strained, it's often the the reason people leave a job. That responsibility, right or wrong, falls on you. To be fair, it's not just your responsibility. Some employees aren't a good fit, resist coaching, or have interpersonal issues with other team members.

A strong culture and opportunities for growth and challenge weigh more heavily with employees than pay. If people are working for a manager who cares about them and their careers and who provides them with challenges in their work, their reasons for staying far outweigh their reasons for moving elsewhere to work.

Personal influence, not positional power, builds connections between employees and managers and commits employees to your company.

Managing as a Tone Setter

Effective coaching is based on building positive working relationships and exercising personal influence with your employees. These efforts are what stimulate the development of mutual trust. One of the critical aspects of the leadership side of management is tone setting. These sections explain what tone setting is and help you do some self-inspection to evaluate your own managing style.

Understanding what tone setting is

Tone setting is when managers understand that their own behavior often sets the tone for the behavior and overall performance for the group(s) they manage. In other words, how your employees work and conduct themselves on the job reflects how you, their manager, work and conduct yourself. And the higher you go up the organizational ladder, the greater the number of people you influence and affect.

EXAMPLE

Show me a manager who, rather than face a problem, looks to find blame when problems occur, and I'll show you a group of defensive employees who often walk around on eggshells. On the flip side, show me a manager who, rather than place blame, always avoids dealing with problems, and I'll show you a group of frustrated employees working in chaos. And another example: Show me a manager who openly complains about management whenever they get frustrated about something, and I'll show you a group that frequently whines and complains, especially about its manager.

These examples illustrate how the tone-setter role can come back to haunt you as a manager. You need to stay aware that your own faults and weaknesses may be magnified within the staff you manage. Of course, even if you lead by positive example, there's no guarantee that you'll get positive behavior and performance in return, but doing so certainly increases the likelihood. Therefore, for managers to exert influence and coach effectively, maintaining awareness of their tone-setter roles is important.

REMEMBER

Over the years, I (Marty) have asked a number of management and employees to identify the leadership-by-example behaviors that managers need to exhibit to set the right tone for their groups. Employees have most often identified the following 16 behaviors:

>> Listens to understand; isn't judgmental

>> Follows through and meets commitments

>> Takes an interest in employees as people

>> Works productively and meets deadlines

>> Is flexible and open-minded

>> Treats others with respect

>> Stays calm under pressure

>> Addresses issues timely and constructively

>> Shares information and stays in touch

>> Collaborates with others

>> Is solutions-oriented and doesn't blame

>> Recognizes good performance of others

>> Displays honesty and integrity

>> Shows interest and enthusiasm for the work of individuals and the group

>> Shows up on time for meetings and other important events

>> Takes a positive focus in interactions

When you make these behaviors regular practices, they earn you respect in return. Most important, they build your personal influence as a manager, which puts you on the road to ensuring the commitment of your employees. It's easier to ask your employees for high levels of performance and professional conduct when you demonstrate these efforts yourself.

Assessing your performance

So how are you doing as a manager at making these behaviors consistent practices? Take this test to see how you're doing:

1. **Evaluate yourself.**

   On a scale of 1 to 5 — with 1 being seldom to not at all and 5 being always — with what frequency do you exhibit each of the 16 behaviors in your management practices?

   After this self-evaluation, if you're open to the feedback, ask your employees to rate how frequently they see you exhibiting each of these leadership-by-example behaviors. As a gauge of how you're doing (and don't shoot any of your employees if they give you a low frequency rating), consider an 80 percent level a competency level (80 percent is a total score of 64 out of 80.) Anything above 80 percent is outstanding.

2. **Be honest with yourself!**

   What's most important here isn't your overall score, which is just a gauge, but the level of your awareness of whether and how frequently you demonstrate behaviors that build your personal influence as a manager.

3. **Focus on when you're stressed.**

   Many managers do well when they're relaxed and composed. It's often during those times of stress that some managers blow it with employees. Try to be more conscious of when those times present themselves and be proactive to do something different. Take a time out, bite your tongue, reschedule a conversation for another time, or make amends immediately.

REMEMBER

The toughest person to manage in your group is none other than yourself. When you recognize this fact, you can work on you, and then you can apply the coaching practices that stimulate high levels of performance and employee commitment.

MAINTAINING YOUR PERSONAL INFLUENCE UNDER PRESSURE

Although many managers want to build positive working relationships with their employees, the nature of the relationship often changes when pressure and stressful situations come into the picture. At those times, their mode of operation shifts to the compliance side.

For example, imagine that yesterday I was willing to be friendly and discuss ideas with you, but now stress has arrived, so today, do what I say! Or yesterday I was willing to show interest in your work and career, but stress has arrived, so now I'm too busy to be bothered with you.

Managers who skip back and forth in their mode of operation limit their credibility for having much personal influence. If you always give orders and push authority, at least your manner is clear and consistent and therefore, easier to deal with. If you shift back and forth, in which case your employees are always trying to figure out whether you're going to be open to listening and engaging in two-way discussions, you'll quickly lose credibility.

Your best bet is to find ways to always build positive relationships with your employees despite stressful situations.

Examining the Collaborative and Assertive Nature of Coaching

Coaching is carried out in an effort of collaboration. *Collaboration* is cooperating and willingly assisting others in some kind of effort. The key is you're working together. It's not all in your control or up to you.

Now moving to the other end of the manager's pendulum, what's not collaboration? Here are some examples of what managers often do that is *not* collaboration:

>> Choosing to be missing in action — totally out of the loop with what employees are doing.

>> Telling people how to do their jobs.

>> Correcting all the mistakes employees make and solve all the problems employees encounter — *for* them.

These examples of not collaborating fit well with the doer approach to management (refer to Chapter 2), which is in many ways the opposite of the coaching approach. Collaboration, on the other hand, is about working with someone else to set plans, solve problems, gain skills, and focus performance in the right direction.

The collaborative nature of coaching recognizes that managers and employees don't have the same level of responsibilities, and it doesn't seek consensus on all decisions. Managers practicing assertiveness and collaboration don't focus on making employees happy or on sitting with employees to help them get all their work done — *hand-holding*, as the expression goes. These approaches focus on communication, on acting and responsibility, and on performance. Instead of coercion or acquiescence in stressful and challenging situations, assertive and collaborative coaches engage in dialog with their employees. Even though these managers are decisive about getting an action done, they are willing to listen and are open to discussion. They're positive, firm, consultative, and understanding in the face of pressure.

Engage in two-way conversations

The collaborative nature of coaching requires two-way conversations. Two-way conversations occur when two people are willing to listen to each other's points of view and express their own points of view. Two-way conversations are discussions, not debates, dialogs, or lectures. They also convey that the employee and what they have to say are important and deserve to be heard with respect. You don't have to agree with each other, but you must be willing to understand one another and maintain dignity in your working relationship.

Remind yourself that you're all adults

Managers can hide behind their position of power when having difficult conversations with their employees. The conversation can sometimes sound like an adult scolding a child, which is not only disrespectful but does little to build an employee's confidence, engagement, and commitment. Remind yourself and your employee you are all just adults trying to do a job. You have your job. They have theirs. This isn't a power play —just two adults trying to do the best they can. When you take this approach, you're using personal influence and building trust and commitment.

Assert yourself

For the two-way conversation and the collaborative nature of coaching to work, managers must be assertive in their manner and actions. In your role as manager, *assertiveness* is your ability to communicate and act in a positive, sincere, and confident manner that maintains respect for others. Assertiveness translates into such actions as communicating directly, using language constructively, addressing problems with a focus on solutions, following through, taking initiative, and leading the way to bring issues to closure.

REMEMBER

Coaching assertively involves flexibility tailored to the individual employee and the situation at hand. This means that managers need to truly understand what makes each individuals tick, what motivates them, and how best to communicate with them, especially if feedback is required. Sometimes this flexibility means being encouraging; other times it means being firm. Sometimes this means being persistent; other times it means being patient. Sometimes this means pushing a person to act; other times it means backing off and seeing what the individual will do. Coaching assertively encourages input and ideas but doesn't compromise high standards of performance. It encourages dialog but not endless discussion with no closure.

INTERNALIZING COLLABORATION

While many managers understand on an intellectual level that coaching is an assertive, collaborative effort that takes place through two-way conversation, they don't act upon it until this understanding reaches an emotional level. Only then are these concepts internalized and truly understood and practiced. The shift begins at times like the following:

- When a disagreement is recognized as an opportunity for listening and entering dialog rather than as a time for arguing or just backing away

- When a manager reacts to an employee's resistance by seeking to find out why the resistance occurred in the first place and how the issue can be settled, instead of using the resistance as an excuse to yell and order or to appease and do nothing at all

- When problems in employees' work are seen as opportunities to ask questions and challenge employees to come up with solutions — versus telling them how to fix their problems or by letting problems linger

When these kinds of shifts take place, you're starting to coach. Your focus shifts as well to be performance-based rather than personal-based, to working together rather than working against, to figuring out what works best to get a job done rather than seeing everything as either right or wrong.

Be assertive not aggressive

Being assertive isn't the same as being aggressive. Although both approaches are action-oriented, they're quite different in their manner and behavior. An assertive manager allows dialog; an aggressive one permits little listening and holds one-way conversations. An assertive manager addresses problems in a solutions-oriented manner; an aggressive one addresses problems in a shoot-first-and-then-blame manner. An assertive manager is direct; an aggressive one is blunt. Being assertive means being willing to take charge; being aggressive means being hard-charging — my way or the highway. In simple terms, assertiveness invites collaboration; aggressiveness seeks compliance.

REMEMBER

The collaborative nature of coaching requires assertive managers, not aggressive ones.

EXAMPLE

TESTING YOUR COLLABORATION SKILLS

To help clarify the value of the assertive nature of coaching, check out the following responses made by managers who approach their roles in different ways.

Here's the scenario: One of your employees expresses an idea for the direction in which they want to see a project go, and you, the manager, don't agree with their idea.

- **Aggressive response:** "That idea will never work. I disagree with it totally. I don't know what you were thinking, and who asked for your ideas anyway!"

  Here, you create a one-way conversation — end of discussion.

- **Passive response:** "Well that idea has possibilities. Maybe we could consider it. If you want to work on it, uh . . . maybe you don't have to. But I do appreciate that you have ideas. But if you want to explore it more, we could."

  Here you create confusion and leave the issue hanging because of an indirect and hesitant response.

- **Assertive response:** "I have some concerns about whether that idea will help the project. Here they are (constructively expressed). What do you think? How do you think they could be addressed?"

  Here you invite a two-way conversation, collaborative problem solving, and an opportunity for closure on how to proceed with the project. By clearly stating your concerns and then asking questions you're inviting a dialog to resolve the issues. So you're not overwhelming the employee, prioritize your concerns and address them one at a time.

Don't be passive or passive aggressive

Passive and nonassertive approaches don't work when trying to achieve collaboration, either. Being meek, hesitant, indirect, and laissez-faire in manner and actions renders coaching useless. The give-and-take and constructive dialog of coaching doesn't occur when managers are passive in their approach with employees.

Sometimes managers are passive, not because they don't care, but they *care too much*. Fear of confronting the employee with constructive feedback can lead to bigger problems down the road if they don't hear what they need to correct to be successful. Doers who are strong technically but lack strong relationship skills are often intimidated and overwhelmed with the task of having any negative conversation. They'd rather ignore it and hope it resolves itself than face a hard conversation.

What's often behind a passive management style is fear — fear of upsetting the employee; fear of them not liking you; fear of them attacking you; fear of it becoming an issue that comes between you; fear that they'll take it personally and become de-moralized; fear of them quitting; and fear that somehow your boss will get wind of this and it won't be good for you.

In my (Leo) work coaching leaders, passive communication is a bigger problem than managers who are too aggressive. There's always a much larger group of managers actively avoiding difficult conversations than there are bullies who are causing trouble.

Looking at an Example of Leave 'Em Alone

The following is a commonplace scenario of good intentions. As you read the story, you may want to analyze the manager's (Maria's) efforts by considering the following questions, each of which I address later in this section:

>> What are Maria's efforts to coach Tim, her employee?

>> What are Maria's efforts to encourage commitment from Tim?

>> (Ah, now the tricky one.) Regarding Maria's decision on making the corrections for the project that Tim is assigned to handle, how would you as a manager deal with this situation?

Tim was eager when he started his new job. A week in Maria, met with Tim and assigned him to handle an important project. Maria gave Tim a general description of what the project entailed and three directions — to do what it takes to get the job done, to come to her with questions, and to complete the project within three months.

As the weeks passed, Maria was pleased with Tim's progress. She noticed that he was meeting with the right people, was often working efficiently, and seemed self-sufficient. Maria held a brief review meeting with Tim a few weeks after the project started, and Tim appeared to be on the right track. Also, every now and then, Maria informally asked Tim how things were going and received an enthusiastic response of "really good."

Tim liked the freedom Maria gave him. Other than an occasional reminder to stay on schedule with the project, Tim appreciated the fact that Maria wasn't a harsh or demanding boss. On the other hand, Tim found that Maria was often tied up in meetings and burdened with her own projects, so Tim learned to get answers to questions elsewhere.

In a little less than three months, slightly ahead of the deadline that Maria had set, Tim informed Maria that the project was complete. When they met to go over the project, Maria's excitement about Tim's work soon turned to disappointment. She didn't like some of the decisions Tim had made, decisions that resulted in the project going in a somewhat different direction than Maria had envisioned.

Maria also didn't agree with some of the methods that Tim used to do his work. She wound up telling Tim that the project needed quite a bit of correction and that because of the tight deadline she would handle it and let Tim work on another, smaller assignment. Tim became deflated and frustrated.

What did Maria do wrong? How could it have ended on a better note? The following breaks it down so you understand what lessons Maria learned and how she might approach it differently next time.

Analyzing the manager's coaching efforts

Maria had good intentions at the beginning. She assigned Tim a meaningful project, allowed him autonomy to run with it, and gave clear directions about when the work needed to be completed. Early on, she met with Tim and did a brief progress review.

After that, however, Maria just left Tim alone, without providing any real coaching. The results expected were never spelled out nor were parameters set for Tim to work within. As for feedback of any substance and progress reviews along the way, well . . . *nothing*.

So after the first few weeks, the two had little regular communication — and don't forget, Tim was a new employee. Maria didn't really take an interest in what was happening for Tim and the project until the deadline. Maria illustrates the classic doer (see Chapter 2) who stays busy with her own affairs until something critical comes up.

Analyzing the manager's efforts to affect their employee's level of commitment

Maria gave Tim meaningful responsibility and initially a sense of autonomy in his work. So you could say that she made an initial effort to involve Tim. She also gave Tim a sense of focus at the beginning by letting Tim know the deadline within which he needed to complete the project.

These two early efforts did scratch the surface of two pillars for achieving employee commitment: involvement and focus. But Maria's lack of ongoing involvement and guidance fell short of building a working relationship and influencing high standards of performance in Tim's case. She failed to lay a foundation on which to build commitment. Maria further undermined Tim's potential for commitment with the decision to leave him out of the correction phase of the project.

Ascertaining how to handle corrections for this project

You have a tight deadline and a project that needs fixing. The quickest course is fix it yourself, as do many doer managers. Although this decision may seem to be an easy solution (and many people, me included, have taken just this course when faced with similar circumstances), it actually has serious shortcomings and may have more difficulties than meets the eye at first glance. There are good reasons, however, not to take the project back, including:

>> When Tim is left out of the effort to correct the project, he can't learn from the experience. And, in a short period of time, trying to match Tim's knowledge of the project is no easy task, even if you have the technical expertise. Also, if you had the time, why didn't you do the project in the first place yourself?

» In determining what went wrong with the project, Maria is focusing on the methods Tim used. From this perspective, you can say that she is placing methods over results — which is common with doer managers, who often worry more about how a job should be done than about the desired outcomes. In this case, it's possible that many of the results Tim produced are acceptable. But not involving Tim in evaluating the results and not focusing on results wastes time and a valuable resource.

» Even if Tim is invited to just sit alongside and watch Maria make corrections, Tim will learn more from the experience than if he isn't involved in the effort at all. In most tough business decisions, two key factors must be considered: the business at hand and the impact on the people involved or affected by the decision. Maria's focus was on the first factor only, the business at hand (how to fix the project). As a result, Tim's potential for future commitment was shot down! The trust and working relationship between Tim and Maria was greatly damaged.

A larger issue is at play here: What is the corporate culture for failure? A friend of mine was highly qualified for a position at a large company but couldn't really answer the question, "Tell me about a time you really screwed up and what did you learn?" She tried to do what many of us would do: give a soft answer about a failure or shortcoming but sugarcoat it as a strength. But the interviewer was looking for a big failure. She didn't get the position and learned that the company really values failure. Success and innovation mean you're going to try things that don't work. Does your company support "small failures" on the road to discovering a new and better solution? Or does it have little to no tolerance for mistakes?

Maria's personal belief, informed from many years at the company, is that there's no room for mistakes or doing things differently. Creating a culture where small failures are the norm, especially when you have a new employee, takes the pressure off employees to get it right the first time. Maria could have had a discussion with Tim on what was expected. Maria could take the step of sharing her failure with Tim with her peers, as a way of initiating a dialog on changing the culture to support creativity and innovation with employees.

Consideration must be given to both factors — making the fixes herself or involving Tim in the revision process — when making critical business decisions, not just one or the other. Involving Tim in fixing the problem and getting the project back on track is a more fruitful, long-term strategy than excluding it for the short-term gain of correcting it.

Coaching focuses on performance but recognizes that people are connected to the work they do. To lay the foundation for building employee commitment requires focusing on developing working relationships and on developing the performance of the individual doing the job. With coaching, they are mutually inclusive efforts.

Introducing the Five Pillars for Building Commitment

Here I introduce *the five pillars for building commitment,* a model for evaluating your coaching efforts to build commitment and foster higher levels of performance. At the end of each chapter, I revisit the pillars to understand how the lessons and examples in the chapter support the five pillars. Here are the five pillars with a description of what they mean:

>> **Focus:** When you consistently focus on personal influence over positional influence, you build commitment. When you're clear in your direction and communication, employees know what's expected and aren't searching for clarity. Clarity is a key element in being effective.

>> **Involvement:** When this pillar is strong, employees feel that they have some say-so over the matters that affect their day-to-day work situations. They have input into the planning, problem-solving, and decision-making that affect their level of responsibility. They feel included. The adage that "people support most what they help create" highlights what the pillar of involvement emphasizes. Your involvement in your employee's growth helps them be involved in taking more responsibility and ownership.

>> **Development:** When this pillar is strong, opportunities for learning and growth are encouraged and supported. These opportunities are both formal and informal in nature, ranging from such activities as a training course to a mentoring discussion between an employee and a senior manager. Helping people continuously strengthen their knowledge, skills, and experience are common practices.

>> **Gratitude:** You're only as strong as your team. When you realize that your success is tied to their success, you become more grateful for the work they do. When you take the time to support and listen to your employees, they become grateful for showing you care.

>> **Accountability:** When this pillar is strong, employees are given responsibility along with the authority to carry it out, which creates in them the desire to produce results with high standards. Lax performance is not tolerated, while measuring progress and reporting results are normal practices. People produce quality results not just because it is expected of them, but, more importantly, because they enjoy experiencing a sense of achievement.

Coaching is your best set of tools for positively influencing employee commitment. All of the coaching skills in Chapter 2 impact one or more of these five pillars for building employee commitment. They, of course, only do so when done as regular practices. People will trust and follow you if your actions are consistent over time.

Chapter **5**

Leveraging Emotional Intelligence

Chapter 4 describes how to move from positional power to personal influence in order to engage and motivate employees in a collaborative relationship. Doer managers focus on executing tasks. Coaching managers focus on developing people to execute the tasks.

This chapter gives you the foundation skills for all coaching and mentoring — understanding and leveraging how emotions impact strong collaborative relationships. This chapter helps you understand what's meant by emotional intelligence and why it's important in coaching and mentoring. I break down emotional intelligence into four quadrants: self-awareness, self-management, social awareness, and relationship management.

Understanding What EQ Is

Researchers Jack Zenger and Joseph Folkman asked more than 300,000 business leaders to rank the top four competencies from a list of 16 key leadership skills. The team then ranked the data from most important to least important skills that leaders need to succeed in their current positions.

The study showed that technical skills, although important, don't differentiate the most effective leaders. A strong grasp of interpersonal communication skills is necessary for motivating, engaging and influencing people.

When I (Leo) interviewed 100 business owners about their biggest leadership challenges, their number one issue wasn't finding better technical experts but rather finding people who can relate and communicate with peers and clients. It wasn't to engineer something or solve a technical problem but to be aware of what's going on with their own emotions, to manage their emotions, to read people, and to have the sense of how to talk to someone — to know when to listen and be empathetic like a therapist; to know when to be direct and as clear as a drill sergeant; and to know how to do it well so you don't tick people off but gain their admiration and trust.

REMEMBER

These skills are sometimes called *soft skills* or *life skills*, but more commonly they are referred to as emotional intelligence (abbreviated as either EQ or EI). *Emotional intelligence* is the ability to understand and manage your emotions and others' emotions to have better interpersonal relationships. EQ is so critical to success that it accounts for 58 percent of performance in all types of jobs.

Differentiating between EQ and IQ

How is emotional intelligence or EQ different than intelligence quotient (IQ)? IQ, the common predictor of intellect, measures your intelligence in rational analysis, reasoning and memorization of data and facts. A person with a high IQ is gifted at figuring things out and solving complex problems. A person with a high EQ is gifted at understanding what motivates and drives people. Both IQ and EQ are important in business.

You want the smartest people in the room to engineer the bridges you drive over, who operate on you when you need surgery, who design a new financial software app, and who build the high-rises that tower 40 stories above the sidewalk. For executing complex tasks, precision and logic are essential skills. You want those technical experts to be sticklers for details. You want them to take ownership of their work. You want them to be uber focused on results and to be accountable to the highest standards of quality control. Technical experts with high IQ are indispensable to any organization.

But when it comes to delivering bad news, resolving interpersonal issues, and motivating other people to perform at their best, math isn't the most useful skill. Technical skills are undeniably important to solving technical problems. But to solve people's problems, you need a different skill set.

Between 1980–2012, the highest growth in wages and demand were in positions that called for high social skills over strictly high math skills. In a 2018 study of 200 organizations, Workday-Bloomberg Building Tomorrow's Talent uncovered that employers are 42 percent more worried about soft skills than technical skills. Studies found 90 percent of top performers have high EQ, and EQ is twice as important as IQ in determining your success. And a team from the University of Virginia Commonwealth amassed years of existing studies in EQ and found that high EQ does have a relationship to strong job performance — in short, emotionally intelligent people make better workers.

Rating your EQ skills

If you want to switch from a doer manager to a coach and mentor, develop your softer side to improve your effectiveness. And here's the great news: Unlike IQ, which is mostly fixed at birth, you can improve your EQ with practice.

As a leadership coach, I (Leo) first ask people to rate the following EQ skills on a scale of 1 (weakness) to 5 (strength). This provides a baseline on what they want to work on. I additionally ask them to solicit input from their manager and peers to understand what skills they think the person should develop.

Rate yourself on the following soft skills attributes. At the end, identify what two areas you want to develop in the next three months:

>> **Interpersonal communication:**

- Engages people easily and takes the time to connect with them
- Prefers direct communication over email, text, and other electronic communication
- Takes the time to listen and understand what's being said
- Gets to the point and clear in email and face-to-face communication
- Is articulate and comfortable presenting complex information to different audiences
- Is persuasive and confident in presenting your perspective
- Asks questions and speaks up when something isn't clear

>> **Time management:**

- Organizes your day effectively and knows how to budget time on priorities
- Actively manages meetings and keeps discussion on track
- Delegates tasks clearly and effectively

- Clearly explains project deliverables, milestones, and responsibilities to staff in the beginning of the project
- Organizes your day effectively and knows how to budget time on priorities
- Doesn't let managing tasks and projects detract from interacting with others
- Is effective at saying no and rescheduling interruptions

>> **People management:**

  - Has strong self-awareness and impact on others
  - Relates well to many different types of people
  - Coaches staff to provide options for solving problems and keeping the project on track
  - Gives constructive feedback in real time
  - Understands and takes the time to mentor people

>> **Conflict resolution:**

  - Takes responsibility for resolving issues in a timely manner
  - Waits until you calm down before addressing conflicts
  - Thinks through the issues and considers everyone's perspective
  - Is aware of triggers and remains calm during the interaction
  - Tries to understand what other people are up against — their obstacles
  - Asks questions to make sure you understand the history or causes of conflicts
  - Owns up to your role in creating or contributing to conflict
  - Focuses attention on the big picture — common goals and overall direction
  - Follows up after resolution to ensure tasks are completed
  - Negotiates adeptly with others

>> **Decision-making:**

  - Is adept at navigating change where there is no clear answer or method for proceeding
  - Takes initiative instead of looking for direction
  - Thinks strategically about the organization's growth
  - Collaborates well with others and brings in their perspective

- Considers possible consequences when making decisions
- Is decisive and doesn't procrastinate on making decisions

>> **Professional development:**

- Is candid about your shortcomings and seeks input to grow
- Develops better peer relationships and learns how to support each other
- Invests in your own professional development
- Builds a strong network of peers for guidance and support

To understand EQ more clearly, the rest of this chapter breaks it into four buckets:

>> Self-awareness of your thoughts, emotions, triggers, and behavior

>> Self-management of your thoughts, emotions, and behaviors

>> Social awareness of other people's cues, emotions, and perspectives

>> Relationship management, which leverages a total understanding of yourself and others to have more successful, productive relationships

Developing Self-Awareness

Socrates said to know thyself is the beginning of wisdom. Your greatest impact as a coach manager is how your words, actions, and attitude influence your employees. Leaders are successful when they're aware of themselves at all times. EQ starts with knowing yourself. Why is that important?

Consider the EQ skills assessment from the previous section. That list is how others view you, but in order for that to be accurate, you need to have an accurate perception of yourself. *Self-awareness* is like standing outside yourself and seeing yourself. It's being able to understand what you think, how you feel, and how you act — as others see you.

Self-awareness is the foundation for developing your EQ. It's also the foundation for being an effective coach manager as the next sections illustrate.

Connecting self-awareness and coaching

You can't help others work on themselves if you aren't doing your own work. When you're more aware of who you are and what forms your thoughts, beliefs, and actions, you begin the work of being an effective communicator, coach, and mentor. Getting to know yourself is a fundamental first step in many ways:

>> You need to first be aware of your thoughts, feelings, and behavior in order to change or modify them to situations.

>> When you improve your self-awareness, you have a better understanding why you react the way you do, which can help explain your modus operandi.

>> By working on your self-awareness you come to empathize with others and see how everyone is similar and different.

Self-awareness has many dimensions. The more you explore the different parts, the more you'll gain in knowing yourself.

Seeing yourself clearly

In my (Leo) experience, a small number of managers know themselves. They've thought a lot about who they are and what's important to them. They've read books on personal growth. They've attended workshops. They have friends who like to talk about their emotions and life goals and challenges. They've seen a therapist more than once. They're very attuned to who they are, how they feel, and how they come across to others.

TIP

But most managers I've worked with have big blind spots into themselves. They're truly unaware of what makes them tick and how they feel. This isn't a book for self-improvement, per se, but I do invite you to peel back the layers to understand yourself. Here are some questions to reflect upon, journal your thoughts, and discuss with a colleague:

>> How has your upbringing shaped who you are?

>> What's important to you in terms of values?

>> Who did you learn most from?

>> What kind of people are difficult to deal with?

>> How much of your day are you preoccupied by negative thoughts?

>> What stands in your way of doing your best work?

>> What gives you energy?

>> What's exhausting for you?

>> Are you introverted, extroverted, or a combination?

>> How do you like to approach projects?

- » Are you a numbers/data person or do you like people/ideas?

- » What bores you?

- » What excites you?

- » Do you prefer when people are direct, even if it's hard to hear?

- » Do you prefer to avoid conflict and just get along with people?

- » Do you forgive and forget easily?

- » Do you hold on to judgments and resentments?

Coaching is an interpersonal skill of working with people, understanding what motivates them, how they work, and how to adapt to different people and personalities.

Chapter 7 challenges you to work with a great diversity of people. Successful coaching and mentoring is about appreciating that people are unique and no one approach works for everyone. The key to unlocking what others think, feel, and act is first understanding how you think, feel, and act. Build awareness with yourself to develop the skills to understand other people.

Valuing your values

Everyone operates from their own belief systems or values. *Values* are those attributes that guide your choices and preferences. They determine what you do for work, how you interact with people, and the choices you make. Values are usually formed early in your life, from your family dynamics and early experiences and role models.

Take a quick assessment of your own values from the list:

1. Underline ten from the list below or write them on a separate sheet.
2. Circle the top five.
3. Ask someone who knows you well to identify your top five values.
4. Compare and discuss.

   - Accomplishment   - Balance

   - Family   - Security

   - Wealth   - Creativity

   - Humor   - Cooperation

- Service
- Accuracy
- Health
- Openness
- Learning
- Abundance
- Passion
- Adventure
- Fun
- Compassion
- Spirituality
- Winning
- Accountability
- Courage
- Honesty
- Humility
- Justice
- Thoroughness
- Love
- Recognition
- Discipline
- Integrity

- Appreciation
- Boldness
- Authenticity
- Consistency
- Credibility
- Respect
- Generosity
- Optimism
- Faith
- Flexibility
- Fairness
- Competitiveness
- Knowledge
- Belonging
- Practicality
- Commitment
- Innovation
- Dependability
- Directness
- Friendship
- Community
- Toughness

To understand how your values dictate what kind of manager you might be, look at these examples. As you check them out, here are some questions to consider for yourself:

>> What are my core values?

>> How do my core values show up in my behavior?

>> What types of people do I get along with best?

>> What common values do we share?

>> What types of people are most challenging for me?

>> How do our values differ?

When you uncover your values and can link them to your thoughts, feelings, and actions, you begin to leverage your EQ in building strong coaching and mentoring relationships.

THE NO-NONSENSE MANAGER

Brenda is a no-nonsense supervisor in a manufacturing facility for mobile homes. She was brought up in a military family, where rules were clear and emotions were not acknowledged. "Toughen up," was what she often heard from her father. Brenda learned early on to be direct, tough, dependable, accountable, hard-working, and practical.

She lives by those values and anyone who works for her can tell you that she can be demanding but fair. She doesn't ask anyone to do anything she wouldn't do herself. Her standards are high, and her team knows they need to execute at the highest level. If they don't, they'll hear from Brenda.

While her direct style works for some people, it doesn't work for people who value friendship, compassion, and flexibility. Luckily, Brenda is very aware of how she comes across and who she is. She's working on adapting her style to be less directive and more of a coach. It's a challenge every day, but the fact that she knows herself gives her an advantage in learning to change and adapt to others.

THE FUN-LOVING MANAGER

Jim is customer service supervisor for a team of eight people. When Jim steps into the room, you know it. He's always positive, smiling, and easy to engage. He's great at drawing people out. He comes from a big family where stories, music, and comedy were common around the dinner table. In high school, he performed in musical theater. Just based on this description, try identifying his core values from the list in the section, "Valuing your values," earlier in this chapter.

You'd be correct if you chose creativity, community, abundance, and fun. He just wants everyone to get along and have a good time. Unfortunately, that's not realistic. Jim has several people on his team who are more reserved and analytical. They get tired of his enthusiasm. Jim doesn't quite understand other people not getting on board with his approach. He's often blind to how he comes across and how his approach might not be appreciated by everyone. Jim has some work to do on increasing his own self-awareness in order to understand and appreciate others.

Identifying your personality

Understanding your personality is equally important. *Personality* is the combination of characteristics or qualities that form an individual's distinctive characteristics. Your values may be the code you live by. Your personality is what others see.

There is no shortage of personality assessments. In my (Leo) experience, they all shed a different light on who you are, your preferences, and what kind of manager you tend toward. Assessments are valuable in helping the individual who takes the assessment gain new knowledge about themselves, which can include helping them determine their right kind of work/role and their suitability for leadership positions, identify their strengths, understanding how they communicate and prefer to be communicated to and how they approach conflict, and generally describe how they show up to others in various situations.

Here's a sampling of common assessments that you can explore on your own to give you new insights into your personality:

>> **Meyers-Briggs Type Indicator:** Also known as the MBTI, the Myers-Briggs Type Indicator is often used by companies during the hiring process. Its questions determine where an applicant falls within four key groupings: extraversion versus introversion, judging versus perceiving, intuition versus sensing, and thinking versus feeling. The results of these groupings place test-takers into one of 16 personality types. With 93 questions in all, it's a fairly long assessment.

>> **DISC:** Based on the categories, Dominance, Influence, Steadiness, and Compliance (DISC), this test breaks into 28 statements each with four options for the test-taker to rate how they identify with the statement, ultimately resulting in one of 12 different personality types.

>> **StrengthsFinder:** StrengthsFinder focuses on your strengths rather than focusing on preferences or behaviors. The test identifies your top five strengths out of a possible 34. This can be invaluable in identifying your career goals and how you might contribute within an organization, based on what you naturally do best.

>> **Enneagram:** Like MBTI, the Enneagram test helps you find your specific personality types. There are nine Enneagram types, and according to the Enneagram Institute, "It is common to find a little of yourself in all nine of the types, although one of them should stand out as being closest to yourself."

>> **Predictive Index:** The Predictive Index measures behavioral drives (Dominance, Extraversion, Patience, and Formality) as well as cognitive ability. PI assessments help business leaders hire the right people based on their fit for the position and coach others to understand differences in behavior.

>> **Kolbe:** Kolbe measures your instinctive way of doing things and the result is called your MO (method of operation). Unlike other assessments, Kolbe informs you how you and your team approach projects and solve challenges.

>> **Platinum Assessment:** This quick self-administered survey helps to quickly identify your general behaviors distinguishing between those who are people oriented versus people who are results oriented on one axis and people who are direct/responsive and indirect/reserved on another axis (see Chapter 10).

The more assessments you take, the more common themes you'll discover about yourself. Not only will you begin to understand yourself better but you'll understand others better, as well.

Understanding Your Emotions

Your ability to interact effectively with employees will be greatly determined by your ability to spot your own emotions as they arise in the moment. It would be great if humans could all be programmed to feel and act in a specific way, but they are complex. Understanding your emotions on a deeper level can help you manage them more effectively when they arise unexpectedly. There will be fewer times when you lose your cool, say the wrong thing, or act in a way that can be counterproductive to building trust and collaboration.

Managing your emotions

Your daily challenge is managing your first impulses based on your emotions. These emotions are deep-seated and often not well understood. When you're faced with working with people who are different than you — in age, color, race, gender, sexual orientation, physical characteristics, and so on — you may experience a negative knee-jerk emotional reaction that no amount of diversity training will eliminate. That's who you are. Emotions are neither good nor bad, but being able to identify them is the first important step.

Additionally, emotions can vary in intensity, or how strongly someone experiences that emotion. A person can be really angry (outraged) or slightly angry (dismayed). That's a big difference. Knowing where you might be on any emotion will help you manage that emotion more effectively and not be ambushed by its intensity.

REMEMBER

The key to managing your emotions is first being able to identify them, even if you don't know the source.

THE BASICS OF HOW THE BRAIN WORKS

Having a basic understanding of the human brain is important. The brain has three main areas, each having developed through evolution:

- **Reptilian:** Also called the *Basal Ganglia,* this is oldest part of brain, around 250 million years old. It controls the regulatory system, breathing, and a person's primal responses to fight or flight.

  When faced with conflict, you want to strike back and shout or go silent and shrink, it's the reptilian part of the brain.

- **Amygdala:** Part of the limbic system, it's about 150 million years old. Emotions and memories reside here.

  When you take something personally, it's the amygdala.

- **Neocortex:** The youngest part of the brain, it's 2 or 3 million years old. Reasoning and rationale thought operate from here.

  When someone says something you understand as language, it's the neocortex.

Everything your brain receives in terms of what you see, hear, feel, and taste first comes through the brain stem, the oldest part. It then travels through the amygdala or emotional part and finally gets to your thinking brain. Your brain is hard-wired to feel first and react before you even think about the right response. Psychologists called this "amygdala hijack," or the tendency for your rational brain to get overridden by how you first feel about something.

Keep a journal and check in with yourself for a couple of days to pinpoint how you're feeling. Check out the following:

- » Figure out what the basic emotion is — angry, sad, afraid, confused, happy?
- » Determine the level of intensity from high to low.
- » Find a list of common emotions to help you identify the feeling (check out https://juliahwest.com/prompts/emotion_intensity.html).
- » Scan your body from head to toe to see if the emotion can be found in a part of your body. For instance, anger commonly shows up as a clenched jaw, tightened chest, and shallow, rapid breathing.

>> Figure out whether there are any specific situations or times when these emotions arise so you can be better prepared to anticipate and manage them when they arise.

Seeking feedback

The fastest and best way to develop greater awareness of how you come across to others is to seek feedback, which can be done in a number of ways:

>> **Enlist the help of a mentor.** Find someone you trust and like to give you feedback on your style and interactions. If you're prone to talking over people and want to improve, ask a colleague who works with you to gently tell you when you talk over others — as soon as you've done it, so you make the connection.

>> **Ask your employees for feedback.** Make it a regular practice to ask employees how you're doing. Assure them it's okay to be honest and that you can take it. By receiving feedback with a healthy attitude, you're also modeling for them how to receive feedback when you're delivering it.

>> **Conduct surveys.** Not everyone is going to feel comfortable sharing feedback on your performance directly to you. Anonymous, confidential surveys — particularly those administered by an outside organization — can be an effective and safe way to give and receive feedback.

When you invest in learning more about yourself, you'll find things you want to change.

Handling Situations — Self-Management

Self-management is how you deal with circumstances after you have the self-awareness to understand how you're reacting, thinking. and feeling. You can't control how you initially feel and think about a situation, but you can control your actions and what you say. As a coach manager, this is a powerful thing to remember. Check out the nearby sidebar for an example.

The following looks at why self-management is so important to being an effective coach and some specific strategies you can use to better manage your reactions.

SELF-MANAGEMENT IN ACTION

Chris was a product engineer in a heavy manufacturing plant. His job required constant communication between different members of the team to collaborate on what the client needs. When I was introduced to Chris for emotional intelligence coaching, I asked him what he hoped to get out of it. He crossed his arms and said, "I think this is stuff is junk (not his words!). I tell it like it is, and I don't give a darn (not his words) if people don't like it. That's their problem!"

I listened and observed Chris getting worked up and defensive. I also knew that his temper and attitude had brought him to my attention. The HR director told me that Chris had a reputation for being difficult to work with and she wanted to see if I could help Chris change.

I could sense that Chris's values included being strong willed, practical, and honest. He wasn't into games, so I took a direct approach. "I get it that you're direct, but how is that working for you?" Chris was caught a little off-guard, but I could see I scored points by being equally direct. He said, "I know I can be too direct sometimes. Look, I wouldn't be here if it hasn't got me into trouble." I then suggested: "I want you to try something just once. The next time you feel upset or angered by someone, just don't do anything. Bite your tongue. And then report to me next time how it went." I knew that Chris would appreciate something action-oriented rather than a touchy-feely lecture about emotions.

The next time we met, Chris said he tried biting his tongue and was surprised by several things: He didn't have to deal with the drama of arguing with someone and getting stressed out; he quickly forgot what he was angry about; the issue naturally resolved itself by not doing anything; he wasn't endangering his employment by reacting in the moment. I then spent the rest of coaching session listening to him vent about other things in his life. At the end, I encouraged him to keep biting his tongue and letting me know how it's going. Over time, Chris became easier to work with, didn't explode as much, and felt better about work.

I talked about the different parts of the brain and how we feel things first. Chris was stuck in the feeling part of the brain that got angry and judgmental and the reptilian part of the brain that just went on attack. What I asked him to do was buy some time for himself to cool down, so he could think it through and use his rational brain. Biting his tongue wasn't his first reaction. It was intentional and applied through self-management.

Connecting self-management and coaching

Coaching is not just being clear about your expectations and asking good questions. It's creating an open and trusting environment for an employee to be honest and committed to their own success. Developing self-management strategies is important for your growth as a coach in several ways:

» You're able to catch yourself in reacting judgmentally or being overly critical and not saying or doing something that will undermine openness.

» You're able to engage your thinking brain to say the right things that are best for everyone, not just what's on your mind.

» You can catch those times when you're slipping into the doer manager role and trying to assert yourself from a position of authority instead of personal influence.

Implementing self-management strategies

Here are some simple but powerful strategies you can use right away to improve your self-management:

» **Understand your triggers.** You're human. Some people are more annoying than others. If you value promptness, people who are always late frustrate you. If you value innovation, people who shoot your ideas down aren't your buddies. Knowing what triggers you helps you factor in how to react to challenging situations. Knowing your work style and preferences can also help you adapt to specific situations. If you're not a morning person, avoid intense discussions first thing; if you don't like surprises, ask for agendas of meetings beforehand.

» **Give yourself a time-out.** If you're aware of your blood pressure rising or chest tightening during a conflict, find a way to give yourself a break, rather than react. Your fight-or-flight instinct can flood you with strong primal emotions, but they will pass if you give them time. Your emotions are temporary and change constantly. In the nearby sidebar example, Chris gave himself a time-out of sorts by biting his tongue. After he had a chance to sleep on it, he cooled down. In fact, he couldn't even remember what bothered him.

» **Remember to breathe.** When you breathe, you deliver oxygen to your brain. Without oxygen, your brain doesn't work well. Your ability to stay calm and rationale suffers with a lack of oxygen. During stress, your breathing often becomes shallow, depriving your brain of what it needs to manage your emotions. Take slow, deep breaths into your nose and out through your mouth to help you manage your most challenging emotions. Try it right now to see how it instantly relaxes you.

> » **Take care of yourself.** Leaders too often sacrifice their personal health to get everything done. They often work late, skip lunch, don't exercise, constantly check their phones, and don't take vacations. Your body is like a battery. You can't be focused, creative, patient, receptive, and productive when you're exhausted and stressed. Eating well, exercising, getting plenty of sleep along with unplugging from work is essential to self-management.

Relating Well to Others — Social-Awareness

Doer managers tend to be focused on work and projects rather than on relationships and people. Coaching managers understand that it's not one or the other. They understand that when you invest in better understanding and relating to employees, you build commitment and get better results. *Social awareness* is increasing your ability to tune into emotions and what might be going on with them: how they react to what you say, how much enthusiasm they exhibit, what their body language displays, what's on their minds, and what's important to them.

As humans, we tend to be self-centric and acutely aware of our needs. Social awareness is switching the focus to what others need to be happy, engaged, and committed to their jobs. People communicate their thoughts and feelings verbally and nonverbally. Social awareness is best practiced by learning to be an active listener.

The following sections explains the importance of developing your awareness of other people to being an effective coach and some specific strategies to improve it.

Linking social awareness and coaching

When you increase your ability to "read" people, you become more effective in coaching and mentoring in these powerful ways:

> » You can change your behavior in the moment based on what someone is saying through their words or body language.

> » People want to be understood above all else. When you learn to understand others, you build trust and engagement in the relationship.

>> Communication can be complex and subtle. You can say one thing and mean another thing. Your body can send different signals than the words you speak. You'll become better at deciphering all the data.

>> When you learn about people on a deeper level, you look beyond your initial assumptions and stereotypes into who they really are. Coaching and mentoring is most effective when they're based on understanding how people are unique and different.

The best place to begin building your social awareness is learning to listen to people. People have a fundamental need to be heard. Learn to be an active listener and you'll build a solid foundation for a relationship.

Encouraging two-way conversations — Active listening

To effectively facilitate a coaching discussion, you need to be an active listener, not a passive one:

>> In *passive listening* is when someone looks at you, sits quietly, and nods their head every now and then to indicate they have a pulse. Little response or interaction takes place. Passive listeners encourage one-way conversations.

>> In *active listening,* sometimes referred to as *reflective* or *responsive listening,* you work to draw out the speaker's message. More important, you provide nonjudgmental verbal feedback to check your understanding of the speaker's message — herein lies the real key to effective facilitation in a coaching discussion. So the focus is *not* on what you think of the other person's message, but on what the person really means. When you achieve this understanding, you're truly listening.

TIP

Active listening is being attentive and engaged in what someone is saying. Doer managers who are prone to interruptions and like to multitask aren't active listeners. It takes practice and discipline to be focused as a listener. Here are some tips:

>> **Clear out distractions.** Find a time and place, if you can, where you can listen without being distracted. If you're rushed for time, distracted, exhausted, or not feeling well, focusing will be difficult.

>> **Let people talk.** You may be tempted to want to solve someone's problem and jump in and cut them off before they've had a chance to talk. Let people talk. Be okay with not talking. Be comfortable with letting them pause and

think. The biggest gift you can give someone is letting them hear themselves. They can't do that if you're talking.

>> **Rephrase for meaning.** Try to capture the essence of what's someone said by paraphrasing rather than repeating. It helps both of you understand what is being communicated. Oftentimes, when people hear a summary of what they thought they said, they're surprised by what others heard. It gives them an opportunity to correct themselves to be clearer. Paraphrasing helps them.

>> **Drop your assumptions.** Active listening means you're practicing being present in the moment. You're focused on the conversation as it's happening. You aren't mentally recycling your past interactions with the person or not really listening because you have a different perspective. Holding on to negative feelings is natural, but doing so isn't helpful in when active listening and trying to understand what someone is communicating.

>> **Clear up confusion.** If your attention has drifted during a critical part of the conversation or the person isn't being clear in what they're trying to say, speak up. Ask them to restate something. Tell them you're confused. Apologize for getting distracted. Active listeners speak up when they get lost.

>> **Be curious.** One of your most important skills to develop is curiosity. As a coach, I'm constantly following my curiosity in a discussion, "That's interesting. Tell me more." "I'm not sure I understand." "What matters to you?" "How did you feel about that?" "Why did you make that choice?" Curiosity opens the doors to understanding people on a level that they may not even understand themselves.

>> **Reflect feelings.** "Sounds like what happened has caused you a good deal of frustration. Is that right?" When emotion, either positive or negative, is prevalent in a message, you can use reflecting feelings to check and show understanding of the emotional meaning in the speaker's message.

>> **Probe.** "Tell me more about how that idea might work." Probing is asking an open-ended question to draw out the speaker's thoughts, like you do when tutoring with questions, but you're also probing when you ask a follow-up question to take the message to a greater depth.

Listening with your eyes

People listen not just with their ears. They also get meaning from observing someone's body language. Body language never lies. The following can help you decipher what someone is telling you through their behavior:

>> **The swallow:** May mean nervousness or displeasure, as in "it's hard news to swallow."

- **The raised eyebrows:** May mean surprise or defensiveness.

- **The squint:** May mean they're confused or questioning what's been said.

- **The slight twitch of the mouth:** May mean discomfort of some news.

- **The stiffened posture:** May signal defensiveness.

- **The crossed arms:** May signal defensiveness or being closed or defiant.

- **Leaning forward:** May signal enthusiasm.

- **The smile or smirk:** May signal acceptance and liking.

- **The glazed look:** May signal disinterest.

- **Looking down or away:** May signal discomfort in a social setting.

- **Fidgeting fingers:** May signal nervousness.

TIP

You can improve your awareness of others by getting a mentor who can help you spot signs in body language and watch movies and television and try to guess how someone is feeling by their body language. If you're not sure what people are communicating, ask them.

EXAMPLE

Lisa and her partner, Bob, ran a commercial real estate brokerage firm. They had an opportunity to pitch a group of owners on hiring them to represent and sell their shopping center. They prepared a sales presentation based on what they understood to be important. Twenty minutes into the PowerPoint presentation, Lisa could see that the owners were bored and distracted. They slumped in their chairs and seemed inattentive. One started to yawn. The others had scowls. She could tell from their body language it wasn't going well. She stopped her presentation and said, "Okay, you don't seem like you're interested. So tell me, what are you interested in." Immediately, they sat up in their chairs, cleared their throats, and looked at each other as if they couldn't believe their disinterest was so obvious. One spoke up, "We're actually more concerned with the schedule of getting out as soon as we can from our obligation." Lisa and Bob switched direction immediately and talked about a plan to speed up the selling process. They won the business.

Reading body language effectively is about paying attention and then following your curiosity by asking questions or probing, based on what you're seeing.

Listening with your heart

When I presented to a conference last year on the importance of listening, a man offered up that people also listen with their hearts: "My wife tells me you look like you're listening, but I can tell you don't care what I'm saying." How many of you can identify with that observation?

EXAMPLE

A COACHING EQ CASE STUDY

I (Leo) worked with an engineer who managed a small team who was very clear about his boundaries. "This is a place of work. I'm not comfortable with getting into emotional issues at work." I asked him if it was a matter of being comfortable sharing his feelings. "With my wife and buddies, but not at work."

As a consequence, he appeared closed down and uncaring. People didn't come to him with their problems. On one hand, it worked fairly well: If you don't appear to care, people won't even bother sharing how they feel and you'll get more work done and get home on time! If you're a patient listener and let people talk, there's the potential it can monopolize your time. And if you're really empathetic, a line can form outside your door. But when people didn't come to him with project problems, he realized he was also out of the loop when it mattered. He wasn't sure how to strike a balance between caring and not caring. He felt wrong if he did and wrong if he didn't.

I then gave him an assignment that may seem overly simplistic, but surprisingly effective: Start each day at work by asking an innocuous question like, "How was your weekend?" This wasn't a big ask and so he did it. What he found over the course of five months was that by asking about little things that weren't too personal, things shifted for him. People started to see him as more approachable. They started to bring him in on issues they were having about real work on their projects. As he invested more time talking to people, they became more interesting to him. What started as an academic exercise became part of his daily routine of connecting with people in a way that he hadn't imagined. He learned, "It's not just asking once and checking the box but taking a genuine interest in their lives."

After he came to know someone's story, he'd ask about updates that showed he cared enough to remember the details of their last conversation — seeing how their son's first job was going, if they had finished a wood puzzle they were making for a granddaughter, or if the CAT scan had revealed any more cancer in their wife. "I'm not a big pet person, but for some people it's their world. Just because it's not important to me doesn't mean it's not really important to other people," he says. When people feel more connected on a personal level, working together is easier and smoother. "I've learned that by taking time to talk about personal things, they feel like a person rather than a number."

He had previously drawn a hard line between work and personal life. "I used to think of employees as resources. I valued them for how much they could produce and the quality of their plans," he says. That strategy served him as a manager but not as an effective leader.

The foundation of EQ is empathy, or the ability to put yourself in the place of someone else to better understand their thoughts and feelings. If you expand your view to include how others may perceive a situation, you can improve the outcome of an interaction. You move from a self-centered approach to an other-centered approach. When you consider how others feel and think about a situation and adapt your approach to include them, they feel acknowledged and respected, have a sense of ownership, work harder and longer, and produce better work. There's no need to micromanage for results when people are engaged and working to their full potential. If the connection between empathy and output is so strong, why is it so difficult for some people to embrace? One of the obstacles to greater empathy in the workplace is that some people draw a strong line between their professional and personal lives. Those who live on the left side of the brain tend to be more guarded and less open about their feelings, so it's difficult for them to hear someone else express theirs.

Leveraging Relationship Management

Relationship management is about how you leverage self-awareness, self-management, and social awareness to build and maintain strong relationships. When you're more aware of yourself and others, you're smarter about what to say and do in a variety of situations.

The following discusses the importance of making the right moves with employees and peers as well as some specific strategies that will keep your relationships strong.

Connecting coaching and relationship management

The foundation of effective coaching and mentoring is relationships. How well you manage your relationships with your employees will drive their motivation, engagement, and commitment. People remember how they're treated. If you treat your employees with respect and are clear in your communications, they'll exceed your expectations.

Keeping track of your interactions

If you want your employees to be respectful and professional to customers and their peers, take a close look at your own behavior. Chapter 4 stresses the importance of setting the right tone as a coach manager. What kind of example are you setting for your employees to follow? Do you gossip or demean people from time to time? Maybe you treat it like a joke. Watch yourself and your actions. Employees are more likely to do as you do rather than do as you say. Back up your talk by modeling the behavior you want to see in others.

Employees either learn to trust or distance themselves from you based on how well you manage the interactions you have with them. Your effectiveness as a coach is largely based on how you treat your employees. In Chapter 9, I (Leo) equate relationships to piggy banks. You build wealth by making deposits and not taking withdrawals. The same goes for people. When employees feel disregarded, disrespected, or ignored, they feel those actions as withdrawals in their emotional bank account. They aren't inclined to do their best work or show initiative.

On the other hand, if you take time with them and show you're interested, you're filling your accounts with employees with deposits. Here are some specific ways you can build trust and cooperation with employees by making more deposits than withdrawals in managing your relationships:

>> **Start conversations with questions.** Be curious about understanding people and situations rather than thinking you have all the answers. Self-awareness will help catch early signs you may be reacting without knowing all the facts. (See Chapter 11 for more on the power of good questions.)

>> **Be honest.** Just because you have the title of manager doesn't mean you have some superpower that other people don't possess. Be honest in managing your relationships that you're doing your best and don't always know the best path forward in any situation. Learn to take feedback well.

>> **Practice clarity.** Many managers don't like conflict so they avoid stating what needs to be said. Chapter 14 has some solid tips for sharing constructive feedback and being clear in your communications.

>> **Do what you say.** Doer managers may say they want to develop their staff, but they don't prioritize taking time to coach and mentor employees. Actions speak louder than words. When managers break coaching appointments or don't take the time, trust erodes. Chapter 3 stresses the importance of investing time in coaching employees by following through and doing what you say you're going to do.

Here I share an example of someone I (Leo) coached and how he developed stronger relationships with employees by applying what he learned by coaching him in EQ.

Case study #1: Terry

When I first met Terry, he was one in a team of eight emerging leaders in my leadership class. I was struck by his eagerness to learn. Here was someone who realized that he didn't have all the answers about leading people. Not knowing and being vulnerable enough to admit it turned out to be one of his greatest strengths.

Terry was one of the smartest and most competent architects I'd met. He was great at designing and executing every detail of a project. Clients loved him. He relied on two skills from his toolbox: work hard and control everything. He was convinced there was just one way of doing things: his way. After all, it had worked well up to this point in his career. But that was when he had his own boutique firm, could do whatever he wanted, and directed people to follow his orders. Not exactly an empowering place for new leaders who had ideas of their own.

When he moved to a larger firm, his job changed from doing to leading. He was told in his first review that while he was technically strong and great with clients, this job required him to grow his team. He needed to guide and coach them — a very different muscle for Terry. He had to let go of being the author of his own work but support and guide what others produced.

After two years of hard work I outlined, he was named principal. He said, "Once I realized my identity wasn't 100 percent defined by my technical skills, I found great satisfaction in helping my team grow. When I realized how powerful that was, it was the best feeling. Like giving gifts is better than receiving. Like feeding the hungry. Seeing what we can do together." His big reward at the top was seeing how far his influence had changed not only his team but himself.

Here's specifically what Terry did to use his newly developed EQ skills to make fewer withdrawals and more deposits in order to improve his relationships:

» Self-awareness:
- Became more aware of his own self-talk: "I'm right. You're wrong. You're too stupid to understand my point."
- Admitted he didn't have all the answers and was open to change and learning.
- Spent time reflecting on himself and his goals.
- Started seeing himself as others saw him.

>> **Self-management:**

- Started slowing down his fast-paced walking in the office so he looked more relaxed and accessible.

- Bit his tongue and stayed silent when he wanted to say what he was thinking.

- Took more deep breaths.

- Got a mentor to help him spot when he overreacted and gave him feedback.

>> **Social-awareness:**

- Stopped talking and listened more to what people had to say.

- Discussed how meetings went with his mentor to improve spotting body language

- Observed how employees performed when he stopped being the smartest person in the room.

>> **Relationship management:**

- Changed his thinking from himself to considering others.

- Made decisions based on what's in the best interests of the team.

- Praised people instead of criticizing them.

- Quick to admit when he would slip into his old habits.

Terry grew as a leader by paying attention and working on his EQ. I conducted a survey of how people felt about him prior to any training and after EQ coaching. Terry's scores dramatically jumped up by practicing.

EQ is a skill that can be developed over time. You can learn how to listen, communicate, and think strategically and be an effective coach and mentor.

EQ and the Five Pillars of Commitment

Developing your EQ is the single most powerful thing you can do to reinforce the *five pillars for building commitment* (see Chapter 4) and revisit this chapter as a foundation for all your coaching and mentoring:

>> **Focus:** EQ is all about focusing on what is happening in the moment and responding appropriately. The more you focus on learning about your

emotions and others, the more adept you'll become at managing interactions and building trusting relationships.

>> **Involvement:** People want to be seen and heard for who they are. When you increase your EQ, you're able to understand employees more clearly. And that leads to greater involvement and engagement among your employees.

>> **Development:** When you develop your EQ, you're modeling the importance that your employees should also develop their EQ. Team dynamics and performance increases when people learn about each other, respect others, listen to others, and manage themselves to work together and do the best work possible.

>> **Gratitude:** EQ is about strengthening your ability to communicate and relate to other people. The better you know your team members, the more appreciative they'll be that you see each of them as individuals.

>> **Accountability:** When people feel understood and respected, they do their best work. They don't need to be told to be more accountable; they have a greater sense of ownership and pride for the work they do.

Coaching and mentoring is about connecting with people. Building your EQ will help you bridge differences, overcome challenges, and engage people in their work.

2
Facing the Changing Workplace

Chapter **6**

Accepting Change

The only thing you can count on is that everything changes. This chapter walks you through the significant changes in the workplace in terms of technology, demographics, and culture. This chapter also help you adapt to the reality of constant change and understand how best to adapt to the needs of today's employees.

Understanding What Has Changed and What Will Change

Grasping how the world is constantly changing isn't easy when you're in the present moment. Looking back to see what life and work looked like in the past gives you a greater appreciation that change is real. And it prepares you to better grasp what lies ahead and the future. These sections look more closely as what life looked like and where we are headed.

Looking back 20 years

The first edition of this book was published in 2000, and a lot has happened in 20 years. To appreciate how much has changed, the following list focuses on a few things that are present today in society that didn't even exist 20 years ago:

>> **Shopping moves online.** You can get anything delivered to your door with a click, cheaper than most retailers, the next day with free shipping. Amazon rules the market, building massive distribution centers in urban areas, and college graduates work as drivers. Amazon's former CEO, Jeff Bezos, becomes one of the richest billionaires on the planet. Shopping malls are dying as consumers habits change.

>> **Everyone is an entrepreneur.** Airbnb revolutionizes the vacation rental business by creating a platform for anyone to rent their whole or part of their residence to complete strangers. Uber and Lyft make it possible for anyone to make a living driving their own car and giving people rides. Consumers rate their purchase decisions and rate companies on a star system for everyone to see. High school dropouts can make more money as social media influencers than people with MBAs.

>> **Smartphones rule.** Not only do phones allow people to call, but they also let people text, FaceTime, and send pictures that are so high quality, professional photographers use them instead of fancy SLR cameras. They hold people's calendars, emails, and applications for everything from learning how to play ukulele, navigating directions, and countless other productivity and mindless activities.

>> **Social consciousness becomes corporate.** MeToo, Black Lives Matters, and LGBTQ movements have made diversity and equity urgent priorities for hiring and training initiatives.

>> **Everything is in the cloud.** Work used to be done in an office on multiple machines and stored on disks and file cabinets. Now everything can be done anywhere on a portable laptop and stored in the cyberspace known cryptically as the *cloud*. Fear of saving information online has been replaced with acceptance by many.

>> **People work in their pajamas.** Policies covering dress codes have relaxed with a younger generation redefining business casual to include T-shirts and shorts. When the Covid pandemic forced people to work from home and meet through Zoom meetings, the dress code became even more casual. Dry cleaners saw a big dip in business.

>> **The world heats up.** Global warming and climate change take center stage around the world. The market for solar panels and electric cars has exploded. Hybrid cars are more present, and electric cars have made a serious dent in

replacing the combustible engine. Businesses embrace environmental responsibility, reducing their waste and moving into energy efficient buildings.

>> **Organic becomes mainstream.** Health-conscious shoppers can buy fresh, organic food. "Locally sourced" and "non-GMO" have become commonplace labels on packages along with a greater selection of gluten-free foods. Milk comes from soy and nuts, in addition to cows. Conventional supermarkets follow suit so even big box discount stores provide a great selection of healthy food.

>> **Google it.** Google, which launched in 1998, is part of the common language and habits of how to find any information: just "Google it." To learn how to fix a lawnmower, just search YouTube for an instructional video that someone in the world has created and uploaded for free.

>> **Social media permeates.** People don't bother calling one another but get updates from TikTok, Snapchat, Instagram, Facebook, Twitter, and other social media platforms. Everyone is a celebrity and can create their own accounts where they can document and share photos and videos of themselves. Disinformation becomes the norm as people rely on unsubstantiated social media outlets for their news and how they form their views.

>> **Independent contracting grows.** More companies reduce labor costs of providing a salary and benefits to full-time employees by having more work done by part-time employees and independent contractors — many of whom work in countries where labor is cheaper. With the Great Resignation, more employees are opting to work for themselves rather than full time for any one company.

I can go on, but you get the point. A lot of massive changes have shaped the world and how people interact with each other, how they eat, how they drive, where they sleep, what they eat, and how they make a living.

Fast forwarding 20 years: What the future holds

Looking forward what can you expect? How can you prepare yourself? Here are some predictions for society and the workplace:

>> **Whites will be the minority.** The 2020 U.S. Census data projects that the nation will become "minority white" in 2045. Whites will comprise 49.7 percent of the population in contrast to 24.6 percent for Hispanics, 13.1 percent for Blacks, 7.9 percent for Asians, and 3.8 percent for multi-racial populations.

>> **People will live longer and work longer.** Advancements in medicine and health will keep people alive and healthy longer. People will continue to reinvent themselves past the traditional 65 retirement age, either because they can't afford not to work or they want to stay engaged longer.

>> **Technology will replace workers.** Artificial intelligence and advanced technology will replace workers as well as create new opportunities.

>> **The workforce will become more global.** Outsourcing, remote workers, and contractors from anywhere in the world will continue to shift the traditional concept of full-time employees working at the same office at the same time.

To understand how quickly things are changing, just look at the last few years.

Recognizing How Covid-19 Changed the Way People Work

Nothing could prepare people for what happened in 2020. The entire world raced to understand what the Covid-19 pandemic was and what kind of precautions to take. Businesses closed. People stayed home. People stayed away from each other. People wore masks. Mass vaccinations became available. Many took it seriously. Some thought it was a hoax. By June 1, 2022, the United States had recorded nearly 85 million Covid-19 infections and more than a million deaths. The impact continues to live on in the following ways:

>> **Uncertainty:** Even as people and businesses return to some form of normal, it's not certain what the future holds and whether another strain isn't lurking somewhere that will become a new pandemic.

>> **Alienation and stress:** When people suffer through a health crisis that disrupts schedules, social connections, and rhythms of their lives, they can feel overwhelmed and stressed. The World Health Organization (WHO) categorized employee burnout as an "occupational phenomenon" in 2019.

>> **Caregivers:** Social distancing impacted every part of people's lives and placed a greater burden on caregivers. Parents had to accommodate their work schedules to home school their children, who had to stay at home. Family members who became ill had to be quarantined inside the home. Caregivers for elderly parents had to take extra measures to ensure their safety. All of this happened while trying to get their work done.

>> **Hospitality's hit:** Businesses that relied on social interaction — restaurants, entertainment venues, professional services, and travel — were particularly hard hit. And businesses that supported those businesses were equally impacted and struggle to rebound.

>> **People quitting:** For a variety of reasons, greater numbers of people are leaving their jobs since the pandemic, in what's being called the Great Resignation. According to the Bureau of Labor and Statistics, in 2021, 47.8 million workers quit their jobs, an average of nearly 4 million each month, meaning 2021 holds the highest average on record, topping the 2019 average of 3.5 million. Nearly 80 percent of those who exited the workforce were women.

REMEMBER

To successfully grow from a doer to coach/mentor, you need to understand that not only are these challenging times, but the future isn't likely to get any easier. What does this mean for your development? What's important to keep in mind that will help you navigate the challenges?

IN THE BLINK OF AN EYE

Change isn't always slow and incremental. If you track how rapidly the Covid-19 virus spread, you can grasp that cataclysmic change can come at any time. No one could have anticipated what happened in a few short months. The lesson here is to remain nimble and adaptive to unplanned events. The Centers for Disease Control documented the outbreak of Covid-19 pandemic: www.cdc.gov/museum/timeline/covid19.html — :~:text=January 10, 2020,-nCoV) on its website.

In just three short months in 2020:

- **February 11:** The World Health Organization (WHO) announces the official name for the disease that is causing the 2019 novel coronavirus outbreak: Covid-19. The new name of this disease is an abbreviated version of *coronavirus disease 2019*.

- **March 15:** States begin to implement shutdowns in order to prevent the spread of Covid-19. The New York City public school system — the largest school system in the United States, with 1.1 million students — shuts down, while Ohio calls for restaurants and bars to close.

- **April 4:** More than 1 million cases of Covid-19 had been confirmed worldwide, a more than tenfold increase in less than a month.

Embracing Change

Flexibility is the key to embracing all these challenges. What you thought was true yesterday may not be true tomorrow. The only thing you can count on is that things will change. As the Greek philosopher Heraclitus said, "No man steps in the same river twice."

TIP

As you're finding out how to be a coach or mentor, keep these things in mind:

>> **People have a lot on their minds.** People have had to worry about their own mortality and the health of family and friends. Relationships have been strained and people don't leave those worries at home when they show up. Employees' minds are not only on their jobs.

>> **Uncertainty and disruption take its toll.** For many people, the sense of security and certainty have been forever altered. They don't feel like they can count on much these days, which makes it hard for them to have the energy, focus, and enthusiasm for their jobs.

>> **People are exercising their options.** People have a greater sense of urgency. Because they can't count on much and life is short, they feel empowered to make bolder, riskier moves in their career. They may feel more inclined to start working for themselves, take an indefinite break, work more than one job, switch careers, change companies, try another job temporarily, or job share. Uncertainty and fear have emboldened people to take more chances. If they aren't getting enough direction, feedback, and support, they may try something else.

>> **Social values mean more.** More people, particularly younger people, only want to work at places that are aligned with their values and champion social justice, equity, inclusion, and climate change. The George Floyd murder and Black Lives Matter movement ignited social justice as a defining event for many younger people. They actively seek workplaces that are committed to diversity, equity, and inclusion and business practices that align with creating a healthy planet.

REMEMBER

If you add up everything, you can see that the challenges of work aren't just isolated to not having enough time to do a task or not knowing how to give someone negative feedback. People need help to manage both work and life. You can play a critical role by giving people support and direction. And when you do that, you also play a pivotal role in recruiting and retaining talent, which helps your organization be more productive and profitable.

Designing for a Changing Workplace

Change is inevitable. Being flexible and open to change is the key to working with it, instead of fighting it. This philosophy is just as important in successfully coaching and mentoring a diverse workforce. What does today's workplace look like to reflect today's realities? I (Leo) took a tour of a client's new office to get a glimpse.

EXAMPLE

Tim Ganey heads the Portland Oregon office of DLR Group, a national integrated design firm. Three years ago, things were different: The office of 50 people was crammed together in a downtown office building. They had just signed a lease to move into a new space, which would need extensive remodeling. Business was good, the firm was growing, and everything looked promising. And then Covid hit.

Like everyone else during the pandemic, all their employees worked from home. The work never went away and the firm still remained profitable. With people working from home, it bought time to leave their old space and design and build out their new space. The design firm works with a variety of clients, including several global technology companies, who were also trying to adapt their work environments for a hybrid environment where many people wanted to work from home.

If you walk through DLR Group's new office, here's what you'll find:

>> **The floor plan is open.** The design team wanted to build in flexibility into the entire design. Few of the walls are fixed, so spaces can be changed as needs change. If people find they need more room, a mobile partition can be moved. As more employees return to the office and want more privacy, DLR Group is adding office phone booths as needed for quieter videoconferencing.

>> **All the furniture and workstations are modular.** Right now, some desks are strategically located six feet apart from each other. As people's comfort levels change, there's the opportunity to increase density by moving the desks closer. The design accommodates the shifting needs and preferences of their employees.

>> **Working remote is an option.** DLR Group is currently working within a hybrid model where some people elect to work from home on certain days whereas others prefer the office environment. Some studies have shown that people aren't as productive and efficient working from home. DLR wants to encourage collaboration with a flexible policy that allows people to work

from home while also coming into the office for at least three days a week, understanding that the policy could change in the future to respond to a changing world.

» **People have dedicated workspaces.** Some offices opt for *free or hot-desk workstations* where people don't have an assigned desk. Workstations are based on staff input, and the design team created a model where the majority of workstations are dedicated and a few are unassigned. In addition, people can work on a laptop in many alternative communal spaces in the office — again, giving people flexibility.

» **The areas are collaborative.** Tim points to the folding partitions, soft chairs, and teleconference equipment and smart boards that make it easy for people to gather and share ideas, whether they're in the office or working remotely. Creative types and many younger employees enjoy working closely with other people — something that's really suffered through the pandemic. The solution ultimately provides the ability to collaborate in-person and/or virtually with the same or different project teams by leveraging technology, blending digital and analog workflow.

» **The office includes areas for social gatherings.** To help make the office more inviting, workers can gather, eat, drink, and socialize in bright, casual places. There is a dedicated room for working mothers, as well as a workout area, and a wall for employees to hang their bikes.

Ganey says that more people are coming back into the office. Working from home has its challenges with video fatigue, lack of social connection with peers, and the tendency to blur work and living, where many employees end up working odd hours.

The design reflects the changing needs of today's workplace in several significant ways:

» The space is designed to adapt to changes in how people work and interact. An emphasis on modular and changeable fixtures allows for maximum flexibility.

» The designers understood that workspaces need to be more than just work. Creating a fun and inviting environment for connection and collaboration was a critical factor in the design.

» The design acknowledged that employees have choices in who they work for and listening and accommodating the needs of employees is key to retaining them.

Looking at Change and the Pillars of Commitment

Here is how change affects each of the five pillars for building employee commitment (see Chapter 4):

>> **Focus:** Begin by understanding that times are challenging and it's difficult for people to always focus and bring their best efforts when they're weighed down by other demands in their lives. If you bring empathy to your role as coach, you build trust and commitment.

>> **Involvement:** When you work with an employee, you come up with solutions that work for both of you. By being flexible and open-minded, the employee feels heard and respected.

>> **Development:** Just as you're learning to embrace and adapt to change, your employee needs to learn to adapt to shifting situations and priorities. Adapting to change and staying focused on the goals is a key to developing as a leader. You're setting an example for your employee by modeling the behavior.

>> **Gratitude:** The gratitude pillar is strengthened when you genuinely care about your employees. They'll be grateful for the support, which builds loyalty to you and the company.

>> **Accountability:** This doesn't mean you can't hold people accountable. Your arrangements need to be clearly articulated and revisited. If your policy states the expectation of coming in three days a week, state why that's important for everyone to support.

IN THIS CHAPTER

» **Seeing what diversity means**

» **Exploring unconscious bias**

» **Breaking down DEI**

» **Coaching individual differences**

» **Focusing on the issues of performance to manage — and behaviors not to tolerate**

Chapter **7**

Coaching for Diversity

S ince this book was first published more than 20 years ago, no one chapter needed more updating than this chapter on diversity. Although the advice was solid, people's understanding of what diversity in the workplace has grown exponentially. With a rapidly changing workforce and a big push for companies to be more inclusive of minorities and underrepresented groups, diversity has gone from a back-burner topic to a front-burner focus in a few short years.

For people who have felt left out of opportunities, it's about time. For those who have traditionally held positions of authority and are trying to catch up, diversity can feel like a lot all at once to absorb. What's the right term? How should you feel? What do you call people? How can I be respectful and get work done?

This chapter demystifies common terms like diversity, equity, and inclusion and finds a practical, grounded way to coach and mentor every employee so they feel like they can be themselves and contribute fully.

Defining Diversity

Diversity means difference or variety. Put two people in a room together and you have diversity. No two people are exactly alike. The ways in which people are unique are limitless.

Diversity goes beyond race, color, ethnicity, and gender though. Organizations that are trying to be diverse by recruiting and hiring more women and non-white people are missing the larger concept. Diversity is a much bigger idea and more nuanced than you might think.

The first step in understanding diversity is examining the different ways people perceive differences in each other. The following sections illustrate the importance of forming perceptions.

Seeing the entire iceberg

Dr. Shirley Davis, author of *Diversity, Equity, and Inclusion For Dummies* (John Wiley & Sons, Inc.), compares diversity to an iceberg. Scientists say that 90 percent of an iceberg is beneath the surface — invisible to the naked eye. You can only see the 10 percent of the iceberg that's above the waterline. Similarly, you can only see 10 percent of what makes people diverse when they're perceived by what you can see. The rest of what makes people unique is below the surface. Figure 7-1 shows how much of people's common perceptions of others only focuses on the small part that can be seen initially.

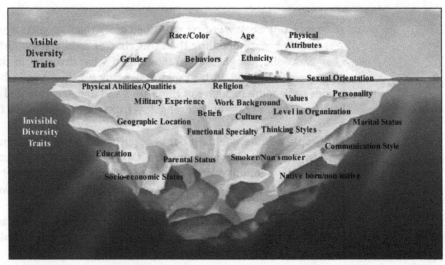

FIGURE 7-1: Just like an iceberg, most diversity traits are below the surface.

Courtesy of Dr. Shirley Davis

Do people really judge others just by what they see? To drive this point home, look at the research to understand people's reliance on what they see and provide some common examples that will make the point clearer. People send and receive information to each other in three ways:

- **» Visual:** What's conveyed through someone's body language

- **» Voice:** What conveyed through the sound of someone's voice

- **» Verbal:** What conveyed through the words someone uses

What form of communication has the biggest impact on people? Research has shown that people pay attention to body language more heavily than what someone says or how they say it. It turns out people pay more attention to what they see than what they hear. Professional actors and politicians have figured this out a long time ago and are very aware of their posture, expressions, gestures, and eye contact in convincing an audience.

The fact that much of people's perceptions of others is based on what they see supports Davis's iceberg analogy (see the previous section). You are hard-wired to interpret the world and quickly size up people with your eyes. Follow the story in the nearby sidebar to see if it hits home.

EXAMPLE

MISSING EVERYTHING BELOW THE ICEBERG

Dani has been set up on a blind date, but she knows absolutely nothing about him. They arrange through text to meet at a coffee shop. Dani arrives early at the coffee shop and waits expectedly, watching every man who walks through the door. Finally, a man comes through the door who is about her age and is quickly scanning the room. In about three seconds, Dani has quickly assessed what she can see:

- Attractiveness

- Dress

- Face and eyes

- Hair

- Height

- Physical condition

- Posture

- Race

- Weight

(continued)

(continued)

Generally positive — she's not sure about those shoes — and he hasn't even come to the table! She's looking how he walks across the room, how he carries himself and his overall energy: excited, a bit tentative. Dani shakes his hand and wishes his palms were drier and his handshake firmer. She now has an opportunity to look more closely at his face, smile, and eyes. He seems not altogether present and distracted. And he hasn't even opened his mouth!

When he does begin to talk, Dani focusses on the sound of his voice, the volume, the speed, the tone, the clarity, and whether he has an accent. Slightly nasal and higher than she likes. Dani hasn't heard a word he's said. It's all white noise because in a matter of a few short minutes she's formed a strong opinion on whether or not there's going to be a second date.

What Dani's missing is that her date has been doing the same assessment of her. After all, it's not just up to her if there's going to be a second date!

What Dani did is focus almost entirely on the top of the iceberg — only the part she could see. As Davis says, that's only a very small part of who people are as individuals. If you weight your perceptions of people mostly on what you see, you miss all the other parts that make people different, special, and interesting.

What if Dani had first connected with her blind date through email and then through the phone? She might have started by focusing on the content of his words, what he valued, what he believed, and what kind of person he is through his responses to questions and stories he shared. Without the heavy filter of visual information, Dani would have focused on getting to know her date as a whole person, not just on the 10 percent she first saw.

Leaving your judgments at the door

Humans are hard-wired biologically to quickly judge situations and people with our eyes. Our early ancestors stayed alive by visually scanning for threats. And in a way, people are still doing that — looking to avoid danger and find safety all around them. I (Leo) was walking down the street one day when a young woman with a glazed, frantic look started running toward me. My first impulse wasn't to get to know her better, to find out more about the 90 percent of the iceberg I couldn't see. My number one goal was to make sure she didn't mean me any harm. She was having a rough day, strung out on drugs. I was able to defuse the situation and move on, but it took some quick thinking to assess and manage that safely.

REMEMBER

Despite the best intentions, each person will form a quick judgment about everyone they meet — both positively and negatively. That's not a bad thing. How does that apply to what you're trying to do here — to be good coaches and mentors and to motivate and engage employees to fit in and bring their best efforts? You need to ensure your first impressions and reactions don't keep you from prematurely judging people you manage. Your employees need to feel comfortable approaching you for questions, direction, and support. If your intention is to listen, empathize, and support employees, your judgments, while natural, may not help you do that.

Inviting Others to the Party

We tend to be attracted and comfortable with people who look like us, act like us, and believe the same things we do. People are tribal by nature, seeking community based on our similarities. I (Leo) have been part of a poker group for more than 20 years. We share a lot: white, older than 60, married, college educated, mostly retired from professional careers (except me!), comfortably middle class, left leaning politically, mostly atheist/agnostic, and dads — our sons grew up together. We like good beer and food, like to garden, and enjoy similar music. We reminisce about concerts we attended, lousy jobs we had, and memorable poker hands from past games. We update each other on how our 30-some children are doing, what kind of season the Portland Trailblazers will have, and upcoming colonoscopies. Our common backgrounds and experiences bind us together.

Over the years, we've had different people drop into our games: Duc, a 40-year-old single web designer, originally from Thailand, single, rode a motorcycle, taught us some new games we still play; Murry, an 85-year-old retiree, Jewish from Brooklyn and resident of a senior center in Florida, a widow, taught us some good jokes and that you're never too old to play poker with the boys; Dan, 60ish, drummer in a band, married, no kids, walks with a prosthetic leg taught us you only need enough money to be part of our game.

There's nothing wrong with finding your tribe whether it's a LGBTQ punk band or a Republican women's knitting group. It's natural, but tribalism can keep us isolated and resistant to learning about others and letting them in. Social media and political battling don't help. The world and workforce are increasingly becoming more diverse and less tolerant of diversity, at the same time. When the world is full of threats and uncertainty, people find safety in sticking to their tribes. There's safety in numbers.

REMEMBER

The question is what role will you play? How will you adapt to it and contribute? As a coach and mentor, you have influence in how team members interaction—much like a volleyball coach sets the tone for the team. By virtue of your position, you're a role model. Employees are looking at you for cues. If you've accepted the job of coach and mentor, it's your responsibility to make sure everyone gets to play and participate. Understanding what might keep people off the court is an important first step.

To be an effective coach and mentor for others, start by looking at yourself. The following helps you become more aware of the thoughts and feelings that may be barriers to be open and understanding of other people.

Letting go of unconscious bias

Chapter 5 stresses the importance of building your emotional intelligence as a foundation in becoming an effective coach and mentor. And the first and most powerful way to do that is to know yourself by improving your self-awareness, particularly those thoughts, feelings, and behaviors that you're not even aware of.

REMEMBER

Unconscious bias (also referred to as *implicit bias*) is an opinion, positive or negative, that you have about a group or person that you may not even know you hold. Because it's unconscious, you're often not even aware of your opinion or judgment. Bias is an inclination that results in judgment without question, often based on incomplete or inaccurate information. On one hand, quick judgment without question can protect you from dangerous situations. But if you hold on to the judgment without question, it can negatively impact your ability to understand, relate, and interact with people on your team.

Bias is natural. People make judgments all the time. Was I biased toward the stranger on the sidewalk? Absolutely. Am I biased toward my poker group? You bet. People make judgments each time they have to choose a middle seat on a plane. People are biased against the young woman with a crying baby and biased in favor of the young woman who seems content to listen to her headset. When bias is about your physical safety and health, bias is useful. When bias is based on other factors, it's smart to be aware of what's going on in your brain.

Table 7-1 looks at ten common biases from Davis's book, *Diversity, Equity, & Inclusion For Dummies.*

TABLE 7-1

Ten Common Biases

Name	Definition	Example
Affinity bias	A tendency to be drawn to people who remind you of yourself	Jake, a father of two, finds it much easier to make small talk in the break room with Mary, who has children close to the same age as Jake's, by asking about her kids' activities. He finds it much more difficult to connect with Julian, a single gay man with no kids who just moved to a hip neighborhood downtown.
Anchoring bias	An inclination to rely too heavily on one piece of information	Melanie is working on performance appraisals for three of her team members. This is a fast-paced office filled with ambitious, hard-working people. Like nearly everyone else on her team, Philip and Samir usually log an average of 60 hours a week on their timecards, while Janice rarely logs more than 45 and never more than 50. Even though Janice always works a full-time schedule or more, Melanie wonders whether she's pulling her weight.
Attribution bias	Giving dominant identities (such white, male, straight, and able-bodied) more credit for their accomplishments and less blame for their mistakes	Karen works on a project team with all males. When she shares her ideas with excitement or she shares her disagreement in a passionate way, she is told by her male peers to stop being so emotional. When her male counterparts share the same excitement or vehemently disagree about an approach taken on a project, nothing is said. When it came time for performance reviews, that same feedback showed up on her review.
Confirmation bias	Favoring data that supports a pre-existing conclusion over data that invalidates that conclusion	Sehr usually hires people from Ivy League schools but, under pressure from her boss, took a chance on Adam, who graduated from a state university nearby. Adam has done great work during the past 12 months, and most of his clients really like him. But when one client complained that his work sometimes lacked the polish of his peers, Sehr declined to give Adam the promotion that most new employees receive after their first year.
Negativity bias	The tendency to pay more attention to negative data than positive data	Donald is finishing up Victoria's performance appraisal for the past 12 months. Victoria's projects throughout the year were consistently on time, well under budget, and executed with high quality. But Donald can't stop thinking about her poor choice of words when speaking to a journalist six months ago, which earned the company some bad press in an industry journal. Under the category of "Excellence," Donald rates Victoria as "Fair."
Performance bias	Judging people from dominant groups (for example, white, male, heterosexual, or able-bodied) based on potential, while judging others solely based on accomplishments	During a calibration meeting, Marceline starts to notice that all the young men who are up for promotion are described with aspirational phrases like "I think he'd be really good at that" or general descriptors like "very bright" or "solid work ethic." However, when it's time to evaluate a young woman's performance, questions arise, such as "Has she done this kind of work before?" Often, the women's promotions are put off for another year until they can prove themselves worthy.

(continued)

TABLE 7-1 *(continued)*

Name	Definition	Example
Priming effect	Altering your reaction to current stimuli based on exposure to previous stimuli	Before a presentation on the company's performance the prior year, Monica overhears a vice president say that the company "only exceeded our target by 5 percent" in a resigned tone. Meanwhile, Jourdain is told by another senior executive that "not only did we meet our goals, but we exceeded them by an incredible 5 percent margin!" When sitting together in the presentation and the data is revealed, Jourdain wonders why Monica isn't more excited by the good news.
Recency bias	The ability to recall events in the recent past more readily than those that took place some time ago	Rashid tends to procrastinate when filling out performance appraisals, a task he dislikes. His report on Shilpa, a member of his team, is due tomorrow. He quickly fills out the Summary section, noting the three most recent projects she has worked on. He neglects to review the self-appraisal she has submitted, which outlines in detail an enormous success that she orchestrated nine months ago, a project that doesn't appear in Rashid's finished report.
Stereotype threat	The tendency to typecast yourself based on common beliefs about your group identities	Sonya is the only woman in her team of five. Whenever her boss, Roger, asks for a volunteer to take notes during meetings, all eyes turn to Sonya. She knows that the stereotype women are expected to exhibit is supportive, nurturing, and communal teammates as opposed to strong, dynamic, assertive leaders. Because of this, she doesn't want to be pigeonholed as the note-taker and, like the others, remains silent. But when Roger asks her directly, she fears that refusing to take notes will give the impression that she isn't a good team player. After a long silence, she says, "Sure, no problem."
Urgency bias	The inclination to focus on work with high short-term impact even at the expense of more meaningful work, with long-term consequences	Grace, who leads the events team for a large association known for its annual conference each year, has just received some upsetting news. Tameka, her deputy conference manager, has been urged by her doctor to apply for long-term disability effective immediately, and the conference is happening in two weeks. No one else on the team can fill Tameka's shoes in that time. Grace begs her HR director to skip some of the steps in the typical recruiting process. "You don't understand," she says. "I need another Tameka, and I need her yesterday."

To help understand your own bias, try asking yourself:

>> What pattern am I seeing in my thoughts, feelings, and reactions?

>> Where did this bias come from?

>> Does this person or situation remind me of something from my past?

>> Am I being influenced by one of my group identities or tribes?

Bringing home bias

Bias is natural and shows up all around us. There's been a great deal of attention on helping white males, who are often in positions of power, become more aware and appreciative of diversity. That's critical to making the workplace more inclusive. Seeing how pervasive bias in every population helps us understand it's a more universal challenge.

Leo shares this insight: My barber is a 60-year-old woman, who was born in Taiwan and has lived in the United States since her 20s. I sat down to get a haircut one day and she was livid about her last customer: a 13-year-old boy who had recently immigrated from Iran with his family and knew very little English. "How am I supposed to understand how to cut his hair. If you come here, try to learn the language!" she said angrily in her own broken English and heavy accent. Intolerance toward someone who isn't like you is a historical and universal phenomenon, not just a problem in the American workplace.

Marty shares this insight: Think back to times when you entered a situation, and, for whatever reason, you felt different than the other people involved. Write down the feelings that you had about being different in those situations. Having done this exercise with many people through the years, I've found that the vast majority respond with comments such as these: strange, isolated, apprehensive, inhibited, awkward, and uncomfortable. What do these feelings have in common? They all have negative connotations. In fact, say the word "different" or "differences" and, more often than not, people have a negative reaction to it.

If you try to pretend you don't have negative feelings, you're not being honest with yourself. Understanding and managing your bias is a tricky, long-term project — not a quick-fix.

Understanding what DEI is

DEI stands for diversity, equity, and inclusion. You may have heard of it or even attended a seminar. Here's what it means:

>> **Diversity:** It includes race, gender, age, but can also include diversity of physical abilities, skills, aptitudes, experience, values, and communication styles. It's the whole iceberg — both what you can see and what you can't. Understanding and celebrating diversity is essential to building strong relationships with people who are different from you.

>> **Equity:** It's a process of leveling the playing field so that everyone has equal access to the same opportunities. Historically, not all demographics or groups have had the same opportunity. Equity is ensuring that all employees are

treated equally and not discriminated against. Equity isn't about giving certain groups special privileges, but understanding that people have different needs. Coaching and mentoring can be a great resource for an employee who wants to fit into the organization but is struggling from no fault of their own.

>> **Inclusion:** It's the environment people work in. Do they feel valued, respected, and included? You can have a very diverse workforce that doesn't work very well together. As a manager your tone, actions, and words set the stage and mood for the kind of place you want to create. The more understanding you can be, the more effective you'll be as a coach and mentor and model for others.

We may be different in many ways, but we are united in wanting:

>> To be treated with respect

>> To feel included and part of a team

>> The same kinds of opportunity and support to be successful in our jobs

That's your job as a coach and mentor, no matter what it looks like.

THE INVISIBLE 90 PERCENT

Coaching and mentoring requires an investment to know employees on a deeper level, as this case study illustrates.

Diversity is not just what you see; it's all the other stuff beneath the waterline. As a coach or mentor, you can only help people be their best when you know them in all the ways that make them unique. This bears repeating: There is no one-size-fits-all approach to coaching and mentoring. Building your emotional intelligence is your single best strategy to your growth and success (see Chapter 5).

Look at just two employees, who are of the same age, gender, and race. They could even wear each other's clothes.

• **Joe:** He's quiet, reserved, and likes to work uninterrupted. He lives alone with his cat, spends his spare time playing online video games, and thinks the pandemic was actually a blessing. He prefers to work at home and stay to himself. He started with the company after graduation, and he's never had another job. As a project engineer, he's very reliable and thorough. He's constantly being brought in on projects to share his historical knowledge. On the other hand, he can be difficult to work with because he doesn't like innovation and is critical to new ideas. He favors solutions and approaches that are tried and true. He doesn't tend to voice his views, but instead he'll protest by sending snarky emails shooting down ideas or quietly protest by putting off projects.

As a coach, you're trying to get the best out of Joe and stretch him as a project engineer. You want him to take more risks or at least verbally present his point of view so others can understand he's not trying to be difficult. You also want him to come into the office to interact with the team, even though that's not his preference. He's resistant to coaching because he doesn't think he has a problem.

- **Jack:** Jack is another project manager on your team. He's the opposite of Joe: He thrives interacting with people, bouncing ideas off each other, sharing stories, and laughing. He's married with three young kids. The pandemic wasn't a blessing — it was stressful to coordinate childcare/education, social connections were compromised, and he really missed interacting with colleagues in the office. His work suffered. He felt drained and overwhelmed and didn't bring his best work. Jack's isn't the best technical project manager, but he's great at bringing people together and motivating them. His nickname "Sparky" describes his personality: bigger than life, enthusiastic, and positive. He's always the first person to sign up for any communication course, even though he could probably teach it.

As a coach, you're trying to get the best out of Jack by helping him get back on his feet. As a positive, can-do personal, Jack is just trying to work harder to get back to his old self. He doesn't know how to say no because he hates letting people down. He's resistant to taking care of himself, even though that's what he needs to do.

The quiet contributor and the sparkplug. Both invaluable members of your team in their own diverse ways. Both wildly diverse in other ways:

- Communication style
- Emotional intelligence
- Home/hobbies
- Marital status
- Parental status
- Personality
- Political beliefs
- Work challenges
- Work style

The key is to get to know people and their stories — to take an interest in them and be curious about what you don't know.

Being Aware of Assumptions — Trouble Ahead

An *assumption* is something that's accepted as true and as fact without being proved or demonstrated. Although assumptions may sometimes be useful because they help people make educated guesses when needed, they can also lead to big problems. You've probably heard the old line about what happens when you assume something: You make a derriere out of you and me, or something like that. When you act on an assumption before checking out the truth, even with something as simple as finishing someone else's sentence before the message is complete, you increase the potential for misunderstandings and destructive conflicts.

TIP

In fact, four assumptions that people commonly make are guaranteed to cause friction and hinder productivity if you act upon them as you manage your staff. The following sections explore four types of assumptions in depth so that you can steer clear of them.

REMEMBER

Coaching focuses on people's capabilities and performances, which is key to managing diversity. But before you can focus on capabilities and performances, you have to push your assumptions aside.

Assumption one: Stereotyping

Stereotyping ignores and dismisses individual differences that make everyone unique from one another. Instead, it assigns a prescribed set of behaviors to everyone in a particular group based on personal background, physical attributes, or occupation.

>> **Personal background:** Personal background can include race, ethnicity, gender, religion, sexual orientation, age, or physical abilities and disabilities. When you stereotype, you imagine that all the people of a similar personal background are relatively the same in their thoughts and behaviors.

>> **Physical attributes:** No one person represents thousands or millions of people just because of a shared physical attribute. Although some people may argue that you can find similarities among groups to form a stereotype, doing so can lead to thinking that all people of a particular group fit a certain mold based on certain attributes, not on their capabilities.

>> **Occupation:** Another example of stereotyping is categorizing how people think and act based on their occupation — for example, "All engineers are this way, and all salespeople are that way." Again, even though similarities exist, so do plenty of differences about the people who do these and every other kind of job.

Assumption two: Setting low expectations

The assumption of low expectations builds from generalizing from one specific situation. People often act out this assumption with comments such as, "We hired one person like that once before, and they didn't work out." "Younger employees are so needy." One individual is used to represent countless others, so no one of this group is given the opportunity to succeed or fail on his or her merits.

By the same measure, the opposite can be true. You can set high expectations of a group based on a limited sample. "If you want to get the job done right, always hire a person from this group." Supporting or favoring specific groups over another can blind you to who's really capable and keep qualified, motivated people outside the group from getting a chance.

Assumption three: Believing that differences are negative

This assumption deems that those of a different group have nothing in common with you or that they're too difficult to ever understand, let alone appreciate or respect.

This assumption implies that differences, especially those that you can see, are negative — they're strange, wrong, or harmful. This assumption can result either in individuals verbally attacking the one seen as different or in individuals timidly backing away from the "other," leaving them feeling isolated or excluded.

Assumption four: Equating sameness with equality

This assumption takes for granted that managing everyone the same way is equivalent to managing people with equality and consistency. However, managing all the staff the same way isn't the same as managing them equally. The problem with this assumption is that it ignores individual needs and differences.

REMEMBER

Managing people equally and consistently means that you afford everyone respect, hold everyone to a high standard of performance, and give everyone the guidance and support they need to perform successfully. So, you treat everyone equally in terms of your management *efforts*, but not necessarily the same in terms of how you *apply* those efforts.

For example, a new employee will need closer guidance than a skilled veteran. Some employees need more frequent feedback on how they're performing than others do.

Employees have different needs to achieve job success and are at different levels of skill and experience. If you try to manage them all the same way — using a one-size-fits-all management style — the chance that you may induce employee failure is greater than the chance that you may stimulate success.

ONE STYLE DOESN'T FIT ALL

The following is a story that serves as a lesson about assumptions. It helps illustrate the dangers of managing everyone the same way and assuming that approach is the best way to deal with your staff.

Maria got her first promotion into management a year ago. The management style of her boss, John, was to tell people what to expect and then let them get the job done — a sort of sink-or-swim-on-your-own style. Maria inherited a challenging situation: She was expected to lead her group in developing and implementing some system and process changes designed to increase efficiency.

Maria's group wasn't an easy one to manage. Many members had been in the organization for a while and were quite comfortable with the status quo, so she faced resistance to the changes she needed to make happen. In addition, Maria came from the ranks of her peers, and some in the group resented the fact that she was promoted over them. All of her peers were men. Maria tried not to read too much into being treated differently, but she couldn't help but notice her peers socialized at work and went to lunch together. Whenever she showed up, they grew silent and went back to work. During meetings, her presentations were often met with folded arms and eye rolling.

John managed three other managers in addition to Maria. These three individuals — Mike, Willie, and Hector — were experienced supervisors who ran efficient and stable operations that required little change. Outside of the occasional check-in with each manager to gauge progress and a monthly staff meeting, John let his managers run on their own with little guidance.

However, this style didn't help Maria deal with her ever-mounting management challenges. The more she came to John to seek support, mentoring, and resources, the more John reacted with disinterest and annoyance. The more John heard the resistance that came out of Maria's group, the more he told Maria that she needed to learn how to handle her problems better — and hold the line on costs, too. To make matters worse, John was open friendly to Mike, Willie, and Hector, always making time for them and joking.

By the year's end, while painful, Maria had made a good deal of progress implementing the changes needed in her group. Despite this, in his annual performance review of Maria, John described her shortcomings a manager as he perceived them, and he recommended that she be reassigned to a less demanding role — a nonmanagement position — for which John wouldn't have to hold her hand.

Focusing on John's management efforts, what is going on in this situation?

Maria doesn't fit John's view of what a manager should be, is someone he has low expectations of, and has an obvious gender difference, which is something he's not comfortable dealing with at all. Too often employees believe Maria thinks "who I am is the reason that you don't provide me with what I need to be successful." In the absence of any other evidence, why shouldn't she believe that?

John seeks to manage Maria as he does his three veteran managers. His *laissez-faire* style works fine for them because they need little guidance or support. But more importantly, their situation and challenges aren't the same: They're established, not new; they're accepted and respected by their peers; they aren't trying to make big changes on their team. John isn't seeing that Maria has special challenges — that have nothing to do with her capabilities and talents.

That's what coaching and managing diversity are all about: tailoring efforts to help individual employees succeed in their jobs. Sometimes, that means working more closely with some staff than with others. John was reluctant to provide much coaching for Maria, and his one-size-fits-all style wasn't effective in managing employees' different needs. Moreover, John's bias favors his peers and discounts Maria.

Focusing on Performance and Behaviors

Coaching employees operates with only two safe assumptions — that people mean well, and they want to and try to do a good job. Only their actions determine otherwise, not any outdated assumptions.

Martin Luther King, Jr., had a dream "that my four little children will one day live in a nation where they will not be judged by the color of their skin but by the content of their character." Keep in mind your own unconscious or conscious bias toward the way people appear. Focus on their character in two ways: first on performance and second, don't tolerate behaviors that hinder performance.

Emphasizing performance

Focusing on performance deals with what you're paying employees to do: their jobs. It means putting forth efforts to make employees feel respected and part of the team and to give them the guidance and support they need to develop and maximize their talents and skills.

The coaching approach focuses on helping employees be successful. To help employees be their best, you need to be aware of the issues involved in managing performance. Job performance can be broken down into three main areas: attendance, work and tasks, and job-related behavior.

Attendance

Attendance has two aspects:

>> **Availability:** The first version of this book emphasized "Productivity comes from people performing their jobs, and they can't perform when they're absent." With greater number of employees working remotely, managers have grappled with the idea of attendance. "If I don't see them at their desk working, how do I know they are?" Many organizations are coming to understand that employees can be trusted to do their work and productivity hasn't suffered from allowing people more flexibility. Still, employees are expected to show up sometimes, like client meetings, for instance. You can negotiate when people are available but employees still have an obligation to be available when needed.

>> **Punctuality:** Punctuality or when people show up has also been redefined after the pandemic. People are juggling many commitments, both at work and home. At the same time, few organizations can succeed in a free-for-all, show-up-when-you-want culture. I've noticed that more and more organizations are loose on punctuality. Meetings typically start late, people drop in and drop out, and the meeting typically go over time. If you're not punctual as a manager, don't expect your employees to be punctual. They're only following your example. If punctuality is important, have a team meeting about the rules and expectations and model the behavior you want others to follow. If you set arbitrary rules, you may wind up with compliance rather than commitment, which is the opposite of what coaching seeks (see Chapter 2).

The work and tasks people do

Work-related issues are critical in every job performance situation. These issues deal with the technical side of employees' jobs — that is, products they make and services they perform. The issues involve the following:

>> **Output:** The amounts or volume of work that people need to produce. Output may include sales quotas, production targets, or numbers of service calls taken.

>> **Quality:** How well the job is done? Is the work produced with few errors? Does it meet the expectations of what your organization can stand behind? Does the work help set a new standard in terms of innovation and creativity?

>> **Completeness:** How thoroughly the work is done? Is everything complete and in order? Half-finished products are items that no one wants to receive.

>> **Timeliness:** The work is getting done when it needs to get done. Was it done within the estimated scope of time? Meeting deadlines and working within a budget is an important performance issue.

Focusing on job-related behaviors

This critical issue of performance relates to employees' conduct and relations with others — behaviors needed to do a job well. Of course, these behaviors vary from job to job, but they often involve things such as teamwork, customer service, upholding operational or safety standards, courtesy and respect, and managing others.

TIP

When managing diversity and, of course, coaching, you want to emphasize the issues of performance that yield high productivity and build positive work environments. Stay away from attempting to manage issues that aren't performance-related. For example, when managers mistakenly deal with the following three issues, they may find that their efforts create problems and fail to enhance productivity:

>> **Attitude:** *Attitude* isn't an issue of performance that you can manage. When I (Marty) share this fact with managers, many want to jump out of their chairs and protest — until I ask them to define the word attitude. (They often have a hard time answering that question.) Attitude is how someone thinks or feels about something. It's not the same as behavior. Behavior is tied up in someone's actions; you can observe and manage behaviors.

You know, of course, that attitude often influences people's behavior. However, you can't *see* attitude, even though you have your perceptions or opinions about it. You can't see what's inside someone else's head, and trying to judge a person's attitude, especially when you view it as bad, is minefield territory. So you need to deal with the *concrete* (the behavior you see) and not the *abstract* (the attitude you perceive behind it).

For example, imagine you operate a retail operation and Sue is one of your employees. She has a bad attitude toward "tire-kickers," customers who take a lot of time but don't purchase anything. You've coached her to be courteous, helpful, and responsive to all types of customers — all behaviors that influence performance. Today, a tire-kicker walks into your store, and Sue must deal with this customer. Although Sue has a negative attitude about this customer, she provides courteous, helpful, and responsive service, and the customer eventually walks away satisfied. Although Sue has a bad attitude about tire-kickers — she's even told you about her attitude — she exhibits the proper behaviors. Her performance is good.

>> **Personal background:** An employee's *personal background* — their race, ethnicity, religion, age, gender, sexual orientation, and gender identity — doesn't determine their ability to perform. Skills and behaviors do that. When you base your employment-related judgments and decisions on who a person is rather than on the person's performance, you jump into the discrimination zone.

All civil rights laws exist for a reason — to protect the who-we-are-as-individuals side of us. *Discrimination* in the legal sense is acting in a prejudicial way that hurts or denies someone an opportunity because of their personal background. Although managers know these points of law, enough miss it or disregard it. As a result, they help keep lawyers busy responding to employees who are filing — and sometimes winning — discrimination lawsuits.

>> **Style:** *Style* is the methods or ways (a personal touch) that individuals use when doing their job, and nearly everyone has a different work style. Although certain policies and procedures must be followed in many jobs, a person often has a good deal of latitude in how they follow them. How neat someone's desk is or whether the employee does a task like you would seldom has any bearing on how well an employee performs.

Unless the style harms others, it's not a performance issue. When managers attempt to make such things an issue or insist that employees do tasks in a set way, employees often wind up feeling stifled and taking less initiative. Certainly, this leaves no room for creativity. When managers focus on methods of doing a job (after someone is trained to do it) rather than on the results expected, they create compliance, not commitment.

You don't need to be a cultural anthropologist to manage diversity. You just need to manage people as individuals and focus on their performance. And when you focus your efforts so that your employees feel respected and included and that they have the guidance and support they need to perform successfully, you are not only managing diversity effectively, but you're also coaching and mentoring at the highest level.

Stamping out insensitive behavior

The second factor in managing diversity relates to behaviors — not tolerating any behaviors that hinder performance: behaviors that are disruptive or insensitive and can offend, intimidate, or anger others. Such behaviors have a counterproductive effect — they hinder quality performance and damage morale. The behaviors listed here are also illegal, which makes them prohibitive by most company policies. As such, these behaviors put the manager and the company at great legal risk for harassment, hostile workplace, discrimination, and/or retaliation. That makes it all the more urgent to immediately address with an employee and ensure they don't happen again.

Here are some examples of such behaviors for you to watch for and address immediately:

- >> **Off-color humor:** Jokes and other attempts at humor that are sexual in nature or make fun of a particular race, ethnicity, religion, sexual orientation, gender identity, age group, or disability.

- >> **Ridicule or insult:** Comments or attempts at humor that personally degrade or attack someone else. Even when done in a subtle fashion, such attempts at humor usually hurt and anger those on the receiving end.

- >> **Profanity and vulgarity:** A word here or there usually isn't a big deal, but many people take great offense at the continuous use of profane, vulgar, or lewd language. Be aware of offending someone who is religious by using crude expressions that might seem acceptable to you. The workplace is different than other parts of your world.

- >> **Stereotypical remarks:** Broad generalizations of a subtle but degrading nature about groups of people. Comments that start out as, "Those kind of people are all like this," or "I'm not prejudiced, but . . .," are usually stereotypical remarks that cross the line of respect.

- >> **Subtle-to-overt sabotage:** This includes withholding information, refusing to give help that people need to do their jobs, or causing damage to work items or property.

- >> **Threats:** They include intimidation about someone's job situation or threats aimed at someone's physical safety.

- >> **Slurs:** Slurs are derogatory name-calling that's most commonly aimed at race, ethnicity, gender, religion, sexual orientation, and gender identity.

- >> **Mimicking:** Mimicking usually involves repeatedly imitating another person's accent, especially when English is a second language.

- >> **Exclusion:** This is ostracizing and isolating someone from the work group — a destructive behavior that hinders performance.

The list can go on, but these behaviors have instant negative impact on individuals and the work environment when tolerated by managers. And it's even worse if the manager is exhibiting these behaviors. As a coach, you must recognize that unprofessional and disrespectful conduct has no place in any work environment. These kinds of behaviors aren't what you're paying employees to do. People have the right to feel safe at work.

TIP

When an employee commits these transgressions, take the appropriate action to rectify the situation. Often, the first action may be to try to rehabilitate the transgressor; that is, coach to improve and refocus the person on the right behaviors and performance to do. Set and follow through on consequences if the person still has difficulty performing in a positive and professional manner. Be consistent in establishing and maintaining the kind of environment you want to create.

Leading by example

Your own efforts to become more understanding of your own thoughts, feelings, and behaviors will not only make you a better coach and mentor, but doing so will also inspire others to follow your lead. Here are some last thoughts on how to lead by example:

>> Take the time to get to know people by asking questions and learning their stories. When you learn more about the lives and perspectives of people who are different from you, you make them feel valued and respected. You also broaden your own understanding of the 90 percent of the iceberg you often don't see (refer to the section, "Seeing the entire iceberg," earlier in this chapter).

>> Stretch yourself by expanding your social network to include people outside your tribe. I don't mean inviting a Black employee out to learn what it's like to be Black. That's singling them out based on their appearance only. Stay open to opportunities to expand your network.

>> Many times being more conscious about your behavior helps you avoid pitfalls. Avoid the opposite effect: treating someone differently because they're different. If you've heard that Millennials like praise, for instance, don't go overboard complimenting them at every turn. They're keen whether you're being authentic and would be just as easily turned off to phony praise than appreciate the gesture.

>> Enlist the help of a mentor to help you spot unconscious missteps. This can be a colleague whom you trust to give you feedback on how you might be interacting with someone in a derogatory or inappropriate way. Refer to Part 5 for more about mentoring.

Chapter **8**

Bridging Generational Differences

Generational differences have always been present in the workforce. That's not new. What's relatively new is the intense focus on categorizing and characterizing how each generation is different. As a coach for 20 years, I've (Leo) coached people in their twenties and people in their seventies. I still have problems keeping the terms and time periods of each generation straight. And then there are those *cuspers* — the ones that straddle generations.

Keeping track of generational labels is confusing and overwhelming. Personally, I don't coach differently to different generations. I try to understand how people are different. Period. And I follow the playbook of solid managerial practices contained throughout this book. I don't have a cheat sheet that helps me put someone in a box based on how old they are. In the same way, I utilize the same strategy for coaching people with different genders, races, or ethnicities. I'm sensitive that not everyone's experience is the same, but it doesn't change my overall approach.

That said, I understand you may be frustrated in your workplace when different generations work together. This chapter sheds some light on how to understand generation differences and how to bridge those differences to be an effective coach and mentor.

Defining Generational Differences

Ten years ago, the typical Boomer manager would say one of their biggest challenges is motivating and managing Millennials (also referred to as Gen Y). But as more Boomers retire, Gen Xers are finding challenges working with Boomers and Millennials. At the same time, Millennials are challenged by working with the next generation or Gen Z, in addition to Boomers and Gen X. Ten years from now, Gen Z will be the old generation managing the next new generation. And on it goes.

Here are some things that will never change:

>> Each generation defines itself by being different from their parents in their preferences, styles, perceptions, attitudes, and beliefs.

>> Many people from older generations will struggle with how newer generations are different. Just consider how generations may split on liking or hating Elvis, the Beatles, Bob Dylan, Madonna, Snoop Dog, Adele, Little Nas X, and Billie Eilish.

>> Everyone is getting older by the minute. No matter what generation you belong to, it's just a matter of time before you say, "I feel old."

The reality is that people are working longer in their careers. The typical retirement age of 65 is being pushed out by Boomers who can't or don't want to retire. And Gen X will likely follow suit by working longer. More managers will be managing both younger generations and older generations. That's why having a working knowledge of the basic differences between generations can be helpful.

Breaking down the birth years

The first thing to understand is how generations are commonly broken down into distinct groups. Table 8-1 shows a common breakdown of people by when they were born.

Connecting generations to events

No matter how much you agree or disagree with embracing generational differences, there's a lot to be gained by understanding how your thoughts, beliefs, and *unconscious bias* (ingrained preferences and judgments that you may not be aware of) might have influenced you by the times when you lived, particularly in the formative years of birth through your teens.

TABLE 8-1

The Generations by Years

Generation Name	Birth Years
Baby Boomers	1946–1964
Generation X	1965–1979
Millennials	1980–1995
Generation Z	1996–2010
Generation Alpha	2011 and on

Take this nostalgia test from *Managing Millennials For Dummies* by Hannah L. Ubl, Lisa X. Walden, and Debra Arbit (John Wiley & Sons, Inc.) to help Table 8-2 with the following things in mind:

>> What age were you when the following things were present?

>> How did you feel about it or react to it in the time?

>> How did it influence who you are today?

TABLE 8-2   ## Nostalgia Experience

Baby Boomers	Generation X	Millennials	Generation Z
The Beatles	MTV	Chat rooms	Newtown shooting
Civil Rights Movement	Challenger shuttle disaster	Events of 9/11	Barack Obama
Moon landing	The Cold War	Reality TV	YouTube
Rosa Parks	Atari	Matthew Shepard killing	#Feminism
Sex, drugs, and rock 'n' roll	AIDS	Napster	ISIS
Birth control pills	*Star Wars*	Iraq and Afghanistan wars	Netflix
Gloria Steinem	Rise in divorce	Columbine	Wi-Fi
OPEC oil embargo	Simpson/Goldman murders	Tattoos, piercings, and body art	Marriage equality

(continued)

TABLE 8-2 *(continued)*

Baby Boomers	Generation X	Millennials	Generation Z
John F. Kennedy	Title IX	Facebook	Great Recession
Booming birth rate	Reagan assassination attempt	Twitter	Beyoncé
Vietnam War	Personal computer	Smartphones	Affordable Healthcare Act
Other:	Other:	Oprah Winfrey	Election of Donald J. Trump
		World Wide Web	Urgency of climate change
		Other:	Artificial intelligence
			Black Lives Matter
			TikTok
			Other:

This doesn't mean if you're born in a certain year, you naturally follow some set rule or definition. Sociologists and academia came up with these classifications, but it's only a rough way of examining people in large groups. Some people call these groups *generational cohorts*. In other words, people who lived during the same period grew up in a world that was different in a variety of ways, including the following:

>> **Culture:** Music, fashion, art, movies, literature

>> **Economy:** Recessions, embargos, stock market, prosperity, inequity

>> **Global events:** Wars, natural catastrophes, climate

>> **Politics:** Elections, civil rights, Supreme Court decisions, legislation

>> **Technology:** Personal, workplace, communication, productivity, advances, impact on populations

Just think how a 10-year-old growing up during these times might be influenced differently than someone in their 20s or 50s. The following examples aren't meant to represent different generations, but to help you see how people can be shaped by the circumstances they're born into. People's stories are informed by their relationship with their parents, what kind of upbringing they had, what events happened while they grew up, and what their peers were doing. It's not just one thing, but a composite of different things.

Example of a Baby Boomer

John (born in 1959, Baby Boomer) is on his second marriage. He saw his parents were never happy and he pledged never to not be happy. John considers himself a good, attentive parent to his 25- and 27-year-old children. When he was growing up he never heard "I love you" from his parents and vowed to make sure his kids knew they were loved. He and his ex-wife, Jill, doted on their children and gave them lots of attention and praise for every accomplishment. They didn't want to be seen as a cold parent but more as caring buddy for them. John went to Woodstock and lived in San Francisco during the '60s. He took plenty of drugs in his day and as a consequence supports the legalization of drugs. He and his second wife, Julie, live in an exclusive suburban neighborhood, own a condo in Maui, and both drive Teslas because they believe in doing the right thing for the environment.

John worked as an advertising executive and was behind some of the most visible brands on the market. It was at a time when television was the biggest media outlet for advertisers. He worked long hours to get to where he is. John worked out regularly at his gym and is thinking of starting a consulting/coaching business in the next phase of his life. He's challenged by the choices he sees his Millennial kids making — one is working as a server and wants to be in a band and the other one is taking an indefinite leave from college to do nothing. He loves his kids but is frustrated by their lack of ambition and drive. The idea of pursuing a professional career is repulsive to them. John can't help but view his Millennial coworkers through the same lens. They just don't seem to care about work very much.

Example of a Gen X

Amy (born in 1973, Gen X) learned to fend for herself at a young age. Both her parents worked long hours, so she figured out how to entertain herself. She grew up at a time when technology was making huge advances. Her family was one of the first to get a personal computer. Amy was eager to start making her own money and worked at a friend's restaurant at 14 years old. When she wasn't working, she took figure skating lessons and competed regionally when she was 16 years old.

Amy has a strong work ethic and is responsible with her money. She is skeptical of mass media and prefers to do her own research even today. While she's had a long-time position as Chief Operating Officer at a software company, she's started to consult on her own and is making plans to start her own consulting business.

Example of a Millennial

Sam (born in 1991, Millennial) was 10 when he saw the Twin Towers fall. He didn't understand the impact at the time, but he can remember how much his parents cried. The Columbine shooting was only a few years earlier. With 9/11 everything changed and the world was no longer a safe place. He was always close to his parents, but he never understood working to make some company more profitable. Everything he read online as he grew up shaped his thinking that capitalism was at the root of climate change, inequities in income, and discrimination. Why would he follow his parents path of working all the time a few privileged people could get rich?

Sam grew up on social media, but he can remember the "old days" when he didn't own a cellphone. He dates women occasionally but is curious about his sexuality. He and his friends continually post on Instagram and TikTok about everything they're doing and what they're thinking. He's had a job driving Uber but is thinking of quitting and going back to school. He has had some jobs but never kept them long.

Example of Gen Z

Latifah (born in 1998, Gen Z) can remember when Barack Obama was the country's first Black president and marriage equality was made law. Latifah's friends were from diverse racial and cultural backgrounds. One of her best friends is a Muslim lesbian. Latifah spends a great deal of her time in her bedroom glued to her phone, scrolling through hundreds of messages, and contributing to posts around social justice and LGBTQ rights. She feels both connected through technology but socially isolated and lonely at the same time.

Latifah is torn between finding a job with good pay and benefits and working for a company that's small, local, and socially responsible. The cost of living is so high, and she hopes to buy a house someday. On the other hand, she can't see herself working for a large company that hordes all the profits and doesn't do the right things socially. She screens potential employers by online rating services and what her peers say about them in social media. She is ready to commit and work hard for the right company. Latifah has developed her own skin care for people of color and markets it online. All the profits go to animal rights organizations. She hopes to continue to build that business, even as she develops her career.

Identifying the trends

You can make some generalizations, including the following:

>> Generations raised on cellphones and social media rely heavily on that form of communication. Younger generations are more comfortable texting over a direct conversation more so than older generations.

>> Boomers tend to be more focused on their careers and work. Younger generations put a bigger focus on their personal life and downtime. They don't see a sharp line between work and life.

>> Younger generations brought up in times of social justice place a heavier emphasis on the need for diversity, equity, and inclusion in the workplace. They also tend to want to work for companies that are more socially responsible.

However these are just trends. You may be 60 years old or 30 years old and strongly disagree with these generalizations. Personally, I have friends in their 70s who are very progressive politically and spend as much time on their phones as my friends in their 20s.

Avoiding the Trap of Generation-Casting

Grouping by generation, just like grouping by gender or race, can pose challenges for building trust as a coach or mentor. People react differently to situations. Everyone is unique.

The key to being an effective coach is learning about people in a deeper way than just your initial perceptions. Chapter 7 describes people like icebergs: What you see initially is only a small part of who people are. There's a much more to everyone than their gender, age, race, sexual orientation, and overall physical appearance. Your job as a coach is to question your own initial assumptions and bias you may have toward each person based on what you have read, seen, or heard somewhere.

Here are the problems with generation-casting:

>> **Generation-casting is often a way of bashing.** "You know how those <fill in the blank> are!" Rarely do you hear someone mentioning that someone from another generation as a positive thing. As a coach, your job is to create a positive, healthy tone in the workplace. Bashing someone who is older or younger doesn't create a respectful environment.

>> **Generation-casting is easy to get wrong.** Although you may be influenced by the world you were brought in, you're still an individual with free will. You can choose how you view things and react. A challenging situation for some people can crush them and for others it can be a source of fuel and motivation. When you generation-cast, you're making assumptions that can easily be wrong.

>> **Generation-casting doesn't build commitment.** Your job as a coach and mentor is to help build a foundation for employee commitment. Chapter 4 outlines the pillars of commitment to engage people to do their best work. Putting someone in a box based on their age discounts the complexity of how they may be unique and doesn't help in seeing their potential.

Here are some examples where generation-casting in the workplace can go wrong:

>> Lavishing praise on a 30ish employee at a company meeting because you heard that's what they need to feel important, but missing the part that they hate being the center of attention

>> Bringing together a group of younger employees to innovate around a new customer portal for a website, and unintentionally not inviting an older employee, who is actually more knowledgeable about competitors than anyone else in the company

>> Not seriously listening to your younger assistant about their ideas because subconsciously you think they're too young to be taken seriously

>> Putting together a company retreat and separating employees by age group to sit together instead of considering mixing them up or separating them into groups by their job functions

>> Not confronting a 20ish employee for turning work in on time because you don't want to appear that you're too old and you don't value work/life balance

>> Expecting the Boomers in your organization to be slow learners when a new learning system is introduced

>> Jokingly calling an older colleague, "old man"

>> Assuming that Boomers will be resistant to change and innovation

We are human. Judging others is in our nature. Wanting to hang out and work with people who are more like you than different is natural. But when you judge others unfairly and make people feel not included, you aren't contributing to a workplace that invites and respects everyone. As a coach and mentor, you have a larger responsibility and opportunity to set the tone and lead by example. You don't need to. You can continue to be part of your tribe, but if you want to be an effective, trusted coach to your team, you need to adapt to the reality that people are different and have different needs. That includes seeing people beyond their age.

Figuring Out How to Connect Generational Differences

You may be frustrated when your employees don't put in the effort or just want you to be positive. You may be thinking: "I'm not a psychologist. I have work that needs to be done. I just want some simple advice. That's why I bought this book!" Here are some practical strategies for working with people who are younger or older and bridge those generational differences.

Know yourself

The first and best place to start in building generational differences is understanding yourself more fully. Table 8-1 earlier in this chapter helps illuminate the choices you made in your life and the attitudes you have toward others based on your life story. That's a start but take more time reflecting on what judgments and attitudes about age you bring into any interaction with employees.

REMEMBER

When you increase your self-awareness, you increase your overall emotional intelligence (EQ). You become more empathetic and understanding of other people when you first take the time to get to know yourself. Chapter 5 discuses EQ in greater detail.

Look at these prompts and see how you'd answer them. You don't need to answer them all right now. Any investment you make in looking at yourself pays off:

>> How do you view others?

- Older people have more . . .
- Older people lack . . .
- Older people don't appreciate . . .
- What I appreciate about older people . . .
- What I don't appreciate about older people . . .
- Younger people have more . . .
- Younger people lack . . .
- Younger people don't appreciate . . .
- What I appreciate about younger people . . .
- What I don't appreciate about younger people . . .

- » How do you view aging?
  - How did you see older people when you were young?
  - Did you learn from older people?
  - In what ways were they role models?
  - What's your own view of getting older?
  - What are your fears or concerns?
  - How do you want to be treated or seen?
- » How do you view your current relationships?
  - What relationships do you have now that have an age gap to whom you might coach?
  - Do you treat them differently than someone your own age?
  - What do you think, say, or do that's different?
  - How do you think it might impact your relationship?
  - What do you want to change about your interactions?
  - What questions could you ask the person to help you see them more fully?

Pay attention to other people's stories

You're most effective as a coach and mentor when you take the time to truly understand the people you're working with. Understanding and adapting to different generations is about being curious and finding out more about the stories that have shaped who people are. Some potential questions are as follows:

- » What events do you remember growing up that had a big impact on you?
- » Where were you when <fill in the blank> happened?
- » How has the world changed since you were a kid?
- » Are there things that are hard for you to accept about your age?
- » What were you told as a kid was important?
- » What did you grow up believing?
- » Do you still believe that?
- » What's not important to you now?
- » When you look at people older, what do you think?

>> When you look at people your age, what do you think?

>> When you look at people younger, what do you think?

View it as just one lens

Generational differences are a real thing. At the same time, you don't want to just see people through the lens of when they were born. Challenge your assumptions and bias as a start to look deeper. Push back on colleagues and employees who just label people based on their age. Many other factors can shape personality and work style including:

>> Culture

>> Education

>> Ethnicity

>> Gender identity

>> Health

>> Life stage

>> Parenting

>> Personal relationships

>> Race

>> Religion

>> Sexual orientation

>> Socioeconomic background

Coaching others starts with coaching yourself. Look at any obstacles that may stand between you and your employee to help them achieve both your goals.

Understanding the Role of Values

What happens to people when they're young shapes who they are. People's core *values* are the ingrained beliefs that drive behavior and attitude. Chapter 5 looks at the importance of understanding your personal values as a key to being a better coach and mentor. Your values are influenced by the times you live in. In my (Leo) experience as a coach, understanding someone's personal values is just as important when coaching them as what generation they're part of.

EXAMPLE

Refer to the section, "Connecting generations to events," earlier in this chapter, to recognize how values and environment go together.

>> **John,** the Baby Boomer, values accuracy, competitiveness, commitment, compassion, family, and adventure. He doesn't place as much emphasis on love, optimism, and humility. If you judge him as materialistic and shallow, though, you'd miss that he's deeply religious and reflects on how he can be a better person, father, and partner. He knows that being more loving and accepting is the right thing, but he struggles with it.

>> **Amy,** the Gen Xer, values honesty, independence, dependability, adaptability, and fairness. She doesn't place as much emphasis on adherence to social norms and traditions. She's seen enough change in her life to accept that reinventing yourself from time to time is a good thing. She belongs to a forgotten generation that's often overlooked by media and sociologists who are more focused on the difference between Boomers and Millennials. Amy is used to being left alone and even underestimated. She's confident in her abilities and resilience.

>> **Sam,** the Millennial, values passion, balance, justice, innovation, and friendship. He doesn't place much emphasis on consistency, discipline, and faith. If you judge him as self-focused and without ambition, you'd miss the work he's done developing a social media platform to match young people with mentors all around the world. Sam has a vision of creating community beyond borders, culture, gender, and age.

>> **Latifah,** the Gen Zer, values fairness, justice, and equality. She's motivated to speak out against discrimination and oppression, particularly of people who haven't had a voice. As a young black woman, she's been inspired by strong successful women like Michelle Obama, Sarena Williams, Beyoncé, and Ruth Bader Ginsberg. She resents the label that she's looking for a handout. Latifah just wants the chance to show the world what she can do to make a difference in her life and in the world.

The more you seek to understand people beyond common perceptions helps make you a more effective coach and mentor.

3

Motivating and Empowering Your Staff

Challenge traditional assumptions of what motivates employees by understanding the role of purpose, autonomy, and mastering skills.

Discover some simple, practical strategies that can have a big impact on employee motivation.

Unlock the power of asking the right questions and engaging employees in meaningful dialog that helps them become independent and grow as leaders.

Help employees help themselves by encouraging and supporting growth and development in their careers.

Guide your employees to see the connection between their performance and their long-term personal goals.

Chapter 9

Fueling Employee Motivation

I n the public-speaking world, in which people get paid to talk to people, some speakers and celebrities refer to themselves as "motivational speakers." They appear at professional association conferences, conventions, and company-wide meetings, address large audiences with all the enthusiasm and energy they can muster, and hope that you leave the session feeling motivated.

In the same way, some sports coaches like to give hard-hitting pre-game or half-time speeches to rally their players. The effort usually conjures up an image of Knute Rockne, the famed Notre Dame football coach, exhorting his players to "win one for the Gipper." The players get excited and charge out on the field, screaming the whole way. Evangelical clergy in the religious world and charismatic candidates in the political world may also give rousing sermons to stir their congregations or fiery speeches to rally their political supporters.

Regardless of the arena, these situations are all about inspiration — not motivation. "Motivational speakers" in business and other arenas are really inspirational speakers. If they're able to entertain and excite you, they make you feel good. Movies often aim to do the same thing. It's a form of entertainment.

This thinking is that, if you as a manager can get your employees excited and pumped up, you've motivated them. But you haven't. Motivation is something altogether different: This chapter explains what it is and how you can use it when coaching your staff.

Calling for Action: Understanding Motivation

The focus of motivation is on action. Specifically, look at motivation as meaning something that causes or influences a person to act or perform. As a coaching tool, *motivation* is the creating of conditions that stimulate an employee to achieve a highly productive level of performance.

As a manager, you can influence the conditions that stimulate performance. You can affect people's *motivators*, intrinsic as well as extrinsic factors that drive a person to act or perform. You can also provide rewards to motivate employees, things people receive for achieving something in their performance.

You may have heard the saying that the end justifies the means: As long as you get the results desired, who cares what you did to get there. The manager who uses motivation as a coaching tool, however, cares about both, the means and the end. The emphasis is to stimulate good performance, not just for the short term but on an ongoing basis.

What's behind motivation that makes a person want to meet and even exceed expectations? To understand how motivation operates, look at what diminishes motivation and what builds motivation.

Withdrawals erode motivation

Any attempt you make to motivate people can just as easily be undermined by conditions, circumstances, or events that demotivate. Maya Angelou said people won't remember what you do, or what you say, but they will remember how you make them feel.

TIP

I (Leo) like to equate relationships to piggy banks. If you want healthy, strong, mutually beneficial relationships, make deposits with people by supporting them, having their backs, and giving more than you take. You'll have money in the bank for the occasional withdrawals you'll make. But if you're constantly making withdrawals by taking more than you give, criticizing or not respecting or supporting people, you'll have a negative balance.

Here are some ways you can make withdrawals that undermine not just motivation, but also commitment:

>> Insulting, offensive, or disrespectful behavior

>> Ignoring people or not being available

>> Criticism without ever giving praise

>> Cutting employees off when they raise concerns and giving orders telling them what to do

>> Having angry outbursts and yelling

>> Using sexist, racist, homophobic, or demeaning comments about a group

>> Belittling people and using sarcasm

>> Publicly lambasting someone for a mistake or error in judgment

>> Terminating an employee or two suddenly and without warning to send a message to the rest of the group

>> Promising and not delivering

>> Saying one thing and doing another

>> Not following through

>> Treating people as dispensable

>> Making decisions without consulting people who are impacted

>> Not caring or listening to people

>> Demanding work schedules without acknowledging the sacrifice

>> Barking orders and being impatient

>> Favoring one employee over another without merit

>> Gossiping or talking behind someone's back

You may look at the list and cringe. Maybe you've done one of these things or someone did it to you. People have long memories, especially when they feel they've been wronged or disrespected. Some withdrawals are so big that digging yourself out the hole is difficult. If you can't remember to do the little things to motivate people, it's better to avoid making major withdrawals.

REMEMBER

Motivating by fear tends to breed compliance, not commitment; silence opposing views, not stimulate thought-provoking discussion; extinguish morale, not light it up; and create deference to authority and disrespect to you in the position of authority. Its effect, while often immediate, tends to be short-term. See how well people employees put their hearts and minds into work when they're stressed and fearful. And see how many people stick around or look for work elsewhere. As Chapter 6 discusses, there's been a shift from employers making the rules to employees being more selective on where they work. In today's drive to find and keep good people, organizations can't afford not to treat people well.

Deposits build motivation

When faced with a stressful or challenging situation, step back and determine the results you want to achieve. From there, determine the means to getting to the results desired that will rally your employees *with* you, not against you — for example, collaboratively solving problems, setting goals, clarifying expectations, or conducting progress reviews while staying positive and firm. That is when you use the coaching tool of motivation.

So what are some motivators or rewards that can act as a positive stimulus to employee performance? I've asked groups of managers this very question over the years and let them brainstorm some ideas. Here is the ever-growing list of positive examples of motivators and rewards:

- A good performance review
- Accomplishments recognized by top management
- Article in newsletter recognizing good work or service to customer
- Autonomy
- Being kept informed
- Care and concern from others
- Challenging work
- Chance to be creative
- Chance to create solutions and help overcome obstacles
- Chance to lead desirable project
- Chance to learn new things
- Chance to travel
- Choice of work schedule and vacations
- Conducting training
- Control over how your job gets done
- Cross training
- Education benefits
- Enjoyable assignments

- Extra time off without using vacation
- Family-friendly environment
- Flexible schedule
- Getting an office or a better office
- Gift certificates for appreciation
- Good communication with your boss and a trusting relationship
- Good incentives or commissions
- Good pay raise
- Group barbecue or potluck
- Group recreation or social activity
- Having ideas listened to
- Influencing decisions and direction
- Involvement in higher-level meetings
- Involvement in important decisions
- Involvement in planning
- Job enrichment
- Letter of recognition with a copy to the personnel file
- Lunch or dinner at the company's expense
- Making presentations that provide visibility
- Manager going to bat for you or improvements
- Mentoring

- » New equipment or tools
- » Paid health club membership
- » Paid membership in professional association
- » Parking place
- » Party to celebrate success
- » Personal note for special occasion
- » Positive feedback
- » Profit sharing
- » Promotion
- » Prompt response to proposals
- » Public recognition
- » Publication of group sales or output results
- » Represent company at industry events

- » Sabbatical
- » Seeing ideas put into action
- » Seeing improvement in performance
- » Service recognition award
- » Showing interest in someone's career development
- » Special projects and assignments
- » Spot bonuses
- » Staff support and resources
- » Stock options
- » Support to resolve problems
- » Telecommuting
- » Tickets to sporting event or concert
- » Trophy or plaque
- » Weekend trip at company expense
- » Working with talented, caring people

This list contains both intrinsic and extrinsic motivators and rewards, and, although not all-inclusive, it contains many ideas that managers have some influence or control to use. If you come up with other useful motivators or rewards, add them to the list.

TIP

Draw upon the list. Put it in the forefront of your consciousness! When managers look for ways to positively stimulate employee performance, they often become surrounded by motivated employees and positive performance.

Show Me the Money: Pay as a Motivator

The list in the previous section focuses on creating conditions that positively motivate performance. A few of them involve pay, which begs the question: Is pay an effective tool for motivating employees to perform? Get a group of managers together to discuss this question, and often a great debate begins.

To do the coaching tool of motivation justice, you can't ignore the issue of motivation and money. Scholars and behavioral psychologists who study motivation often have strong opinions on the subject but not usually consensus on their views. The following sections share a collection of views.

Looking at the pros and cons of money as a motivator

When I (Marty) ask managers if money is a motivator, those who say it is bring up the following points:

>> **People perform at what they get paid to do.** Employees don't volunteer to work. They look for opportunities that will pay them well or have good earning potential. If people got paid to play, not many would be showing up to work.

>> **The top performing salespeople are driven by the commissions they can earn.** They want to beat their quotas to earn their pay rewards.

>> **Money is a form of status.** It gives people their sense of importance. If employees feel they're earning less than what their skills or experience call for, they're demotivated in their performance. If they get paid what they feel they're worth, they feel satisfied and desire to do a good job. That's why organizations look to set up competitive salary systems in line with the labor market. They want to avoid having employees feel that their value isn't fairly compensated.

>> **In a materialistic society such as ours, money is a form of sustenance.** People desire it because of the lifestyle it can afford them. They also need it to survive. Thus people are motivated to perform to receive the benefits their pay can buy for them.

>> **Money is a form of recognition and reward.** Receiving a good raise or bonus is a tangible way to recognize contributions of good performance. The financial reward is proof of the good performance delivered, and one many seek to earn.

For all the managers who feel strongly that money is a powerful and important motivator, just as many comment that it really isn't. Here are the comments most commonly said in support of the opposing point of view:

>> **People want more out of their jobs than just a good paycheck.** They want good work and good people to work with. If they had lousy working conditions, a nasty boss, boring work, and other negative factors, you couldn't pay people enough to stay in such a job. Satisfying or fulfilling careers are far more of a motivator than money.

>> **Money breeds contentment and security.** If employees feel they're paid well, they feel more happy and safe in their situation, but that doesn't mean you get any greater performance out of them. Some professional athletes, as an example, when they earn long-term contracts that give them security, no longer perform at the same level they did prior to earning the big contract.

>> **Surveys taken on the subject of what employees find motivating in their jobs usually report pay as low on the list.** Factors like flexible schedule, employee benefits/perks, recognition, challenging work, and a positive culture often rank higher in importance.

>> **When you find employees who do a good job and take pride in their work, you also find that money isn't what's driving them.** They like their work and the sense of accomplishment in it. Tracking and reporting performance can be a powerful motivator, even if you don't reward people for it financially.

>> **When people only perform for money, they aren't really motivated to perform with new ideas or a better product.** You get what you reward. If your company is focused on bottom line results and meeting defined benchmarks, people will work toward meeting those metrics. That's fine if you don't want to evolve as an organization and look at what competitors are doing to serve customers. The drive to produce and deliver quality performance or better ideas gets lost when the focus of jobs is all on money. That's not motivation; it's more like greed.

Motivating through pay — Yes or no?

Money has great potential to motivate employee performance — no one usually turns down money or an opportunity to get it. However, money is often very difficult to use in motivating performance. Here are some reasons why:

>> For most employees, getting a regular paycheck doesn't qualify as something that will greatly influence their performance or productivity. You expect it to happen and notice it only when something impedes it.

>> The importance of money isn't the same for everyone. For some, it may serve as the driving force that pushes them to perform. For others, especially when you see a strong level of dedication, money often isn't the reason why. Wanting to contribute, wanting to support a good cause, and getting satisfaction out of one's work are factors that push this commitment to excel. For these people, the intrinsic motivators, not money, are what motivate them.

>> Most salary systems in organizations are designed to pay people more on their position and power within the organization than on their level of competence and quality of performance. The company president is usually the highest paid employee and because of that position of power, has a greater compensation package than the outstanding widget maker in production. The great widget makers at the line-worker level may do a far better job than the bigwig at the top, but that won't be reflected in their pay.

>> In many organizations, how people move up the salary ladder, based on policy or actual practice, has more to do with time on the job than performance in doing the job. More often than not, people at the top of their salary ranges are the ones who have been with the company the longest.

>> When pay issues come up, they quite often create more distraction than motivation. When employees feel, whether based on perception or reality, that their pay isn't equitable to either other employees at their own company or to similar positions at other companies, you'll often see a lack of focus and outward signs of discontent. If correcting the inequity is justified and you're able to do so, you've most often removed the distraction but are still left to figure out what's needed to motivate that employee's performance.

>> Money can often be a big part of what lures someone into a job, but it's less often a significant factor as to what motivates them to stay. Research done on issues of retention and turnover more often report that the quality of manager, the growth potential in one's career, the challenge and fulfillment in the work, the amount of recognition, and the culture and values exhibited in the organization play a much greater role than compensation as to the reasons why employees stay or change jobs.

>> For the vast majority of employees, what they earn is mostly through their base salary. In most organizations, managers' opportunity to affect someone's pay occurs only once, and at best twice, a year. Therefore, your ability as a manager to use money as a tool for motivation is fairly limited.

>> Where you have the most opportunity to use money as a tool to motivate employee performance is if you can use a variable pay plan. *Variable pay* is earning potential above a person's base salary that varies based on how well certain performance targets are met. Unlike base pay, it's not a set amount each payout because a person's results may not always be the same. Variable pay plans come in the form of commissions, bonuses, and incentives. The word *incentive* is sometimes used as the umbrella term for all these kinds of variable pay approaches.

>> Bonuses can backfire on you. Often, resentments come out when someone feels they should be paid more and others less. Coming up with a bonus structure that's fair is difficult. The deciding factors are too often subjective or don't account for inequities, like people who work on more profitable projects getting more.

>> If you want to help your bottom line and boost morale, get rid of the underperformers. You'll do more to improve motivation to thin the ranks of people who aren't contributing or tend to cause trouble.

When examining factors that motivate performance, you may notice that only about 10 percent have to do with pay. So if you decide to stay away from pay as a potential source of motivation, you still have at your disposal, a profusion of ways to motivate performance. And in many cases, you have more control over the non-pay motivators, anyway.

Identifying What Really Motivates People

If the goal of coaching is to lay a foundation for commitment and collaboration, the old way of managing people needs to change. Punishing people for not meeting expectations and rewarding them for meeting expectations follows the old carrot-and-stick approach to managing people. You didn't treat them as responsible, thinking adults but as widgets in the company. Their motivation came from an external source doing something: praise, criticism, pay, demotion.

As more work shifts from production to the knowledge industry, independent critical thinking is more valuable in the workforce than having employees who are unquestioningly compliant. To build commitment and engagement, employees need to be motivated to use their brains and stretch themselves. Motivation needs to come from an internal source; people need to see personal benefits from doing a good job. Coaching is about helping people to do just that: grow as independent problem solvers and high performers. Their motivation comes from identifying what's in it for them (WIFT) to work harder, other than a paycheck.

The next sections look at three drivers that author Daniel Pink contends are more powerful than punishment or pay in motivating people: helping people find purpose and meaning in their work; supporting people's desire to be autonomous and not micromanaged; and acknowledging that developing their mastery of skills is a fundamental motivator.

Having a purpose

When I (Leo) coach people, I want to know what drives them personally and professionally. How does work fulfill them? What do they like doing and why is that important? What is their passion? What impact does their work have on their clients, team members, and community?

Finding meaning and purpose in work may not have been particularly important to older generations, who were either just happy to be employed or motivated by how much they could make. But purpose has become a huge factor for the people I've coached: many of them between 35 to 55 years of age. The Covid-19 pandemic seems to have sparked a newfound realization among many people that life is short and you better enjoy what you're doing. The Great Resignation with millions of people leaving their jobs is a sign that people are no longer satisfied with just a paycheck. They want more and are willing to take big risks to find more meaning in their work.

As a coach, consider the following to help people find their purpose:

>> **Take the time to find out more about their personal and professional goals.** When you know what's important to people, you can be mindful of aligning them with people and projects that can help them reach their goals. Take them out to lunch and ask them where they see themselves personally and professionally in three years.

>> **Help them set small, manageable goals toward their vision.** I call these goals their *mountain* (refer to Chapter 12). These goals can be finding a mentor, getting training, working on delegating more in the next week, and more.

>> **Ask them what parts of their job they like and enjoy and why.** The answers to these questions give you an idea of what projects with which to align them. Even though you may not be able to satisfy them all of them time, they'll appreciate you're working to give them meaningful work.

>> **Take the time to give employees the big picture so they can see how their efforts contribute to a larger purpose.** Employees often focus on their part of a larger initiatives or projects. They're unaware of how the individual efforts come together. When you take the time to show how they've contributed to the whole, they can be inspired by the role they played and want to work harder in the future, knowing they're part of a project that has a larger impact. Examples can include showing employees how they helped create a playground for kids of all ages and abilities to enjoy, how they contributed to a successful release of new software and what customers say, and how their attitude and work ethic helped the company win a best-place-to-work recognition.

>> **Encourage experienced people to mentor younger people on tasks that they themselves may not feel challenged by anymore.** Doing so gives the more experienced people a sense of purpose to help others grow and keeps them engaged and motivated in their own success.

Supporting their autonomy

Employees can be funny: They want your immediate attention when they have a question or issue, but they mostly want to be trusted and left alone to do their own work. Chapter 13 discusses how to effectively delegate so people learn to do work on their own. The key to effective delegation isn't hand-holding — nor is it totally ignoring them — but it's allowing them to work on their own to solve issues.

REMEMBER

Coaching assumes employees want to be treated with respect and trusted that they'll do their best work. To take pride in their work, they need to feel like they're the authors — not that they are just following orders. Coaching people to meet expectations and acknowledging their desire for autonomy is difficult but essential to help them grow and stay engaged.

As a coach, here are ways you can support autonomy:

>> **Support a flexible work schedule.** Companies that doubted that people would be productive working from home have been pleasantly surprised that employees can be productive without their manager watching them.

>> **Let go of perfection.** Doer managers often fall into the trap of demanding work be done in a very specific way. That style is de-motivating for people who want to put their own stamp on a project. Focus on the result not the method that someone follows.

>> **Tell employees you trust them to work on their own and meet expectations.** Being clear up front by saying something like, "This is an important project and I'm going to leave you alone to figure out how best to get it done. I'm here if you need me; otherwise, you're on your own."

>> **Provide the tools and resources for people to work on their own.** You can support people who may be challenged by demands of other people on their time. You can help communicate priorities and mediate schedules so people can focus on their work.

>> **Regularly check in with employees about how they're doing.** Some people want less autonomy and more attention and support. Everyone has different capabilities and needs.

Recognizing mastery of skills

Since this book was first published 20 years ago, the field of professional development has exploded. People are hungry to learn how to execute technical tasks from bookkeeping to zookeeping, as well as EQ skills like giving feedback, delegating, and managing projects. Just look at all the management and professional development courses on YouTube, LinkedIn, and more. More people are getting their MBAs as they hold down full-time jobs and taking care of their families. And more people are getting into training, development, and coaching as second careers. The demand for employees wanting to improve their skills continues to rise.

ENCOURAGE SCHEMING

EXAMPLE

When my (Leo) kids were grade-school age, they wanted to play soccer. I thought it would be fun to coach them, but I didn't grow up with the game and knew I needed help.

I enrolled in a coaching workshop for other parents who wanted to learn how to coach youth soccer. One exercise really stuck with me. The instructor told us to pair up and grab a soccer ball. The field had a series of orange cones arranged in pairs, two feet apart from each other. The instructions were to pass the soccer ball through the cones to our teammate in a three-minute period. When the time was up, the instructor then asked each team how many times they passed it through the cones. Most of the responses ranged between 15 to 18 times, but one team did it 30 times. The instructor asked what did they did, and they said instead of going through all the cones, they just stayed in one place and passed it back and forth through one set of cones. The instructor pointed out that his instructions didn't dictate teams needed to go through all the cones. The winning team had come up with a creative scheme of winning that fit the instructions. "On the soccer field, you want to encourage 'scheming,' so players come up with their own spontaneous and fun ways of winning," the instructor said.

I thought about my kids, who were very talented schemers in their approach to homework and household duties. They were very good at coming up with ways to do work very efficiently by finding shortcuts. Younger generations of employees have been raised on technology and apps that do things easier and quicker. Encourage scheming in your workplace by allowing people to come up with creative solutions on their own.

In my (Leo) experience, younger generations of employees are particularly eager to learn. They want to move as quickly as possible from newbie to expert. They want to absorb case studies, tools, and strategies so they can be taken seriously and listened to. They want to provide answers and be authorities. At every organization I've worked, the one comment I've heard over and over is the similar: provide training, mentoring, and experience to master skills. Mastering skills and having opportunities to grow professionally is a huge motivator for many employees.

TIP

Here are some ways you can acknowledge mastery of skills as a coach:

>> **Revisit understanding your employees' professional goals.** If you know what engages them, you'll also find out what holes they have in their knowledge and experience. Often, the skills they want to develop are also the ones you want them to develop to be effective.

>> **Help people find mentors for anything and everything.** Mentors can be peers and even junior people who are knowledgeable in certain areas. Refer to Part 5 for more about mentoring.

>> **Give people the time to learn and develop.** *Lunch and learns*, where employees can gather, eat lunch, and share case studies and knowledge, are a great way to bring learning into the workplace. Some firms require employees to teach back what they learned from a training to other employees.

>> **Reward people who put in extra effort by paying for conferences or workshops.** Share resources such as upcoming webinars, links, and books (like *Coaching & Mentoring For Dummies*).

>> **Sponsor sessions in which a project manager discusses a successful recent project.** They can discuss what went well and what they learned and invite discussion and questions.

>> **Find random opportunities to bring junior people into client presentations or work meetings.** Doing so allows them to learn by observing.

MOTIVATING OTHERS TO DO WORK THAT THEY COULD DO

EXAMPLE

Josh loves water — especially stormwater. As a consultant in a national civil engineering firm, when I (Leo) met him, he knew something about how it flows and how to manage it for municipal projects. Well respected by his peers at the city and county, he was a busy guy. But he spent too much time in production software, computer-aided design (CAD), doing work that junior staff should be doing. Why? Because that was the way he approached projects. He knew it would get done right and on time if he was working on every detail in the methodical, step-by-step way with which he was accustomed. That was the way he met his commitments and had a high say-do ratio. That was how he maintained a lot of equity with his clients. For 15 years, it worked. However, although his approach got him that far, it wouldn't get him to where he wanted to go.

I started by asking him to identify what he wanted in his career and life. To engage Josh in the hard work of changing his habits, he needed to understand why it was important. When he identified his personal goals, he would see more *purpose* in changing.

Josh's vision or mountain was to spend more time with his 12-year-old son now before he got much older and didn't want to spend time with his dad. He could already see his son pulling away and wanting to spend more time with his friends. Josh was keenly aware of how important these father-and-son outings were to their relationship.

(continued)

(continued)

In three years, Josh wanted to be doing less project production work so that he could spend more time learning best practices in stormwater management. He was envious of his peers who regularly traveled around the world with a contingent of business and civic leaders to find out what other cities were doing for best practices. He also knew that in order to advance, he needed to develop his network. But it was challenging to find time for lunch or happy hour with colleagues, let alone a trip.

My coaching focused on helping him *master* delegation and letting go of control so he could get to his mountain. Nothing was stopping Josh, except how he had been working. Instinctually, he knew what he should do and what he shouldn't do. He knew the stuff he shouldn't do was weighing him down and keeping him from advancing.

Mastering delegation required him to read my book, *From the Ground Up: Stories and Lessons from Architects and Engineers Who Learned to Be Leaders,* and watch my instructional videos called PocketTools (preview the tools at leomacleod.com). The rest was up to him to do on his own. I encouraged him to be accountable to the work by suggesting this routine:

- Start with one routine task you should delegate.
- Plan each day by identifying if you'll be doing that task.
- Intentionally avoid doing that task.
- Schedule a time to pass off and coach someone else to do the task.
- Coach the employee to do the work themselves instead of taking it back.
- Let go of perfection and encourage purpose, mastery, and autonomy in people he coached.
- Repeat until the new habit pays off and you can see forward progress.

After six months, Josh had reduced his time in CAD from ten hours a week to one hour a week, which left him more time to spend with his son on camping trips and more time with peers on bigger, more engaging discussions about the future of stormwater management. Last time I checked with him, he was looking at joining the civic group to visit Bogota, Colombia. In addition, the principals in the firm praised him for his delegation skills and asked him to share his method with other employees.

I successfully coached Josh by helping him connect with his purpose, identify how to master delegation, and encourage him to figure out a way to let go of control and let others be autonomous, so he could be free to pursue tasks that were more aligned with his purpose.

Understanding Yourself as a Manager

What motivates you in how you function as a manager? In this section, you get a chance to reflect on yourself as a manager and discover what motivates you. I (Marty) use these ideas when I give coaching seminars, and they often spark quite a discussion with managers. (The following ideas about what motivates managers are a takeoff from work done by David McClelland, a psychology professor.)

To assess yourself as a manager, look at three needs or desires that motivate managers in their performance to varying degrees. Here they are with a brief description of each:

>> **Desire for personal accomplishment:** If this is a high need for you as a manager, it means

- You like to have personal responsibility to achieve success with a work effort, such as with a project or important assignment.

- You like challenge in your work and the hands-on aspects of getting things done.

>> **Desire for quality relationships:** If this is a high need for you as a manager, it means

- You like the social aspects of work — the interactions with other people.

- You want people to bond with you, and you want to get along well with your staff. You reason that if people like you and vice versa, people will work well together.

>> **Desire for influence:** If this is a high need for you as a manager, it means

- You like to assert your leadership influence and have a positive impact on others to get things done.

- You like to give people responsibility and prepare and develop them to handle it, and then firmly hold them accountable to produce results.

How strong are each of these needs for you as a manager today in terms of what motivates you in your job? Using the worksheet in Figure 9-1, rate on a scale of one (lowest) to ten (highest), how strong each of the three needs are for you. You may also want to list your reasons.

The Motivators For Managers

		Personal accomplishment	Quality relationships	Influence
Strong	10			
	9			
	8			
Moderate	7			
	6			
	5			
Not important	4			
	3			
	2			
	1			
Your reasons:				

FIGURE 9-1:
The motivators
for managers.

© John Wiley & Sons, Inc.

Then take a look at the following interpretations of your answers. McClelland discovered these kind of findings in his research, and I have seen much the same in my work with managers and executives over the years:

» **If you're a manager whose strongest need is in the personal accomplishment category, you're likely a high achiever.** Your greatest satisfaction comes in checking tasks off your to-do list as you get them done. You like to be hands-on with projects and the one who delivers much of the work that makes the projects successful.

You may also fall short in effectiveness as a manager because often you try to do all the important aspects of the group's work yourself. Delegating, getting others involved, and providing guidance and direction aren't so much part of your *modus operandi*. Getting a group organized and focused are where you run into trouble, but you're a hard worker. Sounds like a doer-type manager, doesn't it (see Chapter 2)?

» **If you're a manager whose highest need is in the quality relationships category, you're certainly a people person.** Staff may often find you quite likable. You enjoy having a social feeling in your work; the relationships with people are where you often get much pleasure.

154   PART 3 Motivating and Empowering Your Staff

As for your ability as a manager to pull people together and set direction, make tough decisions, and hold people accountable for high standards and results, you may tend to fall short. You worry about people feeling bad if you take these actions. As a result, you may get along well with your staff but at the same time frustrate many of them as you shy away from tackling problems and taking charge of your management responsibilities.

>> **If you're a manager whose strongest motivator is the influence category, you fit closest to what makes an effective manager.** You're willing to exercise your influence through others to make performance happen. You get satisfaction by asserting your personal influence, as Chapter 4 describes, and not by pushing your authority or coercing people to perform. Achieving popularity or doing more than anyone else are not your goals; influencing employees to perform well is. When you see individuals and the group achieve their goals and have success, you find that rewarding.

Thus you seek to develop your staff and maximize their capabilities to the fullest in order to produce the results the business needs. You know that motivating staff to get the best out of their performance requires positive leadership. All of which sounds like a coaching manager.

Managing as a coach isn't a panacea, and doing so doesn't make you a superhero who can tackle all the management challenges you face today. The point to keep in mind, as you have probably seen in your own experience, is that managers who have a strong personal influence and work to assert this leadership influence in positive ways tend to be very effective. They're able to focus everyone on the work that needs to get done and involve them in figuring out the best ways to do so.

REMEMBER

Most managers are motivated to some degree by all three needs described in this section. Don't lose sleep if the personal accomplishment or quality relationship needs are currently greater motivators for you. For success in getting the best out of your people's performance — the heart of what motivation is about — you can slowly change your focus in order to increase your ability to motivate your employees.

As you reflect on your own motivators and use that insight to coach others, consider the following observations:

>> How technically brilliant and achievement-oriented you are isn't enough to be an effective manager. A great salesperson doesn't guarantee a great sales manager; a great engineer doesn't always turn into a great engineering manager.

>> How nice you are and how well you like people aren't critical to management success. Far more useful for success is being able to be sincere, direct, positive, and firm — that's managing assertively.

>> Management, regardless of one's style or motivations, is about making others effective and delivering results through them — and hopefully keeping them around for a while so you don't have to start all over so soon.

>> Coaching skills can be learned. As you grow in your coaching skills, you can increase your ability to positively influence employees while maintaining high results.

Chapter **10**

Implementing Key Strategies to Motivate Your Employees

Motivating employees is a coaching tool that focuses on creating conditions that can stimulate high levels of performance. Performance, the focus of coaching, involves *behavior* — yours and your employees' — in the workplace. Even though work life and personal life sometimes converge (and occasionally crash) when people come to work, motivation as a coaching tool concentrates on job performance. You don't need for a degree in psychology, a license to practice therapy, or experience as a parent. All you need is to be a manager who wants to positively influence employee commitment and performance.

This chapter focuses on how you can motivate employee performance with coaching by utilizing these strategies.

Focusing on Performance

No one wants to create unhappy employees; however, the happiness or unhappiness of a group of staff members isn't central. Instead, motivation works best when you focus on enhancing and sustaining performance. Performance is tied to being engaged and finding purpose in work. Employees who are highly engaged and motivated don't always seem relaxed and happy. They're often too focused on their work. Although you don't want to encourage burnout, you also don't want to encourage unproductivity.

Unproductive employees might seem happy, but they aren't challenged or engaged. It's a fine line but an important one to consider: Do you want to coach performance and people challenging themselves or do you want to encourage people being happy?

These sections focus on how you direct your attention on performance and how to do so.

Encouraging the right behaviors

Chapter 9 emphasizes that your actions as a manager need to consistently encourage the right behaviors, so you're reinforcing a positive, productive culture where people are doing their best work. Inadvertently, your responses to situations may be counterproductive to what you really want to see in an employee's performance.

Sometimes managers discourage behavior that they really want to see. Here are a few examples:

>> When employees attempt to inform you of some bad news, you verbally lash out at them because you're upset at what you're hearing — referred to as *shooting the messenger.*

>> When employees attempt to seek your help or counsel with a problem, you react like the situation is a crisis and create stress for everyone near you.

>> When an employee points out a mistake you made or disagrees with an opinion of yours, you harshly attack this perceived insurrection.

>> When employees attempt to offer ideas that you don't like or find contrary to your own, you cut them off before they finish their explanations or react with a comment such as, "That will never work here."

In cases like these, you may have asked for your employees to let you know when something isn't going well, to come to you when they have problems, to speak their minds about an issue, and to offer ideas. When they do, however, your behavior punishes them for doing so. Then you wonder why you never hear about problems until too late in the game or why your employees never have any ideas when you ask for them.

Rewarding the right behaviors

The key to keeping people motivated is to be clear and consistent in your direction. Rewarding the right behaviors also means you keep employees accountable and give constructive feedback when you don't see the right behavior (see Chapter 14).

Sometimes managers go one step further and, usually unknowingly, reward the wrong behaviors. Here are a few examples:

>> Every time Maria in your group makes an error, you say little and correct it yourself.

>> Every time Roger has a temper tantrum you say little because you don't want to upset him further.

>> Every time Kim misses a deadline, which happens often, you say little or even say thanks, implying missing deadlines is okay.

>> Every time you raise an issue with Ivan about how he's not taking responsibility for an assignment, you end up in long discussions about all the challenges Ivan has and work out no plan for correction.

When you avoid dealing with performance issues directly, you encourage the wrong behaviors to continue. When you don't let the employee take responsibility for correcting mistakes, controlling behavior, meeting deadlines, and getting work done — regardless of your intention — the message sent is that nonperforming behavior is okay. Coaching to help employees know what to do, and holding them accountable to do those tasks, are how you start to motivate behavior to move in positive directions.

Rewarding in a timely manner

Time plays an important role in making motivation work. The longer a person has to wait for good performance to be acknowledged or rewarded in some sort of way, the less likely the reward has much lasting effect. For example, if once a year you tell your employees about all the positive contributions they make in their performance and say nothing the rest of the time, your efforts of positive feedback, while nice, mean little to them. Where were you when they were delivering those good results?

A CASE OF MISGUIDED FOCUS

Jane managed a group of four who provided internal services for the employees of their company. Jane's staff was quite frustrated because a sister company in the same large corporation, responsible for processing payroll and personnel information that affected the employees in Jane's company, ran an inefficient operation, made numerous mistakes, and often took weeks or months to correct their errors.

When employees came to Jane's staff with their problems, her staff could do little to help because the corrections of the problems were out of their control. Every time an employee presented a problem, Jane's staff sent off a nasty letter or made a harsh phone call to their counterparts in the sister company with little effect, other than to annoy the staff in the sister company. In return, Jane's staff voiced their frustrations more and more and didn't come across as very professional doing so.

The sister company's operation was located in a different state. Jane had attempted on occasion to talk with managers there about the problems but hadn't been met with a friendly reception — something related directly to the way her staff acted. Jane didn't persist and began to put her attention to what she could do to ease the frustrations her staff felt.

To attempt to motivate this group, Jane started leaving notes, small gifts, or other tokens of appreciation on the desk of each staff member about once per week. She spent time with her staff, chatting about their weekend plans, hoping to show she cared about them. But the group grew less effective at providing internal customer service and more effective at acting unprofessionally with their concerns. How come? Because the motivation had been mismanaged.

Jane's focus had primarily been on trying to make her staff happy. Her focus got away from performance, so the problems that the group faced stay unaddressed. Here's what she could have done differently:

- Jane called an all staff meeting and acknowledged and empathized with her staff about how challenging the situation was. She listened to their concerns and didn't challenge them. She laid out what steps she had taken and was careful not to be overly critical of the sister company.

- Jane then asked each person to think about what was in their control. What was going well that they could be proud of? How did each member of her team define great customer service? She asked someone to help take notes and put the elements of great service on a whiteboard. Her goal was to focus on the positive things they could control despite their feelings of frustration.

- She summed up that she heard their frustrations and would keep them apprised of updates. In the meanwhile, Jane reinforced the group's decision to focus on what they could control in delivering great service. She discouraged feeding into the negativity and kept people accountable by having one-on-one conversations about working together. Jane was also keen to praise team members who rose to the occasion and executed great service.

Jane was awarding and reinforcing the positive behavior she wanted by including people in the problem, listening to their needs, showing support, and keeping people accountable to being professional-despite a tough situation.

In the same way, if once per year you give your employees a raise, it has little effect on their performance the rest of the year — you're not giving them any compensation when the actions occur. A year is a long time to wait for good performance to be rewarded.

Matching Business Needs to Employee Needs

In any kind of business, the employer has needs that it hires employees to meet and employees have needs that they seek to meet in their employment. The employee and employer both have expectations about meeting those needs of one another, but those expectations often go unstated.

One motivational strategy involves getting these two sets of needs known and building bridges between them. When you do, you have a powerful effect on employee motivation while helping the business accomplish what it needs.

Coaching centers on taking a genuine interest in employee's growth and success. How can you know what motivates and interests employees if you don't make the effort? The next sections help clarify how to dig deeper in understanding your employees to match them to the needs of the company.

Discovering your employees' needs

First you have to understand what motivates each of your employees. What are their needs? What's important to them in their job performance? When you can specifically answer these questions, you know what motivates each staff person and you can then tune them into the needs of your group and the business. Whenever you have this overlap occurring — that is, individual needs are being met at the same time that business needs are being fulfilled — high levels of motivation are stimulated, resulting in good performances.

REMEMBER

You won't be able to meet each person's needs — your job as a manager isn't to cater to each person's needs or to try to meet them all yourself. The responsibility is a two-way street. What you want to be able to do is understand what needs each employee has.

Asking what they need — the motivation questionnaire

While you'll get a sense, through your interactions and observations as you spend time with them, of what's important to every employee in their job situations, the most direct way to truly find out about each employee's needs is to *ask*.

TIP

Find out about your employees' needs related to the key issues of their work and job performance — from what they like to do to where they need improvement, from recognition to needs for guidance and support.

Here's a list of questions to ask (the *motivation questionnaire*) that help you uncover those needs in all these areas:

>> What duties and assignments do you find most challenging?

>> What do you most like doing in your job, and what do you least like doing in your job?

>> What working relationships and work situations with other people do you like?

>> In what areas of your job would you like to

  • Have more guidance?

  • Receive training?

  • Gain autonomy?

>> In which kinds of decisions would you like to have input?

>> When you do good work, how do you like to be recognized for it?

>> What gives you a sense of passion, challenge, and/or accomplishment in your work?

>> In which areas do you think you could use some improvement?

>> Based on the needs of the organization and group, in what skills or areas would you like to gain development and experience?

>> In our working relationship, describe the kind of communication efforts you would most like to see happen.

>> Describe a situation or two (tell the whole story) where you performed at a highly productive and effective level.

Setting yourself up for success

Keep the following tips in mind when putting this motivation questionnaire into action:

>> Schedule a time to meet with each of your direct reports. Allow time for an in-depth conversation. A lunch meeting can work quite well.

>> When making the request for this meeting, tell your employees that you're sincerely interested in exploring their job-related needs and desires.

>> Conduct the session as a conversation rather than an interview. You want the feel of the meeting to be relaxed and informal.

>> Use the questions only as a guide. Probe beyond the given question so that you come away with in-depth knowledge.

>> Listen without judgment and periodically provide verbal feedback to confirm your understanding of what you are hearing.

>> Have a good time and be open to where the conversation may go.

Creating a motivation plan

After asking probing questions, you can develop a motivation plan with each employee. The plan serves as a guide to create opportunities for individual and business success. In developing the plan, follow these steps:

1. **Together with the employee, draw conclusions on the important needs of the individual and develop strategies on how to best meet those needs.**

   This can often be done in the meeting in which you ask probing questions or as a follow-up meeting a short time later if time doesn't permit.

2. **Using Table 10-1, list the key needs of the employee.**

TIP

   Use the left-hand column of the motivation worksheet. To be realistic, target only two or three needs. You also want to go after needs through which the greatest possibility exists to create matches with the business needs.

TABLE 10-1   **Motivation Worksheet**

Employee:	Date:
Employee's Needs	Strategies to Motivate

EXAMPLE

MATCHING NEEDS AND FIRING UP PASSION

Brian was a senior software engineer who had been with his company for a year when Roy, his manager, met with him to complete the motivation questionnaire. The conversation went extremely well, and he learned some things about Brian he didn't know before.

As a performer on the job, Brian did a decent job, but nothing outstanding. He was knowledgeable and got his work done but showed little initiative or creativity in his technical project work.

In his conversation, Roy discovered Brian had been working as a part-time college instructor and loved the opportunity to teach others, even in job assignments. He enjoyed learning and sharing his knowledge with others. Doing project work was fine, but not something that greatly excited him.

Roy then shared with Brian a challenge he was wrestling with for the group. He saw a need for someone who could stay on top of all the latest technical changes in their field and, in particular, who could train new engineers in the group and help keep the experienced engineers up-to-date with these findings. These functions would likely constitute a half-time role.

Brian jumped at the chance. Together, he and Roy targeted a motivation plan that adjusted Brian's role to become the group's researcher and trainer on a half-time basis.

Brian thrived in his new role and his performance excelled. Everyone enjoyed their workshops with Brian. He was an outstanding trainer and became a valuable resource for expertise. Even in his project work, he took initiative to mentor junior engineers. Roy, by matching individual needs with business needs, tapped into a passion of Brian's — and the benefits of now having a highly motivated employee really paid off.

3. **After identifying the key needs together, list the strategies or action plans to meet the needs.**

   Use the right-hand column of Table 10-1.

REMEMBER

Don't confuse a strategy with a need. A *need* is something important or desired in the job situation; a *strategy* is the action to take to meet the need. For example, if your employee talks about wanting training in certain skill areas, the need isn't for training. Training is a strategy or action to be taken. The need is to learn and develop skills.

As you and the employee develop the strategies for the motivation plan, do the following:

- Write them in specific, action-oriented terms.

- Include target dates as to when the actions are to happen.

- Ask the employee what steps you can take to help meet the need.

- Ask the employee what support he or she needs from you in order to meet each targeted need.

4. **Periodically follow up, perhaps once per quarter in your checkup meeting (see Chapter 16) to see how the motivation efforts are going.**

   Also, annually update this information with the employee, perhaps at your performance review meeting. Ask the probing questions again to see what other needs come up. Employees' needs and interests do sometimes change as they move along in their careers.

REMEMBER

The employee is the driver, the one to take responsibility to make the plan happen, and your role as the manager is to provide the necessary support, not to do the motivation for the employee. Your role is also to let the employee know the departmental and business needs, and to then work with him or her to create the matches — opportunities for individual needs that help meet business needs to be met. Table 10-2 shows you a motivation plan for John Doe.

Encouraging initiative

Give your employees the freedom to go make something happen. They may run into an obstacle or two along the way, but their passion to take a risk and make success out of it helps them not be deterred along the way. Your role, when you tap into this passion, is to provide support and keep the bureaucracy out of their way.

REMEMBER

Your role as a manager is to first find out what creates this passion for each of your employees, work with them to create opportunities to tap into this passion, and then give them the support needed along the way. When you do, look out! Motivating in this way will lead to outstanding performance.

TABLE 10-2   **Sample Motivation Worksheet**

Employee: John Doe	Date: 01-11-24
Employee's Needs	**Strategies to Motivate**
1. Strong interest in sharing experience and the knowledge gained from it.	1a. Outline a training program for new hires who come into the group. Finalize by 03-01-24.
	1b. Deliver training for recent hires and new hires thereafter. Start 03-01-24.
	1c. In biweekly, one-on-one meetings, manager will share plans and seek John's input and feedback on them. Start immediately.
2. Have skills expanded, get new challenges.	2a. John will mentor Adriana and Bob to cover half his day-to-day responsibilities. Start immediately.
	2b. John will assist on half-time basis as project manager for ABC Project. Start when Adriana and Bob are ready, estimated to be 03-01-24.

EXAMPLE

Stephanie is an environmental planner, whose job is to write environmental impact statements: How do public policies, programs, or publicly funded infrastructure projects affect streams, communities, and the economy? But her own personal passion is health and community — a relatively new area that measures the human health impact of infrastructure projects. Her success is tied in part to the support of her manager, Scott, who sees the long view. He understands the need to make an investment in key people both to keep them around and to distinguish the organization from others. To ensure he continues to be supportive, Stephanie regularly shares updates both on her development and specific steps she's taking to bring in new projects. She also involves Scott and others on her team in developing a health-impact assessment practice area, so everybody is collectively invested in success. Scott makes time to mentor and support her. He listens to her ideas and challenges and offers help when Stephanie asks for it. He reaches out to his peers and his boss to advocate for her. Scott also supports her taking time from other billable projects to work on her project, which isn't profitable yet. Scott coaches Stephanie when she needs to spend more time on other projects. He knows his role is to do everything to support Stephanie's personal passion because she is too valuable to lose.

Understanding What's Unique about People

Motivation is an individual thing. As Chapter 9 discusses, some employees may be driven by money whereas others say money isn't important to them in their job situations. Assuming that a certain strategy works to motivate all of your staff is misguided thinking. In addition, be careful not to base how you motivate your staff on what motivates you, as in the following example.

EXAMPLE

Julie came in with much enthusiasm as the new manager of the Operations Support group. She wanted her three staff members to feel challenged and motivated in their jobs. Although she never asked what each person's interests were, she knew what had motivated her when she was at their level in her career. So Julie started arranging training sessions and special cross-functional projects for her staff to get involved in. Two of his three staff members really enjoyed these opportunities, but not Mac.

Mac found the training sessions and projects as extra work. They were taking him away from his daily responsibilities and backing him up in finishing his work. Instead of adding value to his job, these motivational activities left Mac frustrated. Julie picked up on his dissatisfaction but was puzzled as to why he felt the way he did, especially when the other two team members were enjoying them. For Julie, these activities helped her advance in her career.

What interests you — or the majority of your team — may not be the same as to what interests every staff member. Seeing the world from your own point of view, even under the best intentions, may blind you to what motivates your employees. (Emphasizing the importance of recognizing individual differences, a key part of coaching, is discussed further in Chapter 7.)

REMEMBER

When you get to understand every employee as individuals, you can understand what motivates them in their jobs. Of course, to know how to individually motivate each of your employees, you have to observe, listen, and ask questions, as opposed to assume, tell, and impose your own ideas.

Treating your employees the way they want to be treated

The Golden Rule, "Do unto others as you would have them do unto you," implies that other people like to be treated the way that you like to be treated. In the previous section, Julie misread Mac as someone who'd value training because she personally valued it. Everyone is different and unique. These sections look at a system that helps you assess how someone might be different and what may motivate them.

Introducing the Platinum Rule

In the *Platinum Rule*, Tony Alessandra, PhD, suggests to "treat others the way they want to be treated." If you want to discover what motivates someone, you need to know how they're different. You can start to understand employees by learning how to identify their behavior. Figure 10-1 shows a matrix of four basic behavior characteristics.

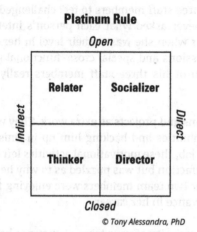

FIGURE 10-1:
The Platinum
Rule.

© Tony Alessandra, PhD

These four characteristics are as follows:

>> **Direct:** This personality trait favors a direct communication style. You know exactly where this type of person stands by their clear verbal and nonverbal expression:

- Is expressive

- Talks and tells

- Is outgoing

- Offers opinions freely

- Takes risks

>> **Indirect:** This personality trait favors an indirect communication style. You don't know always know where this type of person stands by their clear verbal and nonverbal expression:

- Avoids risk

- Is slower to decide

- Is less assertive

- Listens and asks

- Is reserved

>> **Open:** This personality trait values relationships and sharing feelings openly. The focus is on getting along, not just the results:

- Is relaxed, warm

- Likes opinions

- Is relationship-oriented

- Shares feelings

- Is spontaneous

- Is easy going

>> **Closed:** This personality trait is more focused on the work, rather than sharing feelings. The focus is on the work, more than relationships:

- Is guarded

- Acts formal, proper

- Is task-oriented

- Is a thinker

- Is results-oriented

- Is a planner, organized

Applying the Platinum Rule

Alessandra came up with these four different general categories of people that I (Leo) have found useful in coaching people:

>> **Supporter/Relater:** Combines open — a focus on relationships with indirect communication style, which isn't given to assert their opinions:

- Is a harmonizer, accommodating

- Values acceptance and stability

- Dislikes change; slow to change

- Builds networks of friends to help do the work

- Is a good listener; is timid about voicing contrary opinions; concerned with others' feelings

- Is easy-going; likes slow, steady pace

- Is friendly and sensitive; feels no person is unlovable

- Is relationship-oriented

>> **Analyzer/Thinker:** Combines a closed orientation of focusing on results with an indirect communication style that isn't overly vocal or assertive:

- Is an assessor

- Values accuracy in details and being right

- Plans thoroughly before deciding to act

- Prefers to work alone

- Is introverted; is quick to think and slow to speak; is closed about personal matters

- Is highly organized; even plans spontaneity

- Uses a cautious, logical, thrifty approach

- Is thoughtful; no problem is too big to ponder

- Is idea-oriented

>> **Promoter/Socializer:** Combines an open orientation on relationships with a direct and expressive communication style:

- Is an entertainer

- Values enjoyment and helping others

- Is full of ideas and impulsive in trying them

- Wants work to be fun for everyone

- Is talkative and open about self; asks others' opinions; loves to brainstorm

- Is flexible; easily bored with routine

- Uses an intuitive, creative, spontaneous, flamboyant approach

- Is an optimist; nothing is beyond hope

- Is celebration-oriented

>> **Controller/Director:** Combines an orientation on results and work with a direct and expressive communicative style:

- Is a commander

- Values getting the job done

- Is a decisive risk-taker

- Is good at delegating work to others

- Isn't shy but private about personal matters; comes on strong in conversation

- Likes to be where the action is

- Takes charge, has an enterprising, competitive, efficient approach

- Is fearless; no obstacle is too big to tackle

- Is results-oriented

Chances are you have a mix of different types on your team, and that's good! You need the balance of all of them contributing in their own way: the Socializer to suggest getting everyone together to talk about a project, the Supporter to find the common themes, the Analyzer to put the brakes on it to study potential problems, and the Director to wrap up the meeting with action steps and assignments to get it going.

How does this relate to motivation? Ask yourself:

>> What type do you align with most?

>> When is your style most helpful?

>> When does your style get in your way?

>> How do you like to receive recognition or reward?

Think of an employee you manage or a member of your organization with whom you've had challenges and ask yourself the following:

>> How did their communication style differ from your natural style?

>> How might you flex your style and approach to be more effective?

ACCOUNTING FOR DIFFERENCES

Paying attention to people and understanding what uniquely motivates them is critical to being an effective coach manager, as this example illustrates.

Rich managed four different types of people on his team. He could spot their communication styles and work preferences based on their behavior. Rich took this into account when motivating each of them. He didn't use one size fits all but tailored his approach. By the way, Rich is a blend of a Socializer and Director.

Here is a breakdown of the people on Rich's team by personality type. Note how Rich uses his understanding to manage and motivate each person, based on how they value relationships versus results and how direct or indirect they communicate:

- **Beth** (Supporter) always says yes to projects, even if she's buried. Rich appreciates her positive attitude. She's the first one to arrive and often the last one to leave. Rich knows that Beth likes to be known as helpful, but she also doesn't really like the spotlight. He doesn't call out her contributions in a staff meeting because he knows she'll feel bad that others didn't get recognized. Public recognition isn't a motivator for her. Rich knows that Beth likes to blend into the background, just another team member. To keep her motivated, Rich privately acknowledges her can-do attitude, "Once again, you come through!" "You're a life-saver." "What would I do without you?" Rich also has each new employee spend the first day with Beth to get an orientation on the systems. She loves following procedure and is good at it. When he introduces a new employee to Beth, he says, "Beth is our resident expert on our procedures. She'll walk you through how we do things and can answer any questions." He likes to follow up with Beth the next day, taking her out for coffee or lunch to get her assessment on the new hire. This is not only a motivator for Beth, but it's also smart to get the pulse on new employees from your team.

- **Ibrahim** (Analyzer) is the company's brilliant technical IT director. Rich feels lucky to have him, though it can be difficult to communicate with Ibrahim. He's quiet and reserved, and Rich, socializer/director, is more talkative and direct. One thing Rich would never do is publicly acknowledge how awesome Ibrahim is — even in a staff email. Ibrahim values his work, knowledge, and risk avoidance. Rich gets that. To keep him motivated, Rich often asks Ibrahim's opinions on what issues the company needs to consider and what Ibrahim recommends. Rich can tell that even though Ibrahim doesn't like attention, he does like it when at a senior staff meeting, Rich asks Ibrahim's opinion. Acknowledging his intellect and serious side is a motivator for Ibrahim. Supporting Ibrahim's policies with staff is another way he motivates Ibrahim. Rich is very supportive of Ibrahim's interest in attending or presenting at conferences.

- **Sophia** (Socializer) is always at the center of a conversation. As the sales director, she has a gift for drawing people out and engaging them. She is successful because she never pushes a sale but asks a lot of questions and goes out of her way to help clients, even if they don't buy from the company. She frequently socializes with clients and staff. For her, there's not a clear line between work and personal life. To motivate her, Rich knows she appreciates public recognition. "Big shout-out for Sophia for the big sale." Sophia tries to downplay the attention, but Rich can see she not so secretly loves it. Rich sees that Sophia is good at mentoring younger staff and encourages any opportunity. Rich supports her desire to fund company fun events.

- **David** (Director) is his go-to-person when he wants to get a quick assessment of an idea. David gets right to the point and tells it like it is. He's good at reading situations and suggesting a practical strategy that's good for the overall company. David sometimes can be impatient who are indirect (supporters and analyzers), but David is widely liked and respected. Simply by seeking David's advice on topics, Rich is tapping into what motivates him. David likes to be a guy with answers, who can cut through it. In staff meetings, Rich almost always summarizes meetings by asking David what the next steps are. Rich also gives David the most challenging assignments. And while David is more results-driven, Rich knows that David doesn't mind public acknowledgement of his contributions.

Building Pillars of Commitment

The five pillars for building a strong level of employee commitment, covered in detail in Chapter 4, are greatly impacted when you apply strategies for motivation:

>> **Focus:** Creating a motivation plan targets efforts to meet employees' needs. The efforts provide a focus for your employees as to what steps to take to make good things happen in their performance. They know what direction to go and, as a bonus, are motivated to do so because they benefit from it.

>> **Involvement:** For many of the motivation strategies in this chapter, you seek your employees' input or ideas, and then involve your staff in taking on the responsibilities they want to have. Employees help shape their motivation plans and truly own what happens with them. Your role is one of support.

>> **Development:** This pillar of commitment is greatly impacted by your motivation efforts. Much of the work you do in your motivation efforts seeks to develop your employees' skills and capabilities. You're stimulating their desire to grow — that's development at its best.

>> **Gratitude:** Behavior that's rewarded is repeated. When you apply the motivation strategies of giving positive feedback and utilizing various forms of recognition to acknowledge good performance, the gratitude pillar is influenced tremendously.

>> **Accountability:** This pillar for building employee commitment is impacted when you proceed with your follow-up efforts to review progress with your employees on their motivation plans. Because your employees own the plans, the sense of accomplishment and motivation is in their hands.

IN THIS CHAPTER

» **Knowing when to ask questions**

» **Asking effective tutoring questions**

» **Listening actively to facilitate coaching discussions**

» **Overcoming challenges**

» **Influencing employee commitment by tutoring with questions**

Chapter **11**

Teaching by Asking Questions

Your primary role as a coach and mentor is to help develop employees to their full potential. When you motivate them to challenge themselves and learn from experience, you're laying the foundation for commitment. Your employees want to try harder to figure things out on their own, and, in the process, grow in their careers and contribute more overall to the organization.

One of the best ways of teaching is also the oldest: Ask questions. The Greek philosopher Socrates engaged in two-way dialog with his students to spark intellectual curiosity and independent thinking. But you don't have to be the founder of philosophy to tap the power of questions. You just have to remember to use them. This chapter looks at why questions are so important to effective coaching and mentoring, how to ask questions, and when not asking questions is a better strategy.

Tapping the Power of Asking

Doer managers are inclined to tell and direct employees. They often operate from a position of positional authority: don't question, just do it. Although there's a time for being direct and clear about your direction, coaching managers shift the focus to empowering the employee to think for themselves. These sections help you understand what happens in your interactions with employees when you do ask questions and when you don't.

Understanding why questions are so powerful

The organizations that attract the best talent and outperform competitors are organizations that value constantly questioning everything: How happy are employees? What improvements in their products and services do customers value? How do they do better? On a very practical level, questions are part of everyday work. Questions are part of their culture.

Although executive coaches differ in the assessments they use or the style they engage clients, every coach values and uses questions as a foundation for helping people realize their potential. Here are some of the reasons:

>> **Questions promote continual learning.** People learn best when they work at thinking on their own. If your goal is for employees to be more independent, questions challenge and engage them to figure out solutions on their own.

>> **Questions shift responsibility to the employee.** Employees are motivated by finding meaning in their work. When you ask questions, you're supporting their desire to be authors of their own work. You're essentially saying, "This is your work; how would you do it?"

>> **Questions free you.** By encouraging self-learning, people become less reliant on you, their manager. That allows you to focus on higher level tasks, attend conferences, and go on vacation.

>> **Questions often generate surprise answers.** There's more than one way — and often better ways — to solve problems. Questions can unlock new solutions.

>> **Questions increase your emotional intelligence (EQ).** Curiosity helps you learn more about yourself and others. Good questions can provide answers and insights into yourself and others that will help you be a better leader.

>> **Questions help you challenge the bias.** Chapter 7 discusses how many of your biases and assumptions about people are unconscious. Self-reflecting questions force you to look deeper into your beliefs and perceptions. Questions you ask of others help you see their stories, challenges, and motivations.

Knowing what happens when you don't use questions

On one hand, asking questions might seem like a lot of work. Isn't it just easier to just tell people what to do? Here are drawbacks to that approach:

>> The more you tell an employee how to do their job, the less they think and do for themselves. They become dependent on you and don't grow.

>> Motivation suffers when people aren't engaged in their work and simply following directions.

>> When people aren't engaged, productivity drops. People leave and then the organization has to spend valuable time and resources replacing talent.

>> Creativity suffers by everyone doing the same thing. Engaging employees to think on their own often produces new and better solutions that can improve the "way things have always been done."

>> Your time is dominated by micromanaging people to follow your orders and answering questions all day.

>> When you don't ask questions to know people better, you're stuck in what limited knowledge you have of them. You don't understand them and they don't feel heard and respected.

TIP

Many managers tend to overlook or fail to recognize the power of coaching with questions, perhaps because it requires them to shift from the all-telling, all-knowing mode of operation to a collaborative approach. Coaching with questions operates under a simple assumption: Employees are adults and are capable of having thoughts and ideas. Your challenge in switching from doer manager to a coach manager is to listen first, speak second; ask first, offer second. You also need to understand when coaching with questions is appropriate and when it's not.

Using Questions: When and When Not To

Coaching with questions works well in certain situations, but it's not applicable in others. Be aware of when this coaching tool can be plugged in to get value from it and when attempting to use it defeats its purpose. This section gives you a guide to differentiate these situations.

When questions don't work

Although using questions can be a powerful teaching strategy, don't confuse it with teaching in the conventional sense. Even Socrates acknowledged questions and dialog alone had its limitations. After all, employees can't be expected to *know* how to do a task if they don't have the knowledge or experience. To understand when you want to use coaching with questions, take a look at when not to use this tool. Attempts to use the questioning tool in the situations in the following sections can be counterproductive to learning and developing employees.

Playing 20-questions

Did you ever play the game of 20 questions when you were a kid? In the game, someone has something in mind, and through asking questions, the other person tries to guess what it is. Is it bigger than an ice tray? Is it hotter than a hot potato? If you guess right in 20 questions or less, you win.

EXAMPLE

Imagine a manager asked an employee to explain how they'd handle the day's heavy operational issues. The manager greeted each idea that the employee presented with "No, try again." After three tries and having gone through this kind of experience with the manager before, the exasperated employee blurted out, "If there is some way you want me to go about handling this work, just tell me!"

REMEMBER

Be aware when asking questions becomes *torturing* with questions, not coaching with questions. Employees generally don't want to play the game to get to "your right answer." If you have something in mind, say so. Avoid playing guessing games.

Telling employees how they're performing

Chapter 14 dives deeper into giving constructive feedback (which includes both negative and positive feedback), based on your observations of how an employee is performing.

There's value in using questions to engage employees in a collaborative conversation about their performance, particularly as you start your conversation: "How do you think you're doing?"

But it doesn't mean you don't give direct and clear feedback, "Here's my observation." Most managers don't have a problem giving feedback when employees are performing well. However, when the performance isn't up to snuff, many do have trouble giving negative feedback.

REMEMBER

If you rely solely on questions when giving feedback, employees can get anxious and confused. People want to know how they're doing. Although questions are useful, be up front and clear with your feedback. Don't leave the employee with more questions on how they're doing.

Providing necessary information

Part of your role as a manager is to give your employees the information they need to do their jobs well — the little stuff and the big picture stuff. Chapter 13 dives into how to effectively delegate work. A critical ingredient in successfully passing work to someone is giving them the information they need to be meet the expectations. Even though questions are powerful, taking time clearly explain a process, provide detail and documentation, and show examples are critical steps to helping an employee be successful. When to tell and when to ask questions all depends on the specific employee and specific situation.

Giving direction

Giving employees direction isn't the same as being directive. *Being directive* is telling people how to do their jobs and giving them orders — usually actions not well received by most employees.

Giving direction, on the other hand, includes things like explaining what target you want to see accomplished, clarifying where the group should be headed, or describing the parameters and boundaries within which your employees need to work. Employees require and desire direction from their managers.

Asking them how they will meet that direction is where tutoring with questions comes into the equation. Clarifying or giving the direction is best when you explain it.

Asking questions when employees lack the background

When an individual doesn't have the knowledge, skill, or experience to understand or handle a particular issue, asking the person for ideas about how to handle the issue will be met with blank stares. This is a situation in which the employee first needs information in order to proceed effectively. Your role is to explain and teach. After the employee has the essential knowledge or experience, tutoring with questions can work.

When questions work

The following section covers four situations in which questions work well. These opportunities let you challenge employees to think and do for themselves — true coaching opportunities. During these situations, if you tell instead of ask, employees gain little for themselves.

Some of the following situations are also applicable when you've just given negative feedback. In the discussion that follows the feedback, you can use questions to promote a two-way conversation that's often more effective in employee development than simply delivering feedback without dialog (see Chapter 4 for more on two-way conversations).

Analyzing and problem-solving

The process of analyzing and problem-solving is one of the best situations for plugging in coaching with questions. Instead of quickly giving solutions, you're allowing the person with the problem to help create the solution. Solutions often lie with those closest to the problem. Using questions draws those solutions from your employees.

Problems are a normal part of anyone's job. Many employees think their roles are to bring every problem to their managers for them to solve. You may be one of those managers who faces the wave of everyone else's problems falling into your lap. In addition, you may have employees who complain to you whenever something isn't working well. These are problem situations and are, therefore, opportunities to use questions. Instead of feeling the burden of having to have all the solutions, coaching with questions pushes employees to understand how they might solve these problems themselves. Because they're the ones who are closest to the issues in most cases, have them think through how to solve the problems.

Here are some good questions to use:

>> What questions have you asked yourself?

>> If I wasn't around, how would you solve it?

>> What do you think is the issue?

>> What's the next logical step?

>> Where can you get answers?

Evaluating options and making decisions

Employees are sometimes quick to come to you for decisions about what to do in areas that they responsible for. Questions can help them analyze and determine the best course of action. Instead of making quick decisions when you ask for their ideas or recommendations, employees gain decision-making perspectives. The goal is getting employees thinking and making decisions for themselves within their own job parameters instead of expecting you to decide for them. In this way, you expand the parameters of their jobs and grow their capabilities in the process.

Consider using these questions:

» What have you tried?

» What haven't you tried?

» What's the cost/benefit analysis of your options?

» What are your concerns?

» What's the worst thing could happen?

» Are there other models or examples that can help you decide?

» What are the primary criteria you're using to make your decision?

» In a perfect world, what would the outcome be?

» How do your options impact other people?

» Who else do you need to consult with?

» What's your hesitation in deciding?

Doing things better or differently

In many situations, such as when mistakes are made or performance efforts don't go as well as hoped, opportunities exist for employees to learn lessons and correct their course. Using questions to explore what happened and what can be done to make matters work better provides experiences for learning and growth.

Sometimes, managers abruptly react when they see mistakes made. They can be quick to chastise or blame for what happened. This behavior discourages the employee from learning lessons. Some managers just step in and fix the mistakes themselves which, of course, means that employees learn nothing for themselves. Other managers, when employees take initiative that doesn't turn out right, jump on that effort with a harsh and quick reaction. ("What were you doing here! Who told you should take it upon yourself to do that effort!") Such reactions mean good-bye future efforts to take initiative.

Coaching with questions provides good give-and-take conversations in which employees can learn for themselves and improve as they go forward. It allows for the right behaviors to continue with better ways to do them. This approach is much better than blaming, which kills initiative. Even if you're the most patient and understanding manager, employees naturally don't want to disappoint you by making a mistake. If you set the tone that mistakes are part of the learning process, employees will be more inclined to take risks and act independently. Of course, no company can afford for all of their employees to make big mistakes all the time. But companies that factor in trial and error and learning along with performance benefit from a culture of people doing their best work. Coaching and mentoring means you pay attention to employees and provide continual support in their development. You're not a "wind them up and let them go" manager, but you're ever attentive and engaged. You provide instruction when needed. You ask questions and let people arrive at their own solutions when needed. You give feedback and encourage dialog when needed.

Here are some questions you can ask along the way:

>> What did you learn?

>> What steps would you take in the future to avoid these problems?

>> How could you approach it differently next time?

>> What did you learn about yourself?

>> Are there other people you could have consulted with along the way?

>> How could I have done better?

>> In what way could I have helped?

>> If there's a silver lining in this situation, what would it be?

Developing plans

Coaching with questions also is a great tool for helping employees think out plans of action and steps to take in order to tackle a project or assignment. Instead of telling them how they should go about doing their work, you're helping them to think and develop their own action plans.

Instead of leaving them on their own, struggling with how to get started, your questions can guide them to figure out a plan of action. Questions can help them think through, in a logical flow, ways to organize themselves to get the job done. Now they're ready to act on the plans your questions helped them create. Developing a plan by using questions rather than just telling lays the foundation for a collaborative process, in which you're both sharing ideas and knowledge.

USING QUESTIONS TO HELP EMPLOYEES DEVELOP PLANS

To engage people and grow them, use questions strategically. Consider this example.

Marie, who is head of HR, delegated the task to reorganize employee orientation materials to an HR assistant, Donna. Donna was new to HR and Marie knew she'd have to invest in coaching her with questions and telling her information. After Marie spent time with Donna outlining the task and providing important background, she asked Donna to come up with a list of questions on how she might proceed with the project. Marie also took time to jot down some of her own questions to compare with Donna's. After they met and discussed the questions, they brainstormed how Donna could fill in any number of gaps in Donna's knowledge including:

- Who would be using this most?
- How are they going to use it?
- In what format is it most useful?
- How often will it need to be updated?
- Who else needs to be consulted?
- What's the history of the current system?
- What problems have people reported?

They came up with an initial plan to gather more information. Marie could have just told her what she'd do, but in collaborating with Donna, several things happened:

- Unknown problems surfaced.
- People impacted by the system appreciated being consulted with.
- Donna made important connections with people in and out of her department.
- Donna became the expert on employee orientation materials and proactively suggested changes and improvements.
- Marie had worked herself out being responsible for it anymore.

Asking Coaching Questions: The How-To

Not all questions are created equal. The right question can create a spark of inspiration. The wrong question can go nowhere. Knowing what makes a good coaching question for employees is the focus of the next sections. You'll ask better questions in coaching employees if you follow these guidelines.

Comparing close-ended and open-ended questions

Questions are either close-ended or open-ended. *Close-ended questions* are designed to elicit short, definitive responses. Here are a few examples of close-ended questions:

>> Did you take out the garbage?

>> When is the meeting?

>> Where is the meeting on the garbage?

Although the answers can be given in one or a few words, some people still like to expound or ramble when you ask close-ended questions. Nonetheless, they're designed to get you a specific piece of information. Many close-ended questions require a yes/no response.

Open-ended questions are designed to solicit expressions of thought that range from explanations to ideas. These questions must be answered in sentences rather than one or few words. Socrates used open-ended questions when he taught students. He believed that thoughtful questioning enabled the student to examine ideas logically and to test the validity of those ideas on their own.

Following the garbage example, here are few examples of open-ended questions:

>> Why are you reluctant to take out the garbage?

>> What will you do to ensure that the garbage is taken out?

>> How will you keep garbage from coming into the meeting?

When teaching with questions, most of the questions that you ask are open-ended. Close-ended questions are used only occasionally to confirm or clarify a message or to get a specific piece of information. Focus on asking open-ended questions for more collaborative communication. Socrates might have asked his students:

> » Why do you say that?

> » What do you mean by . . .?

> » How does this relate to our discussion?

> » What do you think is the main issue?

> » Could you expand upon that point further?

REMEMBER

When you engage in open-ended questions like these, it changes the interaction and reinforces more of a peer-to-peer relationship. You aren't putting yourself above your employees. You're working alongside them and respecting their intelligence and creativity. If you can discover how to ask open-ended questions, you'll be amazed at how employees will respond by answers and ideas that you could have never imagined. This is coaching at its best.

To see how this works in the workplace, look at the nearby sidebar with Marie who asked a number of open-ended questions. Not all open-ended questions need to be in the form of a question, but they can instead be a request for an exploration, such as the following:

> » Describe what you see as possible causes for this problem.

> » Tell me how you'd implement that idea.

> » Explain the benefits to using that approach.

> » I'd like to hear more of your thinking behind that proposal.

As you can see in these examples, certain key words — such as tell, describe, and explain — create open-ended questions or requests for explanations. Sentences that start with verbs like tell, describe, and explain actually serve as good starting points for tutoring with questions as they solicit explanations and depth of information — the whole idea when using this coaching tool. Who, when, and where at the start of a sentence generally shape questions so that they are close-ended (as in, "Who? Him." "When? Yesterday." "Where? There.").

TIP

Questions that start with *why* are open-ended, but exercise caution with *why* questions. Why? Quite often, questions that start with the word *why* come off sounding accusatory or like you're grilling the person. "Why did you do that?" Such questions often put the other person on the defensive, as though something needs to be justified. So if you feel the need to use a tutoring question or request for explanation that begins with why, either manage your tone carefully or rephrase the sentence to avoid the word. "Please explain your thinking on that issue" is much better than "Why would you want to do that?" What, how, when, and where are often easier for people to answer. You run the risk of confusing or overwhelming people by asking why. Still, use your judgment: Some employees would love to tell you the why behind their decisions.

Focusing on space and time

When asking questions, keep two words in mind — space and tone — as the following clarifies:

>> **Space:** Instead of asking leading-the-witness questions (that is, close-ended questions such as "Do you think that idea is really going to help?" Or "Do you think that if you try it my way, everything will work out for the best?"), ask questions that give employees freedom and space to express their thoughts. For example, ask a question like "How do you think that idea can help?" When you ask questions of this kind — open-ended ones — you're giving the person space to express thoughts. These questions have no right or wrong answers, which is the whole idea when tutoring with questions.

>> **Tone:** Tone is critical to asking questions successfully. An inquisitive and nonjudgmental tone works best, and is much better than an accusatory, sarcastic, condescending, or confrontational tone.

Facilitate and Listen (Don't Dominate or Vacillate)

To make tutoring with questions work in your coaching, you must be an active participant in discussions, playing the primary role of facilitator, which includes actively listening.

In a business meeting, a facilitator guides the flow of the meeting so that it achieves the desired outcomes. Your job as facilitator in a coaching discussion with your employee is to guide its flow and allow the employee to easily express their thoughts and reach a positive outcome with you. Besides asking inquisitive questions, you need to take a few other steps to effectively facilitate the discussion. The following sections show you how.

Seek positive outcomes

To effectively facilitate discussions, you need to know where you want the discussion to go — that is, the *positive outcome* you want to reach. I'm not talking about the specific outcome but a general one. For example, if you're tutoring with questions about a certain problem situation, your positive outcome is to develop a solution. After the general outcome is established, you can then use the two-way discussion to work out the particular solution.

REMEMBER

To guide the flow of a discussion, you need to define the direction in which you want to go. At the start of the discussion with your employee, feel free to explain the positive outcome that you have in mind so that the individual can move in the same direction you're moving.

The key is that you have a positive outcome in mind. Often, especially in situations in which problems are being raised, managers aren't focusing on a positive conclusion. Here are a couple of favorites that I've heard tossed out:

>> "I want you to see how your behavior is inappropriate and causing me and everyone else here so much pain."

>> "I want you to realize how you should never do this mistake again."

If you want to push guilt or encourage defensiveness, these negative statements work well. A statement of a positive outcome, on the other hand, is something like this: "Let's discuss what can be learned from this experience and come up with a plan to make things work better going forward." With this positive focus to aim for, most employees will be happy to talk with you about an issue.

REMEMBER

Don't forget the four situations in which to tutor with questions (see the "When questions work" section earlier in this chapter). Be sure to phrase your statement of positive outcome around the applicable situation you are working with — solutions, plans, decisions, or doing things better. As you start your coaching discussion with the employee, state the positive outcome that applies to the situation at hand.

Go in a logical flow

Open-ended questions help guide the discussion along a reasonable path toward reaching the positive outcome. For example, if your positive outcome is to reach a solution to a problem, follow a systematic approach to get there. Don't explore causes of the problem when you've already developed a solution with the employee. (As in "Hey, why do you think the system keeps going down on your shift?") Or if you're going to discuss the development of a plan with the employee, don't begin by asking questions such as "Now, what would the last step of your plan be?" Instead, move the discussion in a logical step-by-step approach to reach the final stage of the plan.

REMEMBER

Certainly, these coaching discussions don't always flow in an organized fashion. And you do want to be flexible enough to explore an unexpected issue that comes up, if needed. The idea, though, is to think about where you're going with the discussion so that your questions follow a direction to get there. Veering off track isn't difficult to correct when you know the track to go on.

Tune in and listen

To effectively facilitate a coaching discussion, you need to be an active listener, not a passive one. Chapter 5 discusses how active listening can be used as a tool for engaging people and building trust. Active listening means you're engaged and curious in the conversation to understand the employee's thought process and help them formulate their approach. To help guide this flow, periodically explore points to a greater depth (probing), and along the way, check to see whether you understand what the employee means (by paraphrasing or reflecting feelings and other messages). When you make these efforts, your active listening allows the employee to think and sort through thoughts and come up with workable outcomes that they can implement. That's coaching.

Handling Challenging Bumps along the Road

Understanding when it's best to apply questions — whether it's developing plans, creating solutions, learning to do something different or better, or making decisions — is a key part of achieving success with this coaching tool. However, challenges can occasionally happen with some employees. When you hit one of these bumps, resist the temptation to revert to the I-tell-you-what-to-do mode. Not only do you diminish employees' abilities to think and take responsibility for themselves, you also implicitly send the message, "I only give the appearance of being open, but want you to do what I want you to do or tell me what I want to hear." And if this pattern develops when you have a challenging conversation with an employee, it's good-bye to commitment.

So you need to stay the course even when you encounter two of the most difficult challenges in trying to make this coaching tool work. The next sections look at two such challenges and give some tips for working through them.

The "I-don't-know" employee

Ever have a staff member in your group who no matter how good your question is, automatically come backs with "I don't know?" (Sometimes this response doesn't happen initially but comes when you're getting into the crux of the conversation and are seeking the employee's ideas for handling a situation.) In such cases, if you feel like jumping in and saying, "Just do this and get out of here," I'd understand. Unfortunately, doing so discourages employee thinking and encourages more I-don't-know responses in the future.

TIP

Here are some tips to overcome this bump in the road.

>> **Bounce back and wait patiently.** To *bounce back* means to put the authority of solving an issue in the employee's court, by simply saying, "Well, what do you think?" Then wait patiently. Your patient manner is the critical factor in stimulating someone else's thoughts. When you wait patiently, as opposed to anxiously, you allow silence to work as a stimulator for the other person. It says to the employee, "I'll wait for your answer. Feel free to take your time to gather your thoughts."

REMEMBER

Silence with patience also applies positive pressure to the person who has been asked the question. "Hey, my manager really wants me to think and wants to hear what I have to say. I'd better come up with something." If you become anxious or irritated, you shut down any possible flow of conversation.

Use this tip when employees come frequently to ask you what to do, especially if you think they should know what to do (see the nearby sidebar for an example).

>> **Simplify the question.** Sometimes your question may come across to the employee as too broad or difficult, so the initial response may be, "I don't know." This response may follow questions like "What ideas do you have for a solution?" Or "What would your plan be to address this issue?"

So when you get the I-don't-know response, usually accompanied by the blank stare, simplify the question. "Give me one idea that you think will help." The message that you want to impart is that, at this stage, there are no bad ideas. You want your employee to share one that they think will help.

>> **Question the question.** If you're not getting anywhere with an employee maybe you're asking the wrong questions. Don't be afraid to ask, "Am I asking the right question?" "Should I be asking a different question?" Your goal is to engage the employee in any way possible. Maybe their mind is on something else you didn't anticipate.

>> **Draw upon past successes.** Sometimes, you may be aware that an employee has dealt in the past with challenges similar to the one that's currently baffling

them. If so, instead of asking the employee (who can't think of anything) to come up with ideas, shift to analyzing a similar past experience in which the employee achieved success.

You want your questions to encourage the employee to figure out what they did successfully in the past. You can then offer your insights, as needed. By drawing on these successes and tutoring with questions, you can help the employee see which ones can be used in the current situation. Quite often, what worked well once, but was forgotten, can work well again.

>> **Consider what someone else would do.** When an employee is stuck and can offer little more than a pondering I-don't-know answer, you can try shifting the focus away from the employee. Insert a respected source of expertise that you both know or admire. "How would the ideal manager handle this situation?" Or more likely, "If Jane were still here and faced with this challenge, what do you think she would do?" This question allows both you and the employee to remove yourselves from the situation temporarily and become creative, focusing instead on what the employee thinks a proven performer would do.

When you don't like their ideas

The second challenge that causes knee-jerk reactions from managers and defeats the purpose of coaching with questions occurs when an employee shares an idea that you don't agree with or like at all. And to compound the problem, the employee often expresses the idea with a great deal of enthusiasm.

EXAMPLE

BETTER COACHING BY ASKING QUESTIONS

Here's an example of Roberta, a manager who changed her behavior after she discovered how coaching could help her, especially through coaching with questions.

The day after Roberta introduced a new procedure to her staff, Sally came to Roberta, as she often did, and asked, "About that new procedure we're supposed to use today, what exactly am I supposed to do again?"

Instead of repeating what Roberta had explained the day before, as she often did, she bounced back and replied, "What do you think you do?" Then she waited patiently, and after a few seconds, Sally spoke up and explained the procedure step-by-step. Roberta then responded, "Sally, you got it," and Sally responded with a beaming face, a reaction that Roberta had seldom seen. Let employees think for themselves.

TIP

You know that rolling your eyes and snorting won't inspire more ideas. What do you do instead? Here are some ideas:

» **Explore the rationale and consequences.** Find out the rationale behind the employee's thinking. To do that, have the individual explain their thinking directly, by asking or saying any of the following:

- "Explain your thinking or rationale for that idea."

- "What do you see as the pluses and minuses of that idea?"

- "What do you see as the ramifications of going with that proposal?"

These questions help you and the employee look at the thinking behind the idea and analyze its possible consequences, with the employee, through your questioning, leading the way in the analysis.

REMEMBER

By stepping back first and helping the staff person analyze what has been suggested, they're able to conclude what will work and what won't — without becoming defensive. At the same time, by letting the employee think out loud and make their case, you may realize that something you didn't think would work will work after all. Isn't that the definition of open-mindedness?

» **Check your understanding first.** This means, of course, listening all the way through. As needed, ask more questions so that the employee fully explains their idea. Then paraphrase what you hear to see whether you understand the message correctly. "What you're suggesting as the best way to resolve this problem is to run a smear campaign to get the manager in this challenging department fired. Is that right?"

Two things often come out of an active listening effort:

- The employee's idea is clarified. And because you may not have fully understood the idea, after it's clarified, you may realize that it's not so bad after all.

- By paraphrasing, you serve as a sounding board for the employee — who now realizes, through the playback of the message, that their idea isn't a good one to pursue. Even if the employee doesn't come to this realization, and you don't think the idea is a good one, you at least understand where the person is coming from and can proceed with the previous tip of exploring the rationale and consequences or use the next strategy.

» **State your concern and let them address it.** Beyond dismissing the employee's idea outright, the worst thing you can do is to say you like the idea, when you really don't, just so that you won't hurt the person's feelings.

Managing assertively (as Chapter 4 discusses) is a critical part of how coaching works. You don't want to mislead the employee. Instead, constructively state your concern about the individual's suggestion and explain why. Put your explanation within the context of not seeing how the idea will help to achieve your objective or positive outcome. That way, you sound reasonable, as opposed to being biased or a manager who can't listen. You also help align the employee with where they need to go in terms of performance.

When you finish your explanation (and don't be long-winded), say something like "Please address" or "With my concern in mind, explain to me how what you proposed would work." Doing so keeps a two-way conversation going and allows for a good give-and-take dialog, rather than a raucous debate or sparring contest.

This strategy does two things for the employee, as well. It gives the individual valuable input to consider and, if the person still feels the idea has merit, the opportunity to address your concerns and prove the merit of the idea. That's challenging employees to think for themselves at its best — a key part of the mentoring tools of coaching.

The Case of Coaching with Questions

The following shares a live example of coaching with questions:

Sara is VP of security for an IT company. A new protocol for employee background checks was facing resistance by staff for being too invasive. Sara decided to bring up the issue at her staff meeting. John, a long-time employee who hasn't been pleased that Sara was promoted to VP only after three years with the company, is the first to speak up. "So, we're just going to let anyone work here?" She doesn't say anything and pretends not to hear him. Inside, however, she's boiling over. In her mind, this is just another attempt to undermine her authority. She's tired of dealing with John's passive-aggressive behavior and really wants to come down hard on him for his comment, but she doesn't like to make waves either.

Sara shares the story in the weekly executive meeting. Bernadette, the company CEO, offers to meet with Sara to coach her and defuse the situation. Bernadette finds a quiet time to gather her thoughts prior to her meeting. She understands that although she could be doing a lot of things, coaching her direct reports is the best use of her time. If she spends time developing her immediate team of VPs, the VPs will get better at handling their own issues, instead of Bernadette jumping into fix them. Bernadette outlines her desired outcomes of her meeting with Sara:

>> Identify the goal of the meeting collaboratively.

>> Decide on a desired common ground or ideal outcome.

>> Allow Sara to safely vent her feelings and judgments.

>> Separate the facts from judgments and emotions.

This is what a coaching conversation with Sara might sound like:

Bernadette: I wanted to discuss with you the incident with John and help you come up with a way of resolving it so we can get back on track. How are you feeling about the interaction with John? (open-ended question to build trust and allow Sara to vent)

Sara: Really angry and even a little humiliated.

Bernadette: I'd probably feel the same way. (empathizing and acknowledging the validity of her emotions)

Sara: I'm just so tired of his snarky attitude. It's exhausting.

Bernadette: Have you had an opportunity to talk with John since then? (probing question to gather data)

Sara: I haven't. I'm afraid I'll lose it and yell at him. The reality is that we need him. No one knows our system better. I just wish he wasn't so difficult.

Bernadette: What's the ideal outcome of your conversation with John? (moving into outcome)

Sara: That John accepts me as his manager and respects my decisions.

Bernadette: Yeah, that would be nice ideally. In the meanwhile, you have a more immediate goal of addressing staff concerns over the new protocols. (stating clear expectations)

Sara: Correct, I'd like John to act like a team player on finding solutions rather than shooting everything down.

Bernadette: Why do you think he does that? Just to be difficult? (probing question to help Sara look at John less critically)

Sara: I think he sees himself as safe-guarding our system and keeping us safe from threats. He's very much by the book and not afraid of raising issues.

Bernadette: What's wrong with that? (probing question to help Sara see that John was operating from a desire to do what's best)

Sara: As I said, his intentions are good. We need him. His message just gets lost in how he delivers it.

CHAPTER 11 **Teaching by Asking Questions**   193

Bernadette: How do you want John to feel after your discussion? (question to improve the relationship)

Sara: I want him to feel like he's valuable and know that I count on him. Frankly, I can't afford to lose him.

Bernadette: Do you really think his comment was aimed at you? (separating perception versus reality)

Sara: Of course not. It just felt that way.

Bernadette: What would happen if you spoke to John the way you're speaking to me? (helping Sara put it all together with a question without telling her)

Sara: I think he would appreciate it. He doesn't like to beat around the bush, but he also likes to feel valued.

Bernadette: Don't we all! I'll be interested in how it goes. When do you want to touch base again? (move to action)

Sara: Soon.

Bernadette: Can I suggest you get it done instead of sitting and stewing on it? (sharing suggestion to resolve it)

Sara: You're right. I'll do it tomorrow morning and get back to you by the end of the day.

Bernadette: Great. I think you'll do great. You have a good handle on it. These conversations aren't easy, but if you want John to respect you as his manager, you'll need to do more of them. I'm always here if you want to talk these things out. (encouraging, positive talk as a way to end it on a high note)

Sara: Thanks. I really appreciate it Bernadette.

Bernadette's coaching conversation took about 90 minutes, if you consider the time she spent preparing. But note that, other than a follow-up meeting with Sara, she didn't get involved. By coaching Sara, Bernadette kept the issue in Sara's court to figure out. Bernadette used great open-ended questions and helped Sara safely vent and find clarity in resolving her issue.

What's more, Sara will get more comfortable in having these difficult conversations and will need Bernadette's coaching less over time.

Here are the key steps you can take to use this coaching tool successfully:

>> **Aim for a positive outcome.** It's helpful, of course, to have a positive outcome in mind and to state it at the beginning of the coaching discussion. Doing so puts the employee at ease and gives the discussion a sense of purpose. But make sure the outcome you're seeking is truly a positive one.

» **Go in a logical flow.** With the positive outcome as the guiding light for the discussion, organize the questions you ask so that they reach the outcome. This approach allows the two of you to move together. Even if you get off track, you know the track to get back onto, which is much better than meandering and having fragmented conversations.

» **Ask first, offer second.** Give your input in the flow of the discussion and only when it's really needed. Let the employee think first and take the lead in developing ideas. Avoid starting off by giving your ideas.

» **Keep the questions open-ended.** Only use this strategy if you want to stimulate thoughts from the employee and have a lively, positive discussion.

» **Actively listen.** This effort not only helps you understand the employee and have the person feel that they're being heard, but it also pushes you to concentrate and stay in control. That's when your facilitation in this coaching effort really comes to fruition. A participating and nonjudgmental listener truly stimulates a rich conversation.

» **Be sincere and patient.** When you coach with questions, conversations can go from brief to lengthy, depending on the issues involved and the individuals attached to them. As long as you're sincere (not grilling the employee) and patient (not anxious), you'll achieve the positive outcome you're seeking and the commitment of the employee to make it happen. In the long run, and sometimes even immediately, you see an employee who can take responsibility and handle situations confidently. That's a great payoff for your patience.

» **Be yourself and authentic.** Using questions in coaching people doesn't preclude you from being honest about your own observations and insights. Everyone is human. You don't need to pretend to be perfect and say the right things all the time.

» **Be a mentor.** When you use questions and combine it with sharing your wisdom, you can deliver much more than just being a coach who just asks questions. Sharing experiences and lessons learned validates what an employee is going through. It shows you can relate and be a mentor for someone else.

» **Reinforce successes.** When employees walk away from the discussion with a plan or solution to act on, they're on the road to success. Do your follow-ups and see what has happened. Most likely, you'll see success and when you do, shower the employee with positive feedback. The more you recognize employees for applying what they learn and achieving good results with it, the more you ensure that they perform self-sufficiently.

Impacting the Pillars of Commitment

Coaching with questions can positively influence the five pillars for building employee commitment (see Chapter 4). In fact, I ask you to explain how each pillar gets impacted with this coaching tool. (A little coaching with questions for you.) Go one at a time in whatever order you want:

» **Involvement:** How do questions build involvement? Questions greatly involve the employees in developing the plan, solution, or other positive outcome you're discussing. The employees execute what gets worked out in their own performance, instead of the manager doing that for them or constantly telling them what to do.

» **Development:** In what ways do coaching with questions build employee development? It pushes employees to do much of their own thinking for themselves. The purpose of the coaching conversation is for employees to learn and create, and then go perform based on what they created.

» **Focus:** How do questions contribute to better focus? Coaching with active listening and adapting to the conversation helps you focus on the specific needs of each employee. It's not a template-driven formula, but a collaborative, focused approach. In the end, employees walk away with a clear understanding of what they're going to do and how that will help achieve a positive outcome.

» **Accountability:** Which would build more accountability: a doer manager who directs and tells or a coach manager who challenges employees to figure it out themselves? Coaching with questions pushes responsibility to employees. Instead of the manager being the all-knowing, all-telling person, the manager's questions push employees to think of their own solutions or plans and act upon them. By holding follow-ups with you as needed, employees own their results. They get to experience the success of their own ideas.

» **Gratitude:** What is the relationship between gratitude and asking good, open-ended questions? When you ask employees their opinions, you're showing you respect and value them. That makes them grateful and appreciative.

Chapter **12**

Building Career Self-Reliance

Most people seek fulfillment in their work, beyond just the economic support that jobs provide. They want careers that give them satisfaction, challenge, and opportunities for growth. Coaching and mentoring can play a significant role in engaging people in building their careers.

The coaching tools covered in Chapters 2 through 11 not only help drive performance but they also help employees develop their skills and abilities — factors that lead to career growth and satisfaction. This chapter shows you how to support your employees in their career development.

Planning for Changes — Everything from Rightsizing to Downsizing

Changes in the workplace are inevitable, as Chapter 6 explores. The old employment relationship of giving loyalty and getting security has become a scarce commodity. Employers still need commitment even if they can't offer long-term job security — which for some employees has less appeal anyway in today's work environment (see the nearby sidebar in this chapter). At the same time, employees aren't necessarily going to give commitment without something in return — usually something more than just a good salary and stock options. For many employees, career growth opportunity is a big part of that something in return.

REMEMBER

The concept of *a womb-to-tomb career* — going to work for one company and spending the rest of your working career there — is something of past generations. Layoffs have become a common practice and aren't due just to economic slumps. Creative terms from *downsizing* to *rightsizing* have come to mean the same thing: Like or not, you don't have a job here anymore and this is not the place from which you will retire one day. This so-called *rightsizing movement* (although many companies still have not figured out the right size to be) is due to several key factors, including the following:

>> **Mergers and acquisitions:** The practice of buying and selling companies or linking them together has caused job cuts due to redundancy in job functions created from the merger. You don't need two accounting or human resource departments.

>> **Organizational restructuring:** *Restructuring* is the reorganizing of work functions and people in those functions, due to mergers or competitive pressures. Sometimes, this leads to departments being combined, grouped differently, or redesigned in workflow — with fewer people needed to do the work.

>> **Outsourcing:** *Outsourcing* is sending internal functions to outside companies or independent contractors. Reducing employee costs by shifting responsibilities to independent contractors has legal ramifications that need to be fully examined. Still, the move from employees to outsourcing work will only continue.

>> **Investor pressures:** More and more companies seek to go *public*, allowing investors to purchase stock in their companies. However, companies that are public often face pressure to keep the stock price high to please investors. This pressure sometimes leads companies to make changes, including job cuts, to keep costs down and profits up.

>> **Business shifts:** Many companies change their business strategies, emphasizing new products or services and de-emphasizing the old ones. These shifts in strategy, usually in the attempt for growth, sometimes are accompanied by a loss of jobs in the less-emphasized areas of the business.

>> **Technology:** In a survey by the Society of Human Resources Management Association (SHRM), executives predict that automation and artificial

intelligence will replace 1 in 5 jobs. Not only will fewer people be needed to do the same work, but new skills will be needed as roles and responsibilities change. In addition, as more businesses move online, jobs will change with the shift.

>> **Covid-19 impact:** Health concerns of consumers not wanting to be in contact with other people have shifted more work to technology (online shopping and contactless delivery and ordering) and people working remotely, which impacts employment and career trends.

Being an Advocate to Build Self-Reliance

Your role with your employees' career development is one of support. That means you care about what happens with their careers and are interested in assisting where you can in their development, but you're not their benevolent leader or savior who will take care of their careers. At the same time, you don't want to play a totally hands-off role that says, "You deal with your own career growth and don't look to me for support."

In the simplest terms, coaching in the workplace focuses on performance whereas mentoring supports someone's development with the emphasis on their career development and what interests them. But there's not a sharp line between coaching and mentoring. For instance, when you're coaching someone to whom who you've delegated a task, you're focused on how well they meet the expectations. But in that process, you may also be mentoring or educating them on a skill or knowledge they may not possess. You may mentor by sharing a past experience. Coaching and mentoring go hand in hand.

The same is true of building career self-reliance. You may be asking coaching questions and giving direct feedback on their performance, but much of building career self-reliance is playing more of a mentor role: letting employees know you're there as a resource, encouraging self-discovery and reflection, and sharing experiences and resources. Building career self-reliance isn't a skill that you actively coach people to improve. It's playing a supporting role to help them grow on their own, in their own way. Your job as a manager is to educate your employee they have more control of their career than they might think. The next section provides some guidance in making that clear to them.

Focusing on career self-reliance

To best help coach and prepare your employees for today's work environment, help them understand the message of *career self-reliance*. The heart of this message is for them to take responsibility for their own careers; don't expect others to take care of them.

Here are the key points of career self-reliance that you can share with your employees:

>> **They're the greatest determiner of their own career development.** Help them see the fact that the world is ever-changing and less likely to provide one place for their whole working career. Recognize that no one is just going to give them opportunities for growth and advancement. They can get support, but they must be the driver of what they want to achieve.

>> **Build a positive track record.** Point out the importance to make positive contributions in every job opportunity they have, regardless of the kind of situation. They're building skills and meaningful experience, along with a track record of quality performance so that managers in the future — whether within the organization or outside of it — will see them as a valuable performer to have on their teams.

>> **See themselves as a manager.** It can be powerful for your employee to imagine being you, their manager. How would they want to be treated if they were in your role? What would impress them if they had to manage employees? I (Leo) often suggest this perspective switching when coaching employees. If they make their employer happy, they build a reputation as a valuable contributor and elevate their perception within the organization. Are they whining, problematic, and always making excuses? Or are they positive, professional, and always looking to make their manager's life easier? People only really remember how you make them feel. Emphasize this point: How they treat the people in the greatest position to determine their future greatly determines their progress in their careers.

>> **Understand their skills and experience are transferrable.** Make the distinction between the job they currently hold and their long-term career. If they continually invest in building their skills, they'll be valuable not matter where they go. There's too much change in the world and in any one organization to assume they'll be there forever.

>> **Believe in themselves.** With all the uncertainty in the world of work, employees can sometimes be afraid of losing their job. They don't want to speak out, take risks, or advocate for themselves. Unfortunately, a fear mentality doesn't make for a happy, productive employee. Remind them they are valuable to

the firm, as long as they are doing the best they can. I have coached many employees who didn't truly understand how much power they had. If a company hired me to coach someone, it was because they were afraid of losing them. Yet, many employees lack a strong sense of themselves as valuable to the organization. Often, their low self-esteem keeps them from advocating for themselves when they should. Although you don't want to encourage employees to be overly demanding, you also want to encourage employees to believe in themselves and find their voice. In the long run, you'll be building their motivation and commitment to the company.

>> **Look to grow broadly not just vertically.** Employees would do well to measure career growth by more than an advancement up a hierarchy or career ladder (see the nearby sidebar). Recommend they expand themselves in terms of breadth and depth: Lateral moves, taking on new roles, and being involved in special projects are but a few of the ways that they gain valuable experience.

>> **Know thyself.** What are their talents and interests? Suggest that they pursue opportunities that best meet their desires and tap into their talents. At the same time, recognize weaknesses as well as strengths and be willing to work on improving their weaknesses while maximizing their strengths.

REMEMBER

Remember that careers are as much webs as they are ladders in their development. Be open to new experiences and opportunities for learning and training so that each opportunity is a building block for your future.

>> **Build relationships along the way.** Remind them to combine what they know with who they know, making deposits in all their relationships. Get to know the people they work with and, regardless of who they like or don't like, establish working relationships in which others view them as a quality person, not just a quality performer.

CAREER WEBS, NOT LADDERS

How people progress in their careers has changed to some degree. The metaphor used to be the ladder. If you were ambitious, you would rise up the corporate ladder or hierarchy into significant positions of management. Today, you see people progress in their careers like they're traversing a spider web. The following figure gives you a contrasting look at how career paths traditionally flowed, up the career ladder, and how they now often progress in a web-like fashion, going in different directions: lateral movement, moving out, moving out and then up, changing career paths, and growing in job scope

(continued)

(continued)

while still in the same role. The idea of traveling up the corporate ladder in one organization for most of a career occurs less and less these days, and often, a career-web progression is done through changing companies.

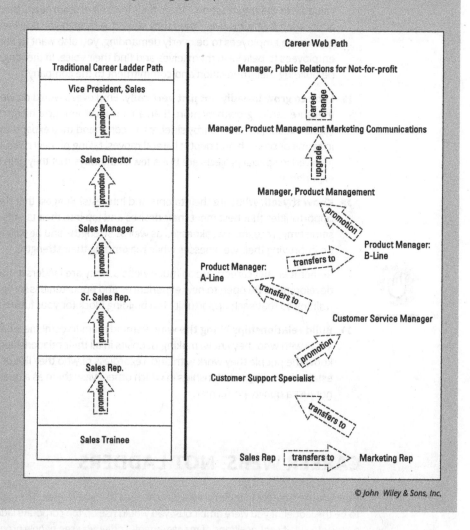

© John Wiley & Sons, Inc.

Considering other trends

As a result of layoffs and job insecurity, other trends have emerged that affect the world of work and careers. Here are a few:

>> **Job hopping is hopping.** People are staying in their jobs for shorter periods and switching careers more often. The statistic that the average person will have more than 12 jobs and three careers in their working life is outdated and continues to change. Short work histories used to be a liability on a resume. Now they're more the norm.

The pandemic disrupted much of the stability that was in the workplace. Boomers have already retired or are retiring sooner, taking different jobs, or switching careers. Demand for talent puts more power in the hands of employees. More people want to enjoy their work situations and are often less tolerant of less-than-satisfactory conditions, such as working for a lousy manager or an organization that doesn't treat them right. With organizations hungry for talent, employees can be lured away with offers for more compensation, greater flexibility, more opportunity, and more progressive cultures.

>> **Work is more team-based and multifunctional.** A generation ago, when people worked in their jobs, they did one or perhaps a few main functions. They served as one piece in the overall puzzle, acting as narrow-based specialists. Even though some jobs still function this way today, you often see people working in teams within work units — and sometimes across departments. The idea of a cross-functional task team is commonly used in many organizations. Work is often project-oriented, instead of being a set of tasks that an individual does, and employees often have multiple functions that they work at.

>> **Emphasis is on technology, information, and service.** The growth industries of the American economy revolve around technology, information, and service — often all three together. Those employees who embrace change in technology and develop their skills and knowledge for the future are investing in their future success.

Counteracting resistance

As you communicate the important message of self-reliance, you may find that some employees don't initially understand the message of working to be career self-reliant, and others may not like it.

WHO'S THE FOOL?

Managers can find themselves in the position of trying too hard to retain employees. When making decisions to keep people, take the long view, as this case study shows.

Tonya supervises a team of project managers, but her biggest concern isn't managing them, but keeping them employed. Client demand for services doesn't end and the team is always short-handed. A good part of the day, Tonya is online, searching for candidates to fill open positions.

One Monday morning, Jeff comes into her office and doesn't even ask whether she's busy. He sits down like he's the one in charge. Tonya is done putting up with his entitled attitude and underperformance. He's always complaining about his workload, even though he never works past 5 p.m. And he's frequently late delivering his work, which is just average at best. Jeff announces, "So, I've got an offer to work at a competing firm for 30 percent more in salary."

Tonya was afraid of this scenario: She doesn't like Jeff but can't afford to lose him. The team is already understaffed with employees burning out. She's silent and keeps her composure, "What are you looking for Jeff?" Jeff responds, "If you can match it, I'll stay. Otherwise, I'd be a fool not to take it." Tonya says she'll think about it. She goes to her manager and explains the situation. He doesn't like it either, but he's more concerned about not disappointing clients by not meeting deadlines and being unresponsive. He leaves the decision to Tonya.

She buckles and decides to give Jeff the raise he demanded, even though he doesn't deserve it. One month later, he quits anyway to join yet another firm that will pay him even more. However, by that time, everyone in the office knows that Jeff got a 30 percent raise because he told a few people and word spread. He wasn't liked by anyone at the firm and people are resentful.

Tonya felt like a fool: She should have never given Jeff his raise and defended her position with her manager, even if it meant disappointing clients. Now she has bigger problems with her entire team upset and demoralized, demanding a pay raise or they'll leave.

Recognizing those resistant employees

You can't please everyone, as the adage goes. Despite your best coaching efforts, some employees won't be on board and resist the concept that their future is chiefly in their own hands. Here are some typical situations you may have already encountered:

>> **Don't-get-it types:** For employees who initially may not understand the message well, you may see them take a wait-and-see approach to everything. Asserting themselves and taking initiative aren't behaviors they usually exhibit in their own careers, let alone in how they work in their jobs. You can coach them to develop by helping them define behaviors that help them succeed and by creating work opportunities that provide challenge to use those behaviors.

>> **Don't-like-it types:** For employees who don't initially like this message of taking charge of their own careers, you often may hear comments like, "I work hard, how come I haven't been promoted?" These employees have *entitlement syndrome,* thinking that they're owed a career with good progression and salary increases because they come to work every day. Don't debate them. Give them time to let the message sink in. In future conversations with such employees, coach with questions, asking them questions such as the following:

- What are you doing to prepare yourself to be promotable?

- What skills are you working to develop?

- What needs do I, your manager, have in running this group, and what are you doing to meet them?

These questions are the beginning of getting don't-like-it-types to take action that moves their careers in positive directions.

Steering clear of potential traps

Despite resistance, don't stop educating your employees with the self-reliance message — continue to have discussions about it. Share articles that help educate your employees about the world in which they work. And above all, avoid these pitfalls in your coaching efforts:

>> **Don't reward noise.** Just because one of your employees wants a certain opportunity or bigger role and complains loudly, you don't have to give the person the opportunity or role. Let the merit of a person's performance determine who is ready to take on bigger or better opportunities.

>> **Don't feel obligated to do something.** As you explore career interests with your staff members, you will hear about their ambitions. Sometimes these are career desires that you currently can't do anything to help the person achieve.

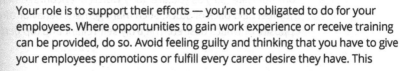

Your role is to support their efforts — you're not obligated to do for your employees. Where opportunities to gain work experience or receive training can be provided, do so. Avoid feeling guilty and thinking that you have to give your employees promotions or fulfill every career desire they have. This action on the part of a manager breeds dependence, not self-reliance. Let business needs, along with employee performance and initiative, be the keys to determine what career opportunities people get to experience.

» **Don't give employees what you think they want.** Sometimes, managers have very good intentions, but those intentions don't translate into actions that their employees appreciate, especially when you insist that employees take on certain assignments or roles that they don't really want — even though you know such opportunities will be good for their careers. Sometimes the actions from managers involve telling employees what they should do and what steps they should take for their careers — even though the advice isn't asked for and doesn't meet with employees' career interests. Avoid making assumptions or thinking you know what's best for someone else.

TIP

Let employees manage their own careers. Pass on your knowledge and experience and mentor with messages that promote career self-reliance, instead of imposing your will on what employees should do with their careers. Give assignments based on the needs of the business and the interests of the employee. To find out about employees' interests, start by listening and tuning into what you see and hear from them.

» **Don't set goals and then not follow through on them.** Sometimes, when managers attempt to support employee career development, they set goals around such issues as part of the performance-review process. These goals often have something to do with getting training in certain areas or getting opportunities for certain work experiences. If the employees don't follow through and meet these goals, some managers think that the staff members have been negligent in their responsibilities, and that's just too bad.

Often, though, opportunities for learning and growth don't happen because managers don't follow through on what they said they would do. When employees are told that the organization won't give the financial investment to go to the seminars agreed upon or that the manager really doesn't want the employee taking on other responsibilities, employees often wonder why the goals were set in the first place. If actions don't follow commitments you make, the message of career self-reliance rings hollow.

» **Don't hold reliable people back.** Don't punish good performers by keeping them in the roles in which they reliably deliver quality performance and subtly blocking opportunities for learning, taking on new responsibilities, or pursuing other internal positions of interest and growth. When employees are no longer challenged and are working for managers whose actions seem to communicate "stay as you are" (any words of encouragement don't matter), they feel held back or stuck. Such management behavior often spurs the opposite of what's desired. The truly self-reliant and top performing individuals won't stay put and will move on to get the growth opportunities you tried to block — often leaving the organization to do so.

>> **Don't appear disinterested.** Giving the message of career self-reliance to your staff doesn't mean that you step away and don't play a role in assisting your employees' career development. Some managers make this mistake: They don't engage in conversations to explore career interests and don't care about opportunities for staff to get training or broaden their experiences. The focus is on having employees do their work — period.

Such disinterest doesn't stimulate employee retention and sometimes serves as an obstacle to employee growth. Good performers look to move to where better opportunities for learning and growth are supported.

Setting a Vision

Your role isn't to manage your employees' careers (you have your own to work on), but rather to coach and mentor them to identify meaningful personal and professional goals. Chapter 9 covers how to motivate employees to engage them and build commitment. If your employee aligns the work they do with their career and life goals, they can find more meaning and purpose in their work. Help employees make the connection that their career and work get the things in life that are meaningful for them: home ownership, family, travel, and so on. Their career at your organization can move them closer to their personal goals. The emphasis is twofold:

>> Helping employees develop the work behaviors and habits to be productive and positive workers for the organization

>> Helping employees develop the skills and competencies to build their careers — even if they don't stay at your company forever

Encourage employees to envision the future they want.

As a coach, I (Leo) like to start my engagements with clients by asking them to define a vision they'll be motivated to work toward. Leaders don't stay in one place, but look ahead. Think of *vision* as where you want to go. Encourage employees to stay at your organization and be realistic that other opportunities may come into play that cause them to leave. The following is the process I use to help clients set a vision for themselves.

Designing the mountain

I've found that three years is a good destination for making career and life plans. One year is too short, and five years is too long. I ask people: "Three years from now, what has to happen personally and professionally for you to be happy with your progress?"

I encourage them to write down everything that comes to them. I call this *designing your mountain*. Like mountains in the near distance, smaller life goals are also easy to maintain focus. Three years is a future you can envision and work toward.

The *mountain* includes their personal goals and professional goals. As their manager, you don't need to know the employee's personal goals, unless they want to share them. What's important is that the employee can see how their work ties into their personal lives.

These sections include ways to help your employees realize their own mountains and some examples.

Letting your employees self-reflect

To help your employees, ask them to reflect on their own:

>> What's important to me?

>> What do I want to achieve?

>> How do I want to be spending my free time?

>> How will my day be broken down by percent of time devoted to certain tasks and responsibilities?

>> How have I set specific metrics to reduce time on technical tasks that others can easily do?

>> Do I have a different title with larger responsibilities?

>> What kinds of projects are rewarding?

>> What clients/customers are great to work with?

>> What initiatives in the office am I spearheading?

>> How does the culture of the office reflect my contributions?

>> How do I show leadership in my industry?

>> Are there specific awards, speaking engagements, or forms of recognition that help me mark success?

Creating their mountains

After your employees reflect on these questions, help them keep the following tips in mind as they design their mountains:

>> **Be as specific and tangible as possible in describing your future life.** What will you be doing? Will it include additional responsibilities? If you want to lose weight, how much?

>> **Don't get caught up in wondering if something is possible or not.** If you're interested in becoming a team manager, go for it! You'll never get there if you don't have a goal.

>> **Use action verbs to describe the action you need to take.** Use words like *be recognized for . . .*, *initiate, earn,* and *take vacation to . . . .*

>> **List any specific accomplishments or outcomes.** Examples may include "Get paper scientific paper published in leading journal" or "Complete my first marathon."

>> **List any changes in mindset, behavior, attitude, or how you're spending your time.** Examples may include: "Have more empathy and be a better listener." "Bite my tongue and hear people out." "Limit my time on social media to one hour a day."

Examples of mountains

Here are three examples of mountains, with the first one being my own:

>> **Example No. 1:** Expert on Emerging Leaders nationally; speak at national conferences; diversify revenue streams; publish a book; create demand; stabilize revenues by finding more consistent sources; collaborate more with people to get energized and expand influence — conference and retreat. More free time to travel and more adventure; own more real estate with my wife, especially a cabin and create passive income; walk the Camino.

>> **Example No. 2:** Assistant Department Head; spend 35 percent of my time in business development and resource planning for future projects (compared to 10 percent now); actively mentor younger designers by knowing the needs of my team and finding opportunities for them to grow each day; build a strong alliance with other assistant department heads so we meet regularly and support each other; improve in financial management and be able to track profitability more consistently. Learn to let go of work and relax; regular practice of meditation; go to meditation retreat in Novia Scotia for a week.

>> **Example No. 3:** Move into an owner role within my company; reduce my project workload by 40 percent; help the owner make strategic decisions for

the company's growth. Grow the company to 75 people sustainably. Play a primary role in screening and hiring people; be a better listener and learn to read body language. Establish stronger boundaries around time and have a much better handle on focusing on highest and best use of time. One major family vacation that we plan each year. Take a Friday afternoon off each month to hang with my son. Go to Hawaii with my wife — alone!

Coaching for Progress

The quarterly checkup review lends itself nicely to having discussions with your employees about their progress toward their mountain — not necessarily every quarter but at least twice a year (see Chapter 16). These meetings also give you a chance to reinforce the importance and meaning of becoming career self-reliant.

As you explore their interests, ask questions, such as the following:

>> Has your mountain changed since you first created it? In what ways?

>> What progress have you made toward your mountain?

>> What competencies, skills, knowledge, and abilities will get you closer?

>> What habits or obstacles are slowing you down from making progress?

>> What experiences would be beneficial?

>> What are you planning to do to prepare yourself for making progress?

>> As your manager, how can I support your efforts?

These questions get your employees understanding your and their roles in this process: Yours is to support, theirs is to work on their own development.

These questions not only stimulate a good discussion and provide insight, but they also allow you an opportunity to mentor and tutor to help prepare your staff to build solid track records in their performance, which will also help them get to their mountain.

REMEMBER

Performance isn't just the work someone does; it also includes behavior. Coaching to improve emotional intelligence (see Chapter 5) and giving timely constructive feedback (refer to Chapter 14) help employees reach their goals.

Continue to drive the point home that employees should take ownership of their careers and their future. This also pertains to acting like a professional. The following sections provide specific insight.

Focusing on professionals

If you have an opening in your group and are faced with two candidates who were equally qualified in terms of their technical competence, who would you select? Tough question, right? Suppose, however, that one of the two candidates sounds bitter, complaining about their past employer, and gives you a list of the duties they don't like, whereas the other applicant consistently expresses themselves in a positive and upbeat manner. Now who would you hire? Easy question, isn't it?

REMEMBER

Just because people have technical skills, knowledge, and education doesn't mean they have the work habits and work ethic that makes for an effective employee. You want to hire people who are both technically competent and professional. In coaching to prepare your staff to manage and achieve success in their own careers, you want to mentor with messages that help them work as professionals, which is about behavior, not occupation. Being *a professional*, as defined here, is about how you work and conduct yourself in getting the job done. It's about your interactions with others and the work ethic you display in your actions.

TIP

To help prepare your employees for building and maintaining success in their careers, mentor them to work as professionals. In your coaching discussion, do the following:

1. **Define what working as a professional means.**

2. **Ask your employees to give you examples of behaviors that fit this definition.**

   Feel free to offer some examples, too.

3. **Ask your employees, of the professional behaviors identified, which do they need to demonstrate in order to be successful in their jobs today and in the future?**

4. **Follow up periodically to assess their progress at adopting these behaviors.**

Spotting 12 behaviors of professionalism

The likelihood is that, together, you can easily come up with ten or more behaviors that fit the definition of working as a professional — and find that all of them are needed to be effective. Here are the 12 behaviors of professionalism:

Exhibiting a can-do manner

This behavior gives you the impression that a positive attitude is behind it. When people show a can-do manner, their body language comes across as alert and receptive — no slouches, grimaces, or rolling of the eyes. The tone comes across as sincere and interested as opposed to monotone or sarcastic. They carry themselves in an upbeat fashion.

The can-do manner shows itself in people's moods. Having good days and bad days is natural, and people who distinguish themselves are those that rise above it. They don't make their problems other people's problems. They don't complain about everything. They don't say whatever is on their minds when they feel about it. They say yes more than they say no. They assure people they can get it done.

Showing a willingness to learn

People are capable of learning but not all are open to it. The ever-changing world of business and the career marketplace requires people to be open and willing to learn. Professionals desire opportunities to receive training and to learn from new experiences. They don't accept that they have all the answers. They see that there's something to be learned new every day.

Having flexibility

Flexibility is the ability to adapt to change from small to big, and to then move forward and continue to perform well. Adaptability is highly valued in today's rapidly changing work environment. Professionals deal with the discomfort and ambiguity that often are a part of change by seeing it as a healthy challenge, not an inconvenience.

Being a team player

Nearly every manager wants a team player, but they're often hard to find. This behavior is about taking individual talents and blending them with others to get work done. It's about being able to help when asked and offer assistance without being asked. Being a team player isn't only lending a hand but also sharing information and welcoming others into the group.

Professionals who are team players are able to work cooperatively versus competitively in collective situations. They're able to fit in with the group and focus on the goals that the group needs to accomplish.

Taking initiative

Professionals who take initiative function as self-starters. They don't waste time in waiting to be told what to do — when they see something needs to be done, they act. Taking initiative also entails the willingness to seek out information and answers, to reach out and connect with others: making that phone call, setting up that meeting, or taking some other action to help make things happen.

Being creative

Being creative isn't about being brilliantly innovative or having the ability to make great inventions. Instead being creative as a behavior of professionals is about offering ideas and about thinking of ways that help get the job done the best way possible. The most progressive companies are fueled by encouraging different ways of thinking solving problems. In 2012, Google studied what makes great teams and found that those teams where people equally shared their thoughts — no matter whether they agreed or disagreed — were the most productive and innovative.

Producing reliably

This behavior is about taking responsibility and being productive; delivering results, not about being busy; getting work done with quality, thoroughness, and timeliness — on a consistent basis. Professionals who function as reliable producers are the employees you can count on — when they take on a job, you have the confidence it will get done well. Excuses aren't part of their vocabulary and repeated mistakes aren't part of their work habits.

Communicating constructively

Communicating constructively is about showing good judgment and awareness in interacting with others. Employees who try to be professional understand that it's important to be liked and respected. They understand that relationships are the key to getting to their mountain.

Professionals express messages the best way possible: Not shying away from the point or looking to be nice, but being direct, sincere, and respectful. It's about recognizing each person as an individual and not expecting that everyone will respond to how you say things the way you would. Concern for individuals is taken under consideration. This professional behavior is also about being able to listen and understand messages that others express without being judgmental — giving others the opportunity to be heard.

Solving problems

Professionals focus on solutions rather than finding fault, blaming others, getting defensive, or complaining about the problem and doing nothing about it. Having a solutions-focus is about engaging in ways to fix the problem. A problem solver uses other professional behaviors in dealing with problem situations — can-do manner, constructive communication, creativity, and initiative. The behavior is about taking action and focusing attention on positive directions to make something come out better.

Being service-oriented

Ronald Nykiel, in his book, *You Can't Lose If The Customer Wins*, refers to an expression that you can't teach pigs to dance. His point is that no matter how much training in customer service you provide, it will do little good if you have employees who aren't service-oriented to begin with.

Being service-oriented is about seeing that your job involves providing quality service to others — external as well as internal customers. It is giving people the help they need in a courteous and responsive fashion. Having the orientation to serve customers well is the best tool for having any kind of job security.

Doing what you say

Employees who do what they say they'll do when they promise are ones you can trust and depend on. They stand out not by overdelivering but by simply doing what they say. There's no shortage of people who say one thing and do another. Their actions don't support their words. Over time, when people drop the ball, they are seen as unreliable. Trust erodes. And without trust, why would anyone follow you? And yet, if you think about your interactions with people, how common are broken promises? Consider the following:

>> The colleague who says they'll get back to you with some good times to meet but never does

>> The staffer who gets overwhelmed with work and lets the project deadline slide

>> The boss who promises you a promotion but keeps pushing it off

Ultimately, people want to know if they can count on you. Your ability to consistently meet commitments is the foundation to building long-term support for your career. Keep breaking your word and see how that works for you in the long run.

Fitting into the culture

Companies have unique cultures. Every employee needs to evaluate whether their company's culture is a good fit for them. Is this a place where they can be successful and supported? Or does it feel like a struggle every day to fit in? Even those employees who align with much of their company's culture understand the limitations. They accept that they won't like everything. They pick their battles. They don't try to make the company change around them. For instance, not all companies encourage creativity and innovation. Some are more focused on repetition and consistency rather than new ideas. Every employee needs to honestly look if their company aligns with their mountain.

EXAMPLE

The talks I (Marty) give about working as a professional are commonly part of presentations about making yourself resilient in your career. One time, after a presentation at a public forum, a gentleman came up afterward and thanked me and asked, "Where were you 30 years ago?" The talk caused him to reflect back on his work career and see the difficulties he'd had in trying to be viewed as a good employee. He could see some of his own inconsistencies in his behaviors and work habits. This list of 12 behaviors provided him a focus to use going forward. I thought, that's a professional — someone who has the humility and wisdom to learn and improve themselves.

Aligning with company goals

If your employee has developed their mountain and believes investing in themselves at your company is good for their career, encourage them to take an interest in what's going on with the company. This coaching opportunity helps them understand the direction of the organization, where it's headed, and what are the biggest challenges. When your employee understands the big picture, they can understand their part. It not only gives them a greater sense of purpose to motivate them (see Chapter 9), but it also gives them insights into how to align their career goals with the organization's goals.

The emerging leaders I've worked with who have risen the fastest in their careers thought and acted like owners already. They spent time asking questions and taking an interest in how the organization operated and learned about their short- and long-term goals. When they were promoted as leaders, it wasn't because they had future promise as leaders. They had already demonstrated their leadership with their actions. The promotion wasn't a promissory note but a recognition of what they already did — acted with other people in mind, questioned what was good for the whole of the organization — and advocated and supported people outside of their team.

If an employee is serious about moving up, suggest they start thinking like an owner. Take them out to lunch and share with them the following:

>> What are the organization's strategic goals?

>> What markets or clients are expected to grow, shrink, or remain the same?

>> What does the organization need to evolve to be more competitive with others?

>> What are the most talked about subjects at the board level?

>> What positions do you see yourselves hiring for in the next year?

>> What economic or market shifts are happening or are on the horizon?

>> How are customers behaving differently in how they're doing business that might affect your company?

>> What are the hot buttons of the most influential stakeholders?

>> What skills will be needed in employees (hint, like them)?

Their mountain represents their future three years from now. They'll have more success reaching their mountain if they know the organization mountain — what management is looking for in the next three years. They'll build more allies and advocates (see Chapter 19) internally if their ideas and strategies align with the organization. They may need to modify their mountain to be realistic, scaling back some expectations. They may need to adjust their timeline to five years, instead of three. But they'll make forward progress that's in the best interest of both the organization and themselves if they're aligned.

Mentoring and advocating

Coaching to build career self-reliance with your employees is an active, ongoing effort for both you and your employees. You're not managing their careers for them. You're mentoring and advocating for them in the following ways:

» You're providing information and discussing mentoring to help your staff members understand the importance of managing their own careers; of working as professionals; and of developing the skills, knowledge, and abilities that help them perform well today and in the future.

» You're working with them to identify areas to work on and to set plans that help prepare and develop them to reach their own mountain.

» You're providing learning and work opportunities that allow for career growth and contribute to business success.

» You're making introductions to help employees expand their contacts and exposure in the organization.

» You're communicating the needs of your department and of the organization overall.

» You're providing ongoing performance feedback.

The following sections provide more detail about how you can mentor and advocate your employees.

Identifying opportunities

Your coaching efforts can also teach them how to learn of opportunities within the organization, including those in your own group, and how to pursue them. Doing so requires them to listen and learn, to take initiative, and to reach out. Here are some additional tips to heed that you can show your employees who want to grow in their careers:

» **Get to know each area of the organization.** Encourage your employees to find out who your organization's executives are, what functions they manage, what messages they hear about where the company is going, and what the important issues are to the business. Understanding these issues helps employees know what's going on in the organization and develop a broader understanding of how things work.

» **Recognize your department managers' needs and challenges.** This strategy applies within employees' own groups but also to other areas in the organization where they may have interest. Encourage employees to talk to other managers and ask questions to find out their needs and challenges, starting with you. As they understand where needs and challenges exist, they know what they can offer to help satisfy those needs and meet the challenges.

>> **Increase visibility and exposure.** This step involves efforts to build relationships and give good performance, not playing politics or kissing up. Encourage your employees to introduce themselves to other staff members and managers in areas in which they have interest to informally talk, keep in touch, and occasionally have lunch. It also involves volunteering to be on special assignments or cross-functional teams to gain exposure and meet others in the organization.

EXAMPLE

Don was a technical contributor and had hopes one day of moving up to become a technical manager. When a cross-functional task team was created to develop some key personnel policies for the organization, he volunteered to be the representative from his department.

Don went forward and made a good contribution to the task team, which took place over the course of the year. He attended all the meetings, followed through on all the assignments, and offered ideas that helped the team do its work. What Don gained most of all from his participation was exposure to different people in the organization, especially the company's management. His contributions were seen as valuable on the team. Toward the end of the year, an opening for a manager's position opened in Don's area. He applied and was selected to take on the role. What he realized was that two actions made a difference in getting this promotion — his reliable performance and his visibility from the task team. All the other internal candidates hadn't taken steps to show leadership or contribute in other areas to help the company.

>> **Build your career portfolio.** Your portfolio is a record of your accomplishments and skills. Performance reviews often reflect what assets you've shown and developed. The idea is to continue to develop skills and to make contributions that build a positive track record. Document this track record: Save products of work and other evidence of the performance contributions made.

>> **Identify opportunities and offer proposals to add value.** When employees understand the organization, understand managers' needs, and have the tools ready to contribute to meet those needs, they shouldn't wait. They should take the initiative and offer ideas and solutions, starting with putting the proposal in writing. In it, ask them to outline the opportunities or needs they see, the services or solutions they have to offer to meet them, and the benefits that the group gains. Then have them sit down with you to discuss the proposal and see what happens. Nothing ventured, nothing gained.

Provide the needed support

Support your employees in networking with colleagues, attending conferences, volunteering in trade associations, attending webinars, and reading articles. The more employees learn to develop their own knowledge, the more valuable they are to you and the organization, and the more they are engaged in their career. They can bring new thinking and insights and contribute in ways you never imagined.

Sometimes these efforts lead to employees taking on new projects or roles within your group and sometimes they lead to handling new opportunities that have them move to other groups. In either case, you've coached employees to take charge of their careers and to make the most of opportunities (empowering them) and have helped influence employees to grow within the organization (retaining their services).

REMEMBER

The fear that some managers face is that if they support employees' growth and teach them how to seek opportunities, they'll lose those valuable employees to other places. Such fear sometimes becomes the reason that little support is provided.

Certainly, sometimes people leave and go elsewhere to work. But if you work for a manager who pushes you to be responsible for your own career yet at the same time takes an active interest in your growth, including your being able to take on opportunities elsewhere in the organization, is this an organization that you want to leave? Not likely.

Sharpening Your Employees' Skills

Coaching your employees to prepare them to manage their own careers also involves developing the competencies to be effective performers. Look at competencies as the skills, knowledge, and abilities to have to perform a job well. Work with your staff to look at what they need in their current roles and what they need for their future interests. (Refer to the "Designing the mountain" section earlier in this chapter for questions that get to the heart of this.)

What are the skills or knowledge areas people should look to develop to enhance their career growth? Start with having them understand what's needed at the organization (refer to the section, "Aligning with company goals," earlier in this chapter). Remember it's their life and career. Coach them to make the connection between developing their skills and deepening their knowledge with advancing their personal goals. The following section provides more clarification and guidance on skills your employees can focus on developing.

Focusing on both technical and EQ skills

Every job requires a combination of technical skills and people skills, which is often referred to as emotional intelligence (EQ — see Chapter 5). *Technical skills* are required to perform the basic functions of a job. *EQ skills* are those that involved interacting and communicating with people. Even professionals who focus heavily in one area, need to do other tasks, such as:

>> A corporate trainer who uses EQ to teach people also needs to understand how to write a learning objective, operate break out rooms in Zoom, and analyze surveys from participants.

>> A mechanic in an airplane factory who uses their hands all day also needs to communicate and interact with team members to resolve issues and be agreeable enough so people want to work with them.

>> A high-tech salesperson who relies on EQ to listen to the needs of prospective clients and read their body language to see if they're interested in buying also needs to know how their technology works and how to input data into a customer relationship management system.

>> An architect who can design a school also needs to get their license, operate modeling software, and delegate work to junior personnel and give them feedback to keep the project on track.

As a manager, you can certainly give your employee feedback on what skills they need to develop. But don't overlook what they're interested in, as well.

EXAMPLE

Judy ran a small commercial insurance company. She wanted to catalog what skills her staff needed to develop, so she sent out a spreadsheet to everyone with the following columns:

>> Skill or task

>> Level of competence (1 to 5 with 5 being highest)

>> Interest in developing (1 to 5 with 5 being highest)

Jim, a new hire, identified a long list of skills with low competence and high interest in developing. Marsha, a senior person, identified a long list of skills with high competence and low interest in developing. Javier, a mid-level person, identified a mix of skills he was relatively competent in and those he wanted to develop.

This simple exercise anyone can do has a number of benefits:

>> It puts the power in the hands of the employee to self-identify what they needed to work on, rather than being told.

>> It gives Judy an indication of how people rated themselves in competency, which could be a good topic for a one-on-one conversation.

>> It gives Judy an indication of people's interest for future assignments, as well as gave her ideas for training and mentorship.

Building skills and knowledge isn't one of the "when I find time" activities. Weave skill building and getting smarter into your day, as you're making your way toward your mountain. The 70-20-10 Model of Learning from George Washington University illustrates that adult learners learn most effectively on the job.

The model breaks down like this:

>> 70 percent (from experiences):
- Learn by doing
- On-the-job training
- *Stretch assignments* (challenging projects that test how far someone can stretch in their capabilities)

>> 20 percent (from others):
- Mentoring
- Internal coaching
- Reflection/feedback
- Curated content
- Social media
- Peer networking
- Peer groups
- Books, resources

>> 10 percent (on your own):
- Workshops
- Outside coaching
- E-learning
- Structured onboarding

Mentorships

Encourage your employee to turn to the people who currently hold the positions they desire; have them observe what skills they use and ask them for advice. Advocate that your employee spend time with people who they can learn from. They may end up enlisting a mentor, ally, and advocate in the process. As Chapters 18 and 19 discuss, mentorship can take many forms and be as organic and informal as needed for people to learn.

Influencing the Pillars of Commitment

Efforts of coaching and mentoring for career self-reliance help employees move forward and take charge of their own careers. They also help stimulate employee commitment. Here is how the pillars of commitment (see Chapter 4) are influenced from your career-coaching efforts:

>> **Focus:** Mentoring with the message of career self-management and with efforts that help prepare employees to manage their own career development gives them a sense of direction and, therefore, focus.

>> **Involvement:** Coaching for career self-reliance encourages employees to take initiative and to seek opportunities that shape their own futures. Success is dependent on their getting involved to help make things happen in their own careers.

>> **Accountability:** Your coaching efforts encourage your staff to take responsibility for their own actions and progress with their careers. Accountability comes from an internal motivation as opposed to a "do as I say" model.

>> **Development:** Your coaching efforts encourage employees to work on growing their skills and behaviors for quality performance.

>> **Gratitude:** As employees move closer to their mountain, they're often grateful for the support and coaching that helped them get there. That support often translates into stronger loyalty to the organization, more commitment, and a longer tenure.

4

Coaching for Performance and Growth

Help managers let go of controlling projects and effectively delegate work to employees to build their confidence and skills.

Provide guidance on how to and how not to give feedback to help employees grow in their position.

Collaborate with employees on setting meaningful, practical performance plans and identifying specific steps to take to develop their knowledge, skills, and abilities.

Plan how and when to structure employee reviews to keep them focused and engaged in meeting the business goals and their own development.

Advocate for employees by continuously coaching for their development and improvement with strategies that build their confidence and keep them engaged.

IN THIS CHAPTER

» Recognizing what effective delegating means

» Understanding the common pitfalls of delegating

» Determining what to delegate and to whom to increase productivity

» Following a formula for clear communication throughout the process

» Overcoming employee resistance to what you want to delegate

» Identifying the factors that cause delegating to fail

Chapter **13**

Delegating and Empowering

When you struggle with not having enough time and not getting as much done as you would like, the advice you may often hear is, "You need to delegate better." While you may agree it's a good idea, but all the reasons you can't delegate better start pouring out:

» "I don't have enough time to teach someone else."

» "By the time I explain it to them, I could have it done."

» "I can't trust that they'll do it my way."

» "The client expects me to do the work."

» "I don't have anyone I can delegate to."

>> My staff isn't skilled enough."

>> "It's what I enjoy doing."

Quite often, at the core of this delegating dilemma is the difficulty of letting go — the belief that your staff won't do the job as well as you need or as well as you could, or that your employees will mess up the job and make matters worse. For some managers, the difficulty in delegating is that employees will do the job very well, which may leave others to wonder why the manager's job is necessary.

Delegating is a great tool to empower employees and increase the productivity and satisfaction of your staff and yourself. This chapter gives you all the tips and tricks you need to start delegating effectively.

Delegating 101 — Just the Basics

A big part of the misconception many managers have about delegating — misconceptions that fuel apprehensions about it and create a reluctance to do it — is the thinking that by delegating you're completely letting go of control. But giving others a share in the responsibility extends influence and creates commitment to the cause. Control isn't lost; you're just letting go of the burden of doing everything yourself.

REMEMBER

Think about it. If you're the only one who can get important work done to maintain daily operations in your group, you bear a heavy burden. If instead, through effective coaching, you delegate some of this responsibility among your staff, and they get the work done with good results, what's happened for you? Less burden — and more control of the operations and of your use of time. That's the whole idea with delegating: You can better leverage your time for higher-level work and extend your influence to greater levels in the organization.

The following sections explain what delegating is, what issues you may encounter (and how to work through them), and what you can achieve by delegating.

Defining delegating

Delegating as a coaching tool is assigning and entrusting assignments and responsibilities to others. Delegating isn't simply about giving people tasks to do. As a manager, you probably ask your staff to do tasks nearly every day. "Jim, can you get me the report on last week's sales figures?" or "Amy, would you check with the vendor on what his volume rates are for discounts?" Don't stop asking your employees to do simple tasks when needed, just recognize that's not real delegating.

Delegating is about the successful transfer of responsibility of a task from you to someone else. Think about it like you're in a relay race and you're passing a baton to a teammate to take it and go over the finish line. In order to let go, several things need to happen:

>> You need to make sure they're ready to take the baton and run.

>> You need to hold on to the baton until you trust they have it.

>> You need to let them go and let them finish the race on their own.

Just like passing a baton, you need to be invested in the process of making the other person successful. Your job is not to simply hand things over in a haphazard way, but also to be *intentional* and *conscious* throughout the process. Delegation is a collaborative effort between you as a coach and the employee. Don't rush it.

You don't have to be hands-on for the right outcomes to occur, but neither are you uninvolved and unaware of what's occurring. If you care about the results of what you delegate, make sure you provide the support needed to help the employee achieve those results. Along with providing the right support comes spelling out clear expectations and maintaining employee accountability. That's what effective delegating means and what empowerment is truly all about. To *empower* your employees take these three actions:

>> Give them the freedom to get a job done (no breathing down their necks).

>> Provide them with the right level of support to get the job done well, including information, training, resources, and so on.

>> Hold them accountable to produce the outcomes needed.

All three actions go together as part of the process. Thus, when you delegate effectively, you empower your staff.

Understanding delegating pitfalls

Delegating is far more than just assigning work for people to do. It's being involved at a support level versus doing the work hands-on yourself. In addition, to make delegating efforts work, you must build on successes with employees, not on failures. Here are the common reasons that lead to delegating failures:

>> **You don't communicate the expected results.** Most employees don't have the ability to read your mind. While most managers tell what they want done when they attempt to delegate an assignment, they don't directly articulate the results they need to see from the completed assignment.

EXAMPLE

Curt needed a spreadsheet created that tracked what management and leadership courses staff have taken. He emailed it to Tim with a simple request, "Please create a spreadsheet of what courses people have taken." Tim, who wanted to be seen as take-charge employee, guessed at what Curt wanted and created a spreadsheet of every course every taken by every employee who had every worked there! It was impressive and included technical training, general administration training, webinars, and anything that could be classified under "courses people have taken." If Curt had spent a little time explaining what he really wanted — one column of "current employees" and one column of "completed leadership/management courses only" in order to decide what the company needs to offer and to whom — he would have received what he wanted, Tim wouldn't have wasted so much time, and both would have felt positive about the delegation experience.

TIP

Don't let your employees find out the real expectations too late: "That's not what I was looking for on this project. That's not how this is supposed to look." Take some time to explain what you need and why.

>> **You tell the employee how to do the job.** When you tell your employees how to do assignments but don't define what results need to be produced, you stifle people's desire and ability to take on responsibility and think for themselves. Managers who function as doers often fall into this trap (see Chapter 2). They focus on the methods of how to get a job done instead of the quality results needed. The following story demonstrates this point well.

EXAMPLE

Sophia was given a project to develop the company's new marketing brochure. Based on her past experience and her creative flair, she was excited to take on this assignment in her new role. Getting involved in work like this was one of the reasons she took this job. Then, however, her manager, Kathy, started to explain what this project entailed. In great detail, she described each step to take in getting the brochure developed and the proper ways to do it. It wasn't a conversation but a lecture. Kathy didn't ask for Sophia's ideas or check for understanding. When Kathy finished, Sophia was overwhelmed, anxious, and unmotivated to tackle the project. Unsure how to start, she avoided it until Kathy asked for the final product. Sophia was clearly upset and Kathy started questioning whether this is the right place for her.

REMEMBER

Employees need to feel ownership of their work, not just copy how their supervisor would do it. People aren't machines. Give them room to put their own stamp on their work, so they have pride and want to work harder.

>> **You don't let go — and even get in the way.** In essence, you're still trying to do the delegated assignment yourself — often under the guise of just trying to help out. This so-called help is neither asked for nor needed. In fact, taking a project back is a surefire way of demotivating someone to do their best work. After all, you've reinforced that you're just going to redo it.

Dan was an accomplished senior manager. Clients loved him for his attention to detail. You never had to worry about Dan doing it right, they often said. But in order to move up into the C-suite, Dan was told he needed to delegate more. He decided to entrust Hilary, a young and ambitious project manager, to a critical deliverable for a client. He spent time with her up front, making his expectations clear. To his credit, he asked her questions and listened to her ideas. Dan even got out of her way to let her run with it. When Hilary turned in the project to Dan to review, he told her, "Good start, but I'll take it from here." Dan needlessly put in extra time to make it into the way he would do it. The fact is Hilary's work was solid, just different. She was demotivated and the fact that Dan couldn't let go of control only hurt his efforts to move up.

REMEMBER

The goal of delegation is to let go of projects and build confidence and competence in your employees. Taking a project back from an employee sends a message that the work isn't good enough. If important changes need to be made, relay that information to the employee. Otherwise, they'll feel like they did all the work and you're getting the credit in the end.

» **The assignment you delegate is beyond the person's capability level.** The assignment or responsibility you delegate is one that the individual isn't ready to handle. It's greater than the person's knowledge, experience, or skill level, and it leaves the employee unable to competently perform and produce the right results.

Employees are often willing to take on duties they aren't really ready to handle, and many are reluctant to speak up even if they know the job is beyond their capabilities. After all, who wants to admit they aren't ready enough to do something? When an employee is given the job with a sink-or-swim approach — throw the person the job and see what happens — it often leads to the employee drowning.

Omar was a star student in college. His professors complimented him and said he would go far in any company lucky to have him. When he landed an entry marketing job at a social media agency, he was thrilled and eager to show his supervisor what he knew. Unfortunately, his supervisor was only a year out of college herself. She was struggling with the workload and some personal problems as well. She met with Omar one morning and said he needed to develop a new social media campaign for a new retail client. "You can handle that, right?" she asked. Omar didn't want to start off on the wrong foot and said yes. She left him to figure it out without giving him any more information. Omar went into panic mode. All his studies hadn't prepared him for this real test. He didn't know where to start, what his supervisor wanted, or even when it was due. But he should be able to do this, right? Omar struggled with even starting. He lost sleep and really started to question if this was a right fit.

When his supervisor came in later that week, Omar's station was cleaned out without any notice.

Many younger employees hate conflict. They also have a strong sense of self. They don't like admitting they don't know something. After all, they grew up with a lot of praise and messages that they could do anything. Spend time with employees to make sure they can handle what you're delegating. Tell them it's okay to admit they don't have all the answers. Ask them questions to make sure they're really ready to take on a project and not wanting to let you down.

>> **The project you delegate is beyond the person's capacity level.** In this case, the issue isn't one of competence level but one of workload. You have a maxed-out employee on whom you pile another critical project. Although many such individuals don't outwardly complain or, when they do, aren't listened to, they suffer with the burden and stress to try to keep up. Overload the machine (your employee in this case) without consideration of its capacity level, and eventually, mechanical failure sets in.

EXAMPLE

Molly was very motivated to become vice president in the regional office of an insurance company. She believed the best way to impress her supervisor was to say yes to everything, and it seemed to be working. Her supervisor said she appreciated her can-do attitude in her last review. But Molly was only human. She had taken on too much and when an emergency on one project required her to work overtime and push off other projects, she missed deadlines. Her supervisor came to her upset, "Molly, this isn't like you. The client isn't happy that you didn't do what you said you would do when promised." Molly crumpled and said, "You're right. I screwed up by taking on too much."

This was a hard and important lesson for both Molly and her supervisor. Delegation is all about clear communication — at every step. And it's a two-way communication, which means both supervisor and employee have a responsibility to be forthright and timely in communicating issues. As a supervisor, make sure your employee can grab the baton before you release control for them to do the job.

>> **You don't provide any review during the process.** In this case, you give the assignment and that's it, abdicating taking any responsibility for what gets produced. Even though you let the staff member have total autonomy for handling the assignment, you don't give any progress review along the way to help the employee and to see how they're performing. You may then wonder why the employee runs into difficulties and why the end results don't turn out very well.

EXAMPLE

Maxine received feedback in her last review that she needs to stop microman-aging her employees and let them do their work. She kept that in mind and tried to delegate future work without meddling, but her hands-off approach to delegating was creating a new problem: The quality of work had suffered. She went to lunch with Diane, a senior leader and her mentor, and shared her frustrations. "I'm wrong if I micromanage and I'm wrong if I don't," Maxine said. Diane listened and then asked, "Are you still doing regular reviews and checking on their work to see how they're doing?" "Isn't that micromanaging?" asked Maxine. Diane explained it's not all or nothing. Employees need feedback to make adjustments, but just not all the time. You need to give them both room to work and guidance as a coach.

REMEMBER

Don't confuse empowering people to take on projects with not offering feedback. Regularly scheduled check-ins are critical opportunities for coaching and mentoring to ensure the employee feels supported and the quality of the work meets your expectations.

>> **You give responsibility without giving support.** When you delegate, support takes on many forms: initial guidance and training, information, equipment, a budget to work with, decision-making authority, or access to staff or material resources.

When support is lacking, you may assign a project, saying "Here, get this project done," and then end the conversation. The lack of support becomes an obstacle that the employee has to expend energy to overcome.

Providing more clarity can help tame the delegated task monkey by reducing the need for constant check-ins and questions. Not only does it free you up to focus on other tasks, but it also provides a road map for the employee for advancement.

TIP

Using the baton metaphor I discuss in the previous section, ask these questions to avoid the common pitfalls of delegation:

>> How can I be clear in my expectations when passing the baton?

>> How can I make sure I let go of the baton so they can run?

>> Is this employee up to taking the baton and finishing the race?

>> What can I do to make sure the process is successful?

Knowing what you gain when delegating

Your growth as a leader in your organization is directly tied to your ability to multiply the efforts of other people. As Chapter 2 explains, the transition from doer to coach is switching how you view your role. As a coach, developing employees into stronger, more independent problem solvers is your job. Here are the reasons why focusing on your delegation skills is the one of the best ways to improve as an effective coach:

>> **It's an easy place to start.** If you're intimidated at all about stepping into a role of being a coach, start with delegation. Talking about project tasks is more

natural and comfortable for most people rather than discussing career and life goals, employee reviews, or performance issues.

>> **You get immediate payback.** When you successfully delegate a task, you're free to handle more important tasks. At the same time, the employee is engaged in the problem-solving process.

>> **You're reinforcing all your coaching skills.** Repetition is the key to acquiring a new skill. Because delegation is a routine practice, you'll strengthen your ability to be clear in communicating expectations, asking questions, listening, and guiding others to solve problems without you doing it.

>> **Your supervisor will see your progress.** As an outside coach hired to develop managers into coaches, I'm always looking for indicators that my coaching is paying off. When the president tells me they can see the manager delegating more, I know I'm successful.

Knowing What to Delegate

Knowing what to delegate (and what *not* to delegate) is a two-step process:

1. **Make a master list.**

Think of this as a brain dump. List all of the projects, duties, tasks, and activities that you perform and are involved with — daily and periodically. You want to keep tasks as small as possible, so list all the activities and work assignments that use up your time — from big to little, from really important to less important. Most managers are able to list from 20 to more than 40 items on this pre-delegating analysis list.

2. **Categorize the list.**

Label each item on your list following these guidelines:

● Items you can completely reassign.

● Items you can share or reassign in part.

● Items you need to keep.

TIP

Ask yourself this question: If I delegate this item to one of my staff, will the time spent up front to provide the guidance and support needed pay off later in productivity, in how the group functions, or in better use of my time? If yes, delegate it. If no, keep it.

You need to keep some items because they truly fall into your domain as a manager. Writing performance reviews, negotiating your group's annual operating budget with your boss, and handling personnel issues are some of the responsibilities you can't give to others to do — even if you want to give them away. Your time and attention are best spent maintaining productive operations and good morale in your group. If not you, who is going to take the lead in the following endeavors?

>> Pushing forward initiatives to improve processes or tackle big operational problems

>> Getting people and material resources that your staff needs to get their jobs done

>> Organizing staff training needs so that they perform effectively

>> Providing technical direction to the group

>> Charting the group's future path

>> Clarifying key work priorities for the group

>> Representing the group's needs with management

>> Challenging and developing staff to perform to their best

REMEMBER

The problem for many managers is that these critical and strategic issues often receive little attention. They get so caught up in their daily tasks, projects, and meetings that a leadership void in the group occurs. Delegating properly helps you begin to focus on more important tasks and fill this void — one so vital to your group's success.

EXAMPLE

What many managers overlook when figuring out what to delegate are the items to share or reassign in part. Items related to the day-to-day operations of your group, which some managers tend to hold onto, are where your greatest potential exists to delegate wholly or in part to people on your staff. Here are some examples:

>> Solving fairly routine customer problems

>> Setting the daily work schedule and workflow

>> Preparing agendas for your regular staff meetings

>> Making decisions on situations that employees face in carrying out their responsibilities

>> Completing functions you're less qualified for or not too good at doing

>> Handling technical duties

>> Compiling data

- >> Composing regular administrative reports
- >> Researching issues that come your way
- >> Training new employees or others in the group
- >> Carrying out important functions for which little staff coverage exists, meaning there's no back-up support for day-to-day operations
- >> Handling vendor-relations issues
- >> Seizing opportunities that build upon others' creative talents or desires
- >> Answering questions you're frequently asked
- >> Dealing with new functions that come about due to change in the workplace

TIP

In many cases, the items you partially delegate can become items that you completely delegate in the future. You do this by adding one piece of the responsibility at a time. Each time the employee masters the new part delegated, you give them another piece to handle. You delegate one step at a time in manageable increments and build off of that success.

REMEMBER

If you assign the whole responsibility or project today — for instance, handle the whole setup and preparation work for an upcoming job fair — the employee could fail. Delegating in increments reduces the chances of failure.

Matching Employees to Tasks

When you know what you want to delegate, you determine to whom you will delegate. Which person will be good for which assignment? Here are some important questions to ask before initiating a delegating effort:

- >> Where does the assignment best fit functionally within your group?
- >> Who has capacity in terms of time and workload to handle the duty?
- >> Who has the interest?
- >> Who has the skill and experience level best for the job?
- >> Whose capabilities do you need to expand to fill coverage gaps in the group's day-to-day operations?
- >> Who needs a new or different challenge?
- >> To whom do you want to give an opportunity for growth?

Notice how one of the factors not listed is "Who has the best track record?" Sometimes managers tend to delegate mostly to their reliable performers. As a result, they don't distribute the workload evenly among all the staff in the group, which has an effect of punishing the good employees. It may also create resentment: among the star employees who wonder why they have to carry the workload for others in the group and among other employees who feel passed over for the most challenging and growth-oriented work. Instead, develop and challenge everyone in your group.

EXAMPLE

The goal of delegating is to empower your employees and help them continue to challenge themselves. However, not all employees are the same. When you're matching tasks to employees, keep in mind their experience and capabilities. To avoid the scenario of the employee constantly checking with you throughout the project, clearly state the level of authority you're giving them in completing the task. Are they seasoned employees who you trust to work independently or are they junior, relatively inexperienced and untested? You don't give the same level of responsibility to everyone. For instance:

» Jerry is a veteran performer and your go-to-person when you can't be involved in a project. Jerry decides on what to do and doesn't need you to inform you at any point.

» Dina is a mid-level employee. She's good, but you think it would be best if she acted and informed you of what she did do, just so you're in the loop.

» Pablo is relatively new. You're encouraged by what you've seen from him so far, but he's too inexperienced to act on his own. You want to mentor him at key stages of the project and want him to come with his recommendations and collaborate on a final solution.

Be clear in your expectations by understanding the capabilities of each employee. Balance giving them authority to act independently with providing mentorship and support, depending on their experience and capabilities. In this way, you'll support their growth and set them up for success.

Putting the Delegating Tool into Action

Successful delegation isn't a one-step process of handing off a task and hoping for the best. It requires six steps to empower employees and get the results you want. You do Steps 1 through 5 when you introduce the assignment; you do Step 6 along the way and at the completion of the delegated assignment.

TIP

Perform Steps 1 through 5 of the delegating tool when you initiate the assignment:

>> Step 1 is when you do most of the talking — you know what the project entails and what outcomes you need.

>> Steps 2 through 5 are best if done interactively. You're checking for understanding and collaborating on the approach. Discuss and negotiate each relevant issue as a two-way conversation. You want the employee involved and helping to shape the project specifics, for that person is the one who must own and drive the assignment.

>> Step 6 is done along the way — the assignment is in progress, so this step involves feedback exchange. Make sure you get your feedback stated directly — especially the positive feedback to acknowledge the successes.

Step 1: Describe the assignment

Kick off the delegating effort by informing the employee of the work you want done. But you go further than that: Tell the *purpose* of the assignment, spelling out why this assignment is important and what you want to see accomplished. In particular, spell out these three aspects of your performance expectations:

>> **Deliverables:** These are the work products, the tangible items to show from the work done.

>> **Quality:** This is providing the picture of what good results in producing the deliverables should look like. You're articulating the standards of performance you want to see happen, not the details of how the job should be done.

>> **Manner:** This expectation applies when the delegated assignment involves much interaction or work with others. State the positive conduct that others should consistently see from the employee in getting the assignment done.

Provide background information and other pertinent news so that the employee has an overview of what the assignment or responsibility entails.

WARNING

Avoid getting overly detailed as you introduce the assignment. Stay away from telling the person how to do the job, which you can discuss in Step 3. Focusing on how to do the job overlooks that people have their own styles of work and may stifle creativity. Stress the results you want rather than the methods of doing the job.

Step 2: Define parameters

Parameters mean boundaries or limits — the worst thing to have happen is for employees to go off in a certain direction or exercise a level of authority and be told afterward that they shouldn't have done what they did. Understanding the boundaries to work within through trial and error can be a painful way to find out what is acceptable and not acceptable to do. It often has an effect of killing initiative.

Here are four areas of parameters to consider:

>> **Budget:** A *budget* is a spending limit. If the assignment involves making purchases or other expenditures, what are the dollar limits for what can be spent?

>> **Timeline(s):** A *timeline* is a deadline for any milestones and for the completion of the job. Sometimes when you're delegating an ongoing responsibility, a schedule must be maintained.

>> **Feedback or information you need:** This information is what you need to be kept in the loop as the project or assignment progresses. This may include certain reports you want or news of certain kinds of situations or problems of which you want to be kept abreast.

>> **Level of authority and decision making:** This is the line for employees at which they can act and decide for themselves and beyond which they need to bring you in to the situation. Refer to the previous section for a discussion about the authority audit.

Step 3: Provide resources for support

Collaborate with the employee on what they need to help ensure success in the project. Sometimes the employee doesn't need much and they are ready and competent to handle what you're assigning. Other times, what you're delegating is a big step forward for the employee, and other times the employee needs some up-front investment of your time and help.

Here is an overview of items to discuss:

>> **Expenses:** As you get into discussing with the employee what is needed to do the assignment, you realize — and allocate — some money to cover additional costs.

>> **Materials:** *Materials* are the equipment, tools, or supplies needed to get the particular job done.

>> **Access to information, resources:** Often, to do the assignment, the employee needs to be given certain information or needs to know where to go to find it as well as who to talk to on issues related to the assignment. Your role is to connect the employee to the "what" and "who" factors needed to get the job done.

>> **Staff:** Sometimes, especially if you're delegating a project in which the staff person is to play a lead role, you want to work out with your employee the human resources needed and their roles for assistance in getting the job done.

>> **Adjustments in priorities and duties:** For the delegatee to take on the project or responsibility you want done, change is sometimes needed in that person's current workload. Such adjustments include shifting current schedules with projects or priorities or assigning some tasks or duties to others on the team.

>> **Training:** Sometimes you need to teach new skills to employees so that they can complete the responsibilities you delegate to them. This may consist of walking them through the job once or twice before you give it to them to handle. It may consist of bringing in someone else who has expertise in the area to do the training.

Whatever the case, after you complete the training, let the employees carry out the delegated duties in their own style. Not everyone does a job in the same way. After they discover how to do a job, allow employees to have the freedom to do it in their own style. That's when the best performance comes. Put your focus less on methods and more on the results you need to see.

>> **Informing others of the employee's new role:** Sometimes, when others don't know that this person is now the responsible party, their tendency is to not give much cooperation or attention until they hear from the horse's mouth (meaning you) about the change. You can provide support by telling everyone that the delegatee is now handling a certain project or responsibility and ask them to give that person full cooperation. This usually removes potential obstacles and provides the authority to go with the responsibility.

TIP

Before you move to the next step in the delegating meeting, ask the employee the following question: "What else do you need in terms of support in order to handle this assignment successfully?" This question serves as a safety net for you. You may not think of all the support issues needed. In addition, asking this question provides an opportunity for the employee to raise any concerns — concerns that you two can address more easily now rather than later.

Step 4: Check for understanding

Before sending the employee off to get to work, make sure they understand what you want. Far too often, you think you've clearly covered everything the person needs to know, and by that person's conversation with you, you think the employee understands too. But what happens then? The employee goes off in a different direction or produces results different from what was needed, and then you find out that person's interpretation and your interpretation of what was to be done weren't the same. This list provides specific insight to help ensure the employee understands what you need:

Ask open-ended questions

To check understanding, ask an open-ended question in a clear and direct fashion. For example, "To see if I was clear on all this, please recap your understanding of what you're being asked to do here and the expectations for it." This helps you see if you need to clarify any misunderstandings *before* the employee gets started on the assignment. It also helps you know if you left any important details out of your discussion.

Other probing questions to ask include the following:

>> What do you see as your first steps?

>> What challenges do you foresee?

>> What resources do you need?

>> What questions do they have?

>> What are their other priorities?

>> What do they need from you?

WARNING

The worst question you can ask is "Do you understand what I'm asking you to do?" Of course, almost every time the answer comes back "Yes," usually with a nod and smile. Unfortunately this close-ended question tells you nothing about the employee's understanding.

Tracking how they respond

Your focus should be on listening closely and observing how they answer these questions. This is an opportunity to exercise your emotional intelligence skills for social awareness that Chapter 5 discusses. Positive signs that the project will go well:

>> They're forthright and ask questions.

>> They're honest about their concerns.

>> They clearly articulate the goals of the project and how they'll approach the project.

>> They seem confident and look you in the eye.

>> Their posture is erect, and they're leaning forward, communicating they're excited to get going.

>> They smile and exude confidence.

WARNING

Warning signs that the project may not go well:

>> Their eyes are glazed over as if they're preoccupied and not engaged.

>> They're quiet and withdrawn as if they're worried.

>> Their posture is slumped as if they aren't looking forward to carrying this responsibility.

>> They don't ask any questions, indicating they may not want to admit ignorance or disappoint you.

>> Their answers are incomplete, indicating they may not understand the scope.

REMEMBER

You can try to engage them with more questions or even be honest and tell them that they seem tentative or they have something on their mind. If you have time, you may reschedule another meeting to go over the scope and approach. They may just need more time to think it through. Not everyone is the same in taking on projects. Coaching for different personalities involves getting to know people over time.

Step 5: Establish checkpoint meetings

This is the last step of the coaching discussion that you cover with the employee before the person gets started on the assignment. *Checkpoint meetings* are progress-review meetings — times set when you and the employee get together to see how the project is progressing. By setting them up front, you're planning together and, as a result, building in milestones and time frames for the assignment instead of leaving timelines vague.

TIP

A good rule to follow in setting the checkpoint meeting times is the more the assignment is new to the employee's skills and experiences, the more frequent the checkpoints. The more the employee has the skill and experience to run with the job, the less frequent the checkpoint meetings.

The checkpoint meeting helps you get the following benefits, which makes them worth your while:

>> **Allows for course correction:** If the employee is off-track or is having problems, you're able to work with the person to get problems resolved. The meeting gives support and helps employees not get derailed from completing their assignment. You're increasing the likelihood for good results and employee success.

>> **Builds accountability:** The checkpoint meeting prevents employees from running and hiding or procrastinating in getting the assignment done. The meeting also reinforces the good job your employees are doing in taking responsibility for completing the project.

>> **Minimizes nagging disease:** Nothing is worse than being delegated a project and having a manager checking up with you daily to see what you have done. Employees usually call this behavior *micromanagement;* another name for it is *nagging disease.* You're nervous about letting go and want to make sure everything is being handled well. Although wanting to check in daily is understandable, the constant doing so is a major nuisance.

Scheduled checkpoint meetings give you the opportunity to be fully informed of what's happening without having to chase after your employees to find out. Set the meetings at the frequency level that meets your needs and the employee's needs, and then leave the person alone to do the job.

>> **Maximizes your investment:** Checkpoints allow you to emphasize quality time with your employees, as I discuss in Chapter 3. The meetings allow you to be involved with what's going on without being too hands-on. They allow you to show interest without having to have daily contact. They allow you to see how spending time getting the employee started is paying off. In essence, checkpoints are the step to ensure that you get a good return on your investment of time and trust with the employee.

TIP

When you hold a checkpoint meeting, consider using the status review format in Chapter 16.

Step 6: Provide feedback and positive reinforcement

The last step of the delegating tool is carried out at each checkpoint and at the completion of the project or assignment. At the checkpoint meetings, give both positive and negative feedback (see Chapter 14). No matter their generation, an employee thrives on positive feedback, especially if it's authentic. Don't be so quick to point out problems or errors. Find what deserves praise and call it out like "I like what you did here."

REMEMBER

Recognize the progress the employee is making and the good results being delivered. This positive reinforcement is a critical element of building success for the employee. Remember, delegating works best when you build upon success, not failure.

Putting delegation in action: Case study

Here's an example of the six steps of the delegating tool in action:

John was the vice president of human resources in his company. He had been having recent discussions with his fellow members of the executive team about developing and implementing a telecommuting program, in which employees work at home for some to all of their normal working hours rather than coming into an office. They looked at it if it could work for the business and as a practice that could help attract and retain employees. From these discussions, John was asked to put together a program that the executive team could review and implement.

John turned to Anne, an HR analyst on his staff, to be his point person for the research and development of a telecommuting program. This project was something Anne had wanted to do, and she had recommended to John that the company should look at implementing such a program. They met, and John utilized the delegating tool in getting Anne off to a good start in the project. Here is what they worked out:

>> **Step 1:** The project was to involve both research and program development — interviewing some employees and managers within the company, visiting other companies, and researching periodicals to learn about telecommuting programs and what might work best for their organization. The purpose of the project was to recommend a cost-effective telecommuting program. John outlined the results he expected:

- **Deliverables:** Two reports, one summarizing the findings from the internal interviews and one summarizing the research from the external sources; a recommended telecommuting policy; and an implementation plan for its rollout. At the end, John and Anne would make a joint presentation to the executive team on their recommendations.

- **Quality:** The recommended policy needed to be clear and concise, addressing cost considerations, what positions would participate, and how the program would work.

- **Manner:** Maintain responsive listening efforts in all the interactions and maintain confidentiality of all findings until they have been reviewed with the executives.

>> Step 2: One parameter was for Anne to do no out-of-town travel for her research on other organizations' practices. Incidental expenses that occurred in doing the research were acceptable. The other parameter was that in her fact-finding, she was to give recommendations and let employees know that she talked only of the possibility of a telecommuting program, not of the assurance of one.

John and Anne negotiated a three-month deadline. By the end of three months, all of Anne's deliverables would be written, and she and John would be ready to deliver the joint presentation. This project was also a good development opportunity for Anne, especially the opportunity to present to the company's executive management.

>> Step 3: John would send out an announcement to all the employees and managers so that they would understand the project. He would also shift some of Anne's hiring activities to Bill, another member of the group. In addition, because Ann was nervous about making formal presentations, John would be involved in the presentation. He also agreed to coach Anne in making presentations as part of their preparation work.

>> Step 4: Almost without asking, Anne summarized to John the essentials and expectations for this project. She was excited by it and took good notes during their dialogue.

>> Step 5: Together, Anne and John set up the checkpoints around the key milestones in the project. For the first checkpoint, they would meet in one week to review Anne's draft questionnaire for the interviews and her proposed list of employees and managers to survey. The next checkpoint was set at a month-and-a-half, the midway point in the project, during which Anne would review her two fact-finding reports. This meeting would also be used to plan what the policy might look like. The last checkpoint was set for one month after the second one, and Anne would come ready with her drafts of the telecommuting program and a plan for its implementation. This would allow enough time to make necessary revisions and prepare the presentation to the executive team.

It might be tempting to rush through the steps of delegation, but keep in mind, the time you invest in doing it right is a long-term investment in your employees taking more responsibility and less time from you. However, even the best plans face challenges as the next section illustrates.

Handling Employee Resistance

Sometimes despite the best of efforts, employees don't want to do the work you want to delegate to them — no matter how nicely you ask or plead. What then? These sections identify the forms that resistance may take and what you can do to deal with it.

Recognizing what causes resistance

Low interest is most often the source behind the resistance. Discover what's effecting the low interest and you uncover what is driving the resistance against what you want the employee to do. This is the key to overcoming resistance and getting performance moving forward.

This lack of interest sometimes is displayed outwardly, "Do I have to do this assignment? Can't you get someone else to do it?" Sometimes it's displayed more quietly, in which the employee nods and smiles when you make the assignment, but little effort follows. Some even take the approach to produce the opposite of what you asked to be done. Others get the job done fine but with a lot of moaning and groaning along the way.

However the low interest gets expressed, the reasons for it most often stem from employees' past experiences. These experiences may have come from working with you, while others have come from managers of long ago. Some people hold on to emotional baggage for long periods of time. No matter who the source has been, here are some experiences in delegating-type situations that have turned employees to the low point on the interest scale:

>> Was given much responsibility but no authority with it

>> Had an annoying manager who kept insisting the job be done their way

>> Was given assignments to use skills that aren't strengths and received no training support to develop them

>> Was offered an interesting project but had it pulled away by the manager because the direction the employee took didn't suit the manager's taste

>> Had a bunch of new duties dumped on the employee with no help to figure them out

>> Took on a challenging project and got chastised on every little mistake made

>> Was assigned a difficult project in which cooperation from others was needed but wasn't forthcoming, and the manager didn't want to be bothered with it

When you come along ready to delegate a new assignment, you encounter resistance. Reminders of the past, plus apprehensions of what could happen now, add up to a lack of interest in your project.

WARNING

Managers often don't explore the reasons behind the lack of interest. Which employee would be easier for delegating an assignment to handle?

>> Employee A: High interest in the job, but skill less developed to do it

>> Employee B: Low interest in the job, but has high skill level to do it

Most managers select Employee A because developing skill level, especially when the person is eager and willing, is easier than motivating someone with low interest. Don't give up on that disinterested employee, however. Keep at him!

Overcoming that resistance

The past experiences that are blocking staff members from wanting to take on what you want to delegate indicate, in most cases, a lack of effective guidance and support with previous delegating attempts. The key, then, to overcoming the employee resistance so they'll perform is to reverse the problems that previous managers created. In particular, these actions may help:

1. **Listen patiently and responsively to discover the employee's concerns.**

    Through your active listening efforts, you may discover a simple reason for the employee's disinterest in what you want to delegate: The individual just doesn't like that kind of work — no apprehensions or past experiences of suffering involved. So even though the assignment is something the person can handle, the employee just doesn't like to do it.

    TIP

    In these cases, take the *such-is-life approach:* Oh well, such is life that on occasion something has to be done in your job which isn't something you're fond of doing. You don't say these thoughts, but with this approach in mind, you can acknowledge the employee's point, nod and smile, and then proceed to working on the delegating plan with that person. In simple terms, don't dwell on an area that isn't that important.

    Keep what you learned in mind for future assignments. But if this is the best resource to take on an assignment you need help with, proceed. It's all part of work and why your employees get paid to do it.

2. **Plan with the employee steps to take to ensure that the right level of support is given for success to occur.**

3. **Explain the importance of the assignment and related big-picture stuff as you develop the plan together.**

4. **If the assignment has meaningful benefit to the employee, spell that out.**

    Only do so if it is truly the case; otherwise, you're selling broccoli to someone who hates vegetables.

5. **Reassign the job to someone else only when you see that truly is the best option under the circumstances.**

   If you do give the project to someone else, off-load something from the other person to this employee. Be firm about your expectation that everyone helps the team and is to pull their fair share of the work.

6. **Follow through on the support efforts you agreed to and be receptive when the employee comes to you with any questions in doing the assignment.**

Using Delegating to Build the Pillars of Commitment

One major benefit you get from delegating effectively is having a positive influence on employee commitment. Here is how this coaching tool affects each of the five pillars for building employee commitment (see Chapter 4):

>> **Focus:** By spelling out your expectations and setting parameters when you delegate, you give employees a clear direction and the sense of importance they need to do the job well. When employees know the high standards you expect, they're more likely to focus on meeting them.

>> **Involvement:** Shaping the initial course of the delegated assignment is done collaboratively between you and the employee. When you use this tool right, you're not assigning work; rather, you're planning together to get work done. The employee takes over from there and works to bring home success. This is involvement at its best.

>> **Development:** Many delegated assignments or responsibilities provide staff with opportunities to grow in skill, abilities, and experience. Through training provided, employee's capabilities develop for the better.

>> **Gratitude:** This pillar is especially impacted through your follow-up efforts in checkpoint meetings (refer to the earlier section, "Putting the Delegating Tool into Action" in this chapter). As you delegate, you positively reinforce the progress your employees make, building on experiences of success.

>> **Accountability:** The progress review nature of the checkpoint meetings serve to reinforce employee accountability. In addition, because you let employees handle assignments when you delegate (your role is to give support), they know from the fruits of their own labor when they're doing well. Self-sufficiency is promoted, and that's a key driver for accountability.

IN THIS CHAPTER

» **Contrasting constructive feedback with praise and criticism**

» **Giving performance feedback effectively**

» **Introducing a tool for tracking your feedback efforts**

» **Facilitating the discussion after the feedback and handling challenges**

» **Influencing employee commitment through constructive feedback**

Chapter **14**

Giving Constructive Feedback

One of the most powerful coaching skills is the ability to give effective *performance feedback* — information given to an employee about how they're performing. This feedback lets the employee know whether the job was done well or whether they needs to improve upon the work.

Giving feedback is integral to developing many other skills, including delegation, emotional intelligence (EQ), and career development. Quite often, doer managers talk with their employees about work issues, but they never directly tell them how they're performing in regard to those issues. Performance feedback, on the other hand, is direct and timely. That is, on an ongoing basis, you let employees know how effectively they are carrying out a specific effort or achieving a specific outcome — right at the time they occur. This chapter helps you build your performance-feedback skills.

Using Constructive Feedback versus Praise and Criticism

Performance feedback can be given in the following ways (don't fall into the trap of giving praise and criticism on employee performance):

>> **Constructive feedback:** It's information-specific, issue-focused, and based on observations. It comes in two varieties:

- *Positive feedback* is news or input to an employee about an effort well done.

- *Negative feedback* is news to an employee about an effort that needs improvement. Negative feedback doesn't mean a terrible performance, rather a performance in which the outcomes delivered should be better.

>> **Praise and criticism:** On the other hand, these are both personal judgments about a performance effort or outcome, with praise being a favorable judgment and criticism, an unfavorable judgment. Information given is general and vague, focused on the person, and based on opinions or feelings.

The following examples help show the difference between constructive feedback (either positive or negative) and praise/criticism:

>> **Praise:** "You did a great job on that project. Good work."

>> **Positive feedback:** "The contributions you made on this project were a big help. I noticed that the work you produced was thorough and accurate. In addition, whenever I needed help in coordinating the team and managing the project schedule, you stepped in and covered for me or gave me assistance, which kept the team and the project on schedule. When team members had questions, you were available to help get them answers. Thanks so much for your contributions in helping make this project a success."

>> **Criticism:** "You weren't much help on this project. You were really ineffective. I hope this isn't the best you can do."

>> **Negative feedback:** "Here are the concerns I have regarding your assistance on this project. As I explained at the beginning of the project, your services were needed to help coordinate the project management in terms of keeping people focused on their assignments and on the schedule. I did not see much effort of coordination occurring. For example, many of the team members came to me with questions about assignments and schedule issues, often after they could not get answers from you. Most of the time, I noticed that you were working on your part of the project, but the interactions with the others

about the overall project and its progress were not evident. When I asked you to cover for me at three of the meetings, each of the meetings ended after a brief time with no minutes or action items produced. Delays have occurred in the project, and we'll now require everyone's attention to get back on track."

The two types of constructive feedback come across as far more objective, specific, and nonjudgmental than praise and criticism. Because constructive feedback is based on observations in specific terms about issues of performance, it isn't a right or wrong. Constructive feedback encourages a discussion after the person gets the feedback. As a result, you and your employee can learn more about the situation and, if needed, set a positive course of action.

Praise and criticism don't encourage this dialog. Although nothing is wrong with praise — employees like to know if they did a good job — it can often be seen as hollow or lacking in substance.

Sometimes managers attempt to soften criticism by first saying, "Now don't take this personally." After that's been said, the employee will likely become defensive. Like praise, in which specifics aren't stated, criticism often leads to a battle between a manager and an employee about whose opinion is right or wrong. Because no observations are provided to give a factual basis to the input — the input is focused on personal judgments — the receiver has a difficult time understanding exactly what he needs to improve upon, and the result can be defensiveness.

WARNING

For effective coaching, therefore, give your employees constructive feedback about their performance, rather than praise and criticism. Praise and criticism don't give the employee valuable information to help them learn.

Performance isn't just about how they met or missed a deadline or how they exceeded or came short of meeting a sales goal. Performance is also how they got the work done and the impact they had on relationships. Did they deliver on time but upset other employees by making them drop their jobs to accommodate last-minute requests? Did they hit their sales quota by focusing exclusively on new clients but ignoring and damaging existing clients? Conversely, did they fall short of hitting their goals but kept everyone, including you, in the loop? Did they slip on meeting some of their timelines to help a colleague who was suffering from losing a parent?

REMEMBER

Performance needs to be holistic and include all the things that make people human. It's not just about hitting numbers. It's also about impacting relationships. Many managers are more comfortable giving performance feedback strictly on output measures and often gloss over the tough conversations about negative behaviors that have a larger impact on morale, motivation, and productivity.

Providing Constructive Feedback: A Step-by-Step Guide

The guidelines for giving constructive feedback are relatively the same, whether you're giving positive or negative feedback. These methods fall into four categories: content, manner, timing, and frequency, each covered in the following sections.

Content

Content is *what you say* in the constructive feedback. To focus on the content, remember these steps:

1. Identify the issue of performance involved.

In your first sentence, identify the topic or issue that the feedback will be about. For example, "I want to discuss with you your progress on the ABC project." ABC project is the issue of the feedback.

2. Provide the specifics of what occurred.

Give the examples or other evidence to provide the picture of what took place in the employee's effort of performance. (Without the specifics, you only have praise or criticism.) Start each key point with an "I" message, such as, "I've noticed," "I've observed," "I've seen," or when the need exists to pass on feedback from others, "I've had reported to me." "I" messages help you be issue-focused and get into the specifics.

By contrast, "you" statements tend to put the employee on the defensive. You want the employee to hear what you're saying. Starting with an "I" makes it clear that it's your perspective and helps the employee listen without shutting down before you've even started.

Manner

Manner is *how you say* the constructive feedback. As you may know, how you say something often carries more weight than what you have to say — manner is an important element when giving feedback. Remember the following when focusing on how you provide the feedback (see Chapter 5 to understand how to be more aware of how emotions play into communication):

>> **Be direct when delivering your message.** Get to the point and avoid beating around the bush. Managers uncomfortable with conflict have difficulty getting

to the point. They creep into the difficult conversation, only making the employee more anxious. Positive or negative feedback should be delivered in a quick, straightforward manner.

» **Avoid "need to" phrases, which send implied messages that something didn't go well.** For example, "Jane, you need to get your reports turned in on time, and you need to spellcheck them." This message isn't really performance feedback. It implies that Jane didn't do something well with her reports, but it doesn't report exactly to Jane what happened. Providing clarity on what occurred is the aim of feedback.

» **Be sincere and avoid giving mixed messages.** Sincerity says that you mean what you say with care and respect. Mixed messages are referred to as "yes, but" messages. For example, "John, you have worked hard on this project, but. . .." What follows is something the person isn't doing well and is the real point of the message. The attempt to be nice first — sugar-coating the message — is negated, and the real sincerity of the message is diluted. (See the nearby sidebar for an example of how to give positive and negative feedback without mixing the two.) The word "but," along with its cousins "however" and "although," when said in the middle of a thought, create contradictions or mixed messages. In essence, putting "but" in the middle tells the other person, "Don't believe a thing I said before."

» **In positive feedback situations, express appreciation.** Appreciation can be expressed in many ways: "Great job," "Thanks for all your help on this project," or "I really appreciate the good work you did here." Appreciation alone is praise. Yet when you add it to the *specifics* of constructive feedback, your message carries an extra oomph of sincerity.

EXAMPLE

For example, "Sue, we had a backlog this past week and without being asked, I noticed you pitched in and helped John get everything caught up. Your handling of all the processing work while John did the callbacks made for an efficient effort and showed good teamwork. Everything you did was accurate, as well. Thanks so much for helping out. Such initiative is a real value to the team."

Here the last two sentences express appreciation after the content of the feedback was given. It also gets at the purpose of positive feedback — to reinforce good performance. Behavior that is rewarded is repeated, so reward the right behaviors.

» **In negative feedback situations, express concern.** A tone of concern communicates a sense of importance and care and provides the appropriate level of sincerity to the message. Tones such as anger, frustration, disappointment, and the ever-popular sarcasm tend to color the language of the message and turn attempts at negative feedback into criticism. The content of the message gets lost in the noise and harshness.

The purpose of negative feedback is to create awareness that can lead to correction or improvement in performance. If you can't give negative feedback in a helpful manner, in the language and tone of concern, you defeat its purpose.

>> **Give the feedback person-to-person, not through messengers of technology.** The nature of constructive feedback is verbal and informal. That can be done only by talking live to the employee, either face-to-face — or by phone when you physically can't be together. Email, text, and voice mail don't work for constructive feedback because they don't allow live, two-way conversation to follow. Nor does the sincerity of the message come across as well, whether it's positive or negative feedback. Talk one-on-one with people when giving feedback.

>> **State observations, not interpretations.** *Observations* are what you see occur; *interpretations* are your analysis or opinion of what you see occur. Tell what you've noticed, not what you think of it, and report the behavior you notice at a concrete level, instead of as a characterization of the behavior. Observations have a far more factual and nonjudgmental aspect than do interpretations.

Compare these interactions: "You've been moody and uncooperative today" (interpretation and criticism). "Today I noticed that you often had your head down on your desk, and you either didn't answer the phone to take customer calls until reminded to do so or you answered on the fourth ring, which has me concerned" (observation).

The same reasoning applies to positive feedback. Instead of saying to an employee, "You were wonderful with that customer today" (interpretation and praise), report the observations of the behavior you saw, "I noticed you answered the customer's questions accurately and in lay terms. In fact, the customer remarked how helpful you were in explaining how our products work. Well done."

Timing

Timing answers this question: When do you give an employee feedback for a performance effort worth acknowledging?

The answer is ASAP (as soon as possible). Feedback is meant to be given in real time, as close as possible to when the performance incident occurs so that the events are fresh in everyone's minds. When feedback is given well after the fact, the value of the constructive feedback is lessened.

CONSTRUCTIVE FEEDBACK SCENARIO

Suppose Sheri is one of your top technically trained staff members. In fact, in her latest project, her technical skills have been put to good use. So far, the work she has produced has been thorough and accurate, and she has been helpful and responsive to other team members when they've encountered problems. At the same time, Sheri's work has been late . . . again. Now she's two weeks past the second milestone. Because she is a key player in the project, her slowness has resulted in a delay for the overall project. You want to make sure the project stays on schedule and meets its final deadline. Now you need to give feedback to Sheri.

What do you say? You want to hit the key guidelines: The issue of performance needs to be clearly identified; you need to be specific, direct, and sincere, with no mixed messages; and you want to give observations, not interpretations.

This scenario is challenging. Does it warrant both positive and negative feedback? To guide your judgment of whether to use both types of constructive feedback (both positive and negative feedback) in the same conversation, do so only when they're relevant to the issue at hand. If you attempt to give positive feedback along with negative feedback when the positive isn't really relevant, you're sugarcoating your message and undermining your sincerity. However, when both are relevant, don't blend their points — that creates confusion and may send a mixed message. Let the points you want to make in each type of feedback stand on their own; don't connect them in the same thought. In your opening sentence, introduce that you have two sets of feedback to give.

Here's an example of giving both kinds of feedback when they're both relevant:

> "Sheri, I want to give you feedback on your progress so far with Project X. You've performed some aspects of the project very well, and I also have one area of concern I want to work out with you.
>
> In the deliverables you've produced for each milestone, I've noticed they've been thorough and completely accurate. The research done outlines the issues we needed addressed with this project. I've also noticed that you have been responsive to fellow team members' questions and challenges and taken time to help them get problems solved. Thanks for the great teamwork.
>
> The issue of concern deals with meeting deadlines. Work for the second milestone was turned in two weeks past due, as occurred with the first milestone. These delays have contributed to delays with our project schedule, and that is my major concern, especially with the need to deliver this project on time."

(continued)

(continued)

As you see in this example, both positive and negative feedback were given because both were relevant to the issue at hand — the progress shown with Project X. No praise or criticism were provided, and each point stood on its own. The manager didn't use transition words, such as "however" or "but," that blend points together and create mixed messages. If you only want to comment on the missing deadlines issue rather than assessing progress with the entire project, you go with just the negative feedback. Remember, though, that if you continuously only comment on what the person doesn't do well and overlook what is done well, you may demotivate the employee and lose the value of your feedback.

Here is another example of where both positive and negative feedback fit together.

> "Tom, I had a chance to read over your assessment report and want to give you some feedback about it. Most of it was good, and I saw one area that could use some work.
>
> Overall, the report is a good start. It gives me a good sense of what is working and what isn't working from your viewpoint.
>
> I'd like you to reach out to other people on your team to get their impressions, so we're getting the whole picture. You may not learn anything new, but if we want them to be part of the solution, we need to hear them out."

WARNING

When giving negative feedback, you may want to apply a different timeline: ASAR (as soon as reasonable/ready — that is, when *you're* ready). Sometimes when an incident happens, you aren't feeling too good about it, and you need time to cool off and get your thoughts in order before you give negative feedback (so that your manner displays a tone of concern). Doing that may mean giving the feedback tomorrow rather than right now, but tomorrow is still timely, and your feedback will come across as far more constructive.

Frequency

Frequency answers the question, "How often should your employees receive constructive feedback on their performance?"

This last guideline is the most important one of all. It's the one that makes all the other guidelines work. So how often should constructive feedback be given? The answer: on an ongoing basis that reflects each employee's actual performance.

Constructive feedback shouldn't be contrived. You use it to acknowledge real performance, and you do so as a regular practice. But be careful not to take the positive for granted. As you look at the performance of your employees, how many produce more efforts and outcomes that warrant negative feedback than positive? Like most managers, more than likely you see more outcomes of positive performance occurring. Yet, often, employees hear about performance only when something goes wrong. If the positive performance is taken for granted, constructive feedback doesn't work because it isn't reflecting most people's actual performance. So regularly giving positive feedback is the secret for coaching success with constructive feedback.

REMEMBER

Be mindful of how often on average you're critical compared to when you're giving someone positive feedback. Doer managers tend to pick at people's performance, without much constructive feedback. People are motivated by doing a good job. If they have areas to correct, give negative feedback. But try to balance the negative feedback with positive feedback so they don't think they're constantly letting you down.

Generally speaking, the newer the employee, the more frequent the feedback. Overall, the idea here is quite simple: Try to catch and respond to employees doing the job *right* just as much as you catch and respond to them doing something that isn't quite right — and don't acknowledge how they are performing only once or twice a year.

Using a significant-events list

A significant-events list (see Figure 14-1) serves as a tool for recording the constructive feedback you give to your employees. It helps you track what's happening in people's performance rather than relying on your memory. And relying on your memory is the most unreliable practice you can have.

REMEMBER

The significant-events list consists of your notes on the performance feedback that you give. Remember to do the following when filling out the significant events list:

>> **When you record the feedback you give, write summary notes.** Two to three lines per incident of performance should do in most cases. Recording feedback should be quick and easy.

>> **Everything that you record on the list has been verbally stated to the employee.** Don't write notes about employee performance that you haven't already communicated to that person — only write what you say. You have no hidden agendas or surprises for employees.

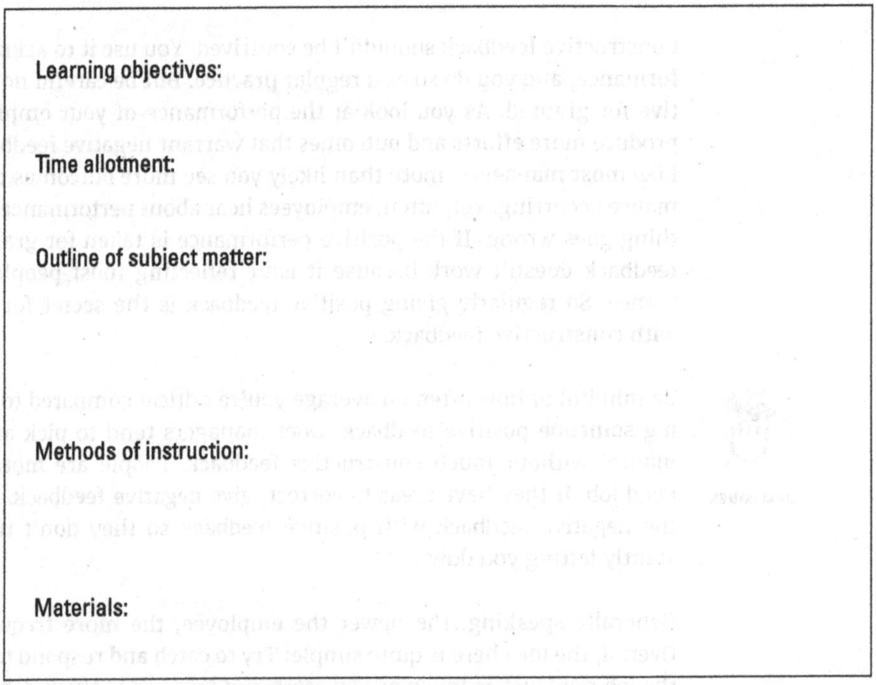

FIGURE 14-1:
Significant-
events list.

© John Wiley & Sons, Inc.

A significant-events list yields some substantial benefits. When you go to write a performance review, typically asked for on an annual basis, your task is an easy one. You merely summarize the feedback you've been giving to the employee all year long. Also, maintaining this tool helps you see trends in employee performance and then set strategies as needed for further coaching efforts. Most importantly, the significant-events list helps you manage the toughest person you have in your group — yourself. With this tool, you can see whether you're giving constructive feedback that reflects each employee's actual performance. This information keeps you honest and helps you avoid the mistake of taking the positive for granted.

Focusing on the Discussion after Giving Feedback

Constructive feedback (either positive or negative) is a direct report to an employee about how they performed a specific task or other incident related to performance. Although the feedback starts out as a one-way conversation — so that you can clearly identify what occurred — the feedback needs to promote a dialog from that point on, which the following sections examine in more detail.

TIP

Often, when giving positive feedback, little discussion is needed; you may even end up talking about other matters with an employee. However, in general, discussion should follow negative feedback. A discussion allows the employee to digest what was heard and then work with you on how to make the situation better as you both go forward.

REMEMBER

After you break the mindset that negative feedback is an uncomfortable thing to do — or that it's just about telling bad news — you'll probably find that it gives you a great coaching opportunity to promote learning and enhance your employees' performance.

In fact, answer this question: If you didn't do something well in your performance, would you want to be told about it? Few people would answer "no" to this question for a simple reason: Most people want to be informed about how they're doing — they just don't want to be hit over the head with the news. Be constructive, not harsh, and then let the discussion begin.

Keeping a positive outcome in mind

When you give negative feedback, enter the discussion phase with a positive outcome in mind, and state it clearly to the employee. Doing so influences the dynamic of the conversation and gives it a positive direction.

For example, after giving feedback, you may say, "I want to explore with you what you can do to stay on schedule and make your total efforts with the project a success." This is a positive outcome, with a focus on solutions, and it invites the employee to participate in a two-way conversation. That's much better than what many managers may say or imply — such as, "I want to know why you can't meet our milestones, and you better not let this project have any more delays. Stay on top of your assignments and spend less time talking with your team members." That's not a good tactic: pushing blame and giving orders. This interaction isn't much of an invitation to a productive post-feedback discussion with the employee.

One of the most powerful ways you can build your competence as a coach is to develop your self-awareness (see Chapter 5). It's often what you aren't aware of that gets you into trouble. Delivering tough news is often fraught with judgments and negative feelings — toward the other person or yourself. You may not be able to forget a snide remark the employee said about you a few months ago. You may be frustrated that the employee doesn't seem like they respect you as their supervisor. You may be telling yourself you're not good at your job. Your unresolved feelings toward the employee or yourself can make it difficult for you to be objective in delivering feedback. Building your self-awareness helps you understand how you're feeling and what you're thinking before you even enter the room to have the discussion.

TIP

After stating your intended positive outcome in a post-feedback discussion, do more asking than telling and more listening than speaking. These steps can help:

1. Initiate employee involvement with a question.

For example, ask "What's getting in the way of reaching the milestones?"

2. Listen to get an understanding from the employee's perspective as to what has been happening.

3. Move the discussion toward the positive outcome you're seeking.

For example, ask "What ideas can you offer to ensure that you stay on schedule for the remainder of the project?" Let the employee help shape the efforts to produce the positive outcome: Often, this means creating a solution.

Offer your input as needed, but conduct the discussion as an exchange of ideas, not as a dictation of your ideas to the employee.

4. Ask what support the employee needs from you.

This isn't an opportunity to take responsibility for a project away from an employee. And it's not an opening for them to dictate everything they don't like about their job. This is a collaborative effort in reaching a SMART solution (see Chapter 15 for how to set SMART goals).

REMEMBER

Two-way discussions push employees to think and take responsibility. And when people help create their own solutions, they're more committed to making them happen. Building self-sufficiency and commitment is what coaching is all about.

After the positive outcome is worked out, bring the conversation to a close. If the matter is important for monitoring progress, set a follow-up date with the employee to do just that.

Dealing with defensive reactions

A handful of employees are sensitive and react defensively whenever you attempt to give them negative feedback. Certainly, defensive people make discussions difficult.

Here are some ways that you can prevent defensiveness, minimize its effect on your meeting, and help you work through a defensive situation, should it arise:

>> **Give negative feedback, not criticism.** Make sure that you follow the guidelines for giving constructive feedback; namely that you're issue-focused, specific, direct, and that you base your feedback on observations. If you fall into the giving-criticism trap, you're often inviting defensiveness, regardless of your intentions. Critical comments with a personal focus based on character-izations, not substance, usually come across as extremely judgmental. If you come across as judgmental with a sensitive employee, the fireworks begin.

>> **Give sincere and straightforward negative feedback.** Time for a little physics. For every action, there's a reaction. In interactions between two people, although you don't control another person, you can influence how that individual receives your message by the way you deliver it:

- Deliver the message with anger or harshness in your tone, and you're likely to get anger and harshness in return.

- Deliver the message in a hesitant and apprehensive manner, and you're likely to face someone becoming quite anxious, wondering what is so terrible that you can't tell it straight.

When giving negative feedback, communicate the appropriate sense of concern in both your language and your tone so that your message comes across with care and importance. You're out to help, not hurt, with your feedback.

>> **Give employees feedback on how they receive feedback.** If you give performance feedback constructively, you have the opportunity to coach your employees on how to receive feedback constructively. Let them know that you are going to give feedback as a regular practice and set the expectation that you want them to receive it well and learn from it. Make sure that you, too, are open to the feedback that you get from them.

As you give constructive feedback, positively reinforce when your employees receive it well. Give negative feedback when they don't receive it well. Remember, state your observations, not your interpretations:

- **An interpretation:** "You react defensively when I attempt to give you feedback on your performance."

- **An observation:** "Sometimes when I attempt to give you feedback about mistakes or areas for improvement in your performance, I notice that your voice gets louder. I'm interrupted before I can finish my message, your face often becomes flushed, and you frown. These behaviors make it difficult for me to give the feedback that I need to give."

Often, it's a good idea not to give feedback on how employees receive feedback in the heat of the moment, but later, as an issue by itself. Then, if the employee reacts defensively and demonstrates the very behavior you're describing, you can report it right on the spot. "Hold on. That's the behavior I'm talking about, and that's what I'd like you to change." People can better understand the behavior you want improved upon when you capture them doing the actions live and, in essence, can show it to them.

» **Aim for positive outcomes.** When giving negative feedback, discussion between you and an employee is a must. Give the feedback at the start of the conversation, and then allow a two-way discussion to automatically follow. No hit-and-run such as, "Here's what you aren't doing well, specific-specific, blah, blah. Now go on and get out of here." If your style is to state the feedback and attempt to end the conversation at that point, regardless of how specific you are, your abruptness can be like a kick in the teeth and invites a defensive person to become quite reactive.

TIP

When you finish giving the negative feedback, state the positive outcome you're seeking and initiate a discussion with a question that invites the employee's participation. Listen patiently and responsively; if you debate, you get defensiveness in return. Stay focused on the positive outcome you're seeking. The whole dynamic of the interaction changes as a result. When you dwell on problems, you get blame going both ways. When you dwell on solutions, you get collaboration and often creativity.

» **Announce the behavior you want to see.** This serves to set an expectation and prepare the employee for the behavior you want exhibited. You state the behavior you want to see before giving the constructive feedback, as a kind of introduction to the conversation. Make sure that you state in positive terms what you want to see rather than the behavior that you don't want to see. Instead of saying to the employee, "When I give you this feedback, I don't want you to react defensively" (guess how the employee will react to that?), you can say in positive terms, "I want to give you feedback about an issue, and I want you to listen patiently and openly the whole time, and then work with me to come to a positive solution."

EXAMPLE

A manager told me that she followed this tip with one of her employees who often became defensive when receiving negative feedback. Although the employed squeezed the arms of his chair very tightly, he stayed in control during the whole conversation. He heard the feedback all the way through and engaged in discussion to help figure out a solution to correct the problem at hand.

Stating this behavior expectation up front allows you to refocus the employee, should defensive behavior rear its ugly head. For example, as the employee starts to get defensive, "Hold on, remember, please stay patient and open the whole time in this conversation."

TIP

>> **Give ongoing constructive feedback that reflects actual performance.**
This tip is the biggest and best one for minimizing, if not preventing, employee defensiveness when hearing negative feedback: Acknowledge all aspects of an employee's performance, not just the problems or mistakes. If you give feedback to your employees only when something goes wrong, you encourage their quick-to-react-and-get-defensive behaviors.

Try to achieve balance in your efforts of giving constructive feedback, and do so on a regular basis so that your employees are used to hearing from you about how they are performing — what they have done well and what they need to do better. They know where they stand and that their positive efforts are not taken for granted. So when you say, "Hey Jane, please come in my office for a few minutes," you don't get a "what-did-I-do-this-time?" reaction.

Building the Pillars of Commitment through Feedback

Coaching can have a great influence on promoting employee commitment. The five pillars that are the foundation for building commitment (see Chapter 4 for further details) are impacted by providing regular and timely constructive feedback. The following looks at how regular constructive feedback — both positive and negative — affects these pillars:

>> **Focus:** Positive feedback reinforces that employees are going in the right direction in their performance — you focus on the right priorities and things that are being done well. Negative feedback helps the employee who is getting off track to refocus and head in the right direction, especially through the discussion that follows the feedback.

>> **Involvement:** Feedback is a direct way to be involved in an employee's growth. When done right, feedback is an opening for two-way dialog and real learning.

>> **Accountability:** When delivered in the right manner, feedback builds accountability by clearly spelling out gaps in performance. It puts accountability in the hands of the employee by providing valuable information on their performance. Most people want to know how they're doing so they can do a great job.

>> **Development:** As employees grow in their knowledge and skill, the appropriate level of positive and negative feedback helps reinforce their development and build the confidence that goes along with the growing competence.

>> **Gratitude:** Positive feedback is one of the most cost-effective ways to recognize employees and let them know that you care about their good performances. Even negative feedback that may be tough to hear initially is often a gift in helping employees grow.

Often these five pillars of commitment come together simultaneously when constructive feedback is given. Giving constructive feedback helps to ensure beneficial results in performance and influences employee commitment.

Chapter **15**

Setting Performance and Development Goals

anaging by plan is one of the fundamentals for effective coaching that drives results. Simply, a *plan* sets a course of action. More specifically, a *performance plan* provides direction for the employee to meet expectations and develop their skills, knowledge, and abilities to grow in their position and career. A well-conceived plan helps the employee focus on the right things, stay involved and invested in high performance, and accountable to sticking to the plan. In short, a good plan reinforces the five pillars of commitment (see Chapter 4).

This chapter illustrates the importance of planning in satisfying both the organization and the employee, why plans often don't work, guidelines for developing a plan that people follow, and some examples to help you build a plan of your own.

Understanding the Importance of Planning for Everyone

Coaching and mentoring employees isn't a one-time event but a continual process. Planning is the foundation of attracting and retaining the best people. Here are some reasons why planning makes sense:

>> **A plan keeps people focused on a common direction toward results.** It provides alignment so people are working together, all doing their part to one end.

>> **A plan allows you to integrate intention into your daily schedule.** I (Leo) often use plans to coach people to change a habit or build a skill. If people understand the larger picture, they're more motivated to commit to the hard work it takes to change.

>> **A plan informs action.** What's the best use of your time? Is this task or strategy taking you closer or further from our desired outcome? A plan guides activity toward the right result.

>> **It provides a benchmark of your progress.** If you've set goals with a timeline for progress, you have a common document that serves to remind you what you intended and what you achieved. Often plans change, but you can only learn from change if you know where you started and where you intended to go.

I've worked with clients who adamantly oppose any kind of planning. You can't even say the word casually without upsetting them. It may be that the way they run their business works for them. But I believe a plan, particularly a performance plan to guide employees, brings together so many elements that are essential to keeping and growing talent. Imagine these two different scenarios:

EXAMPLE

>> Naomi works for a small industrial manufacturer. After she was hired, she was told what to do, but there has been no attempt to set goals for her or to engage her in her career development. She has never received any feedback on her position other than, "You're doing great." Although she likes her job, she has no sense of direction. She doesn't know where she's going and she wants to know what she can improve. Her manager is more of a doer manager. He's a nice enough guy but isn't the kind of person who likes to have a thoughtful, intentional conversation that includes goal setting and feedback. He says they're a waste of time and no one follows them anyway. Naomi is at the point of looking for another job elsewhere and reaches out to her friend Melinda. Naomi and Melinda meet for a drink after work.

>> Melinda works for a mid-sized software development company. She couldn't be happier. The company is all about developing people. They post the key drivers that everyone should be looking to follow on a large sheet in the hallway. People are always huddled around it and talking about how things are going and what needs to improve. Melinda had three meetings with her manager in the beginning of the year to set her performance goals and development goals. They spent time looking at the key drivers as they did that. She meets with her supervisor quarterly for updates on how she's doing. Naomi asks if Melinda's company has any openings. Melinda inquires with her manager, who immediately asks for an introduction.

REMEMBER

Finding good people is the number one priority for organizations these days. Keeping employees engaged and happy is essential to ensure they don't leave. Naomi's current employer doesn't understand that. That organization seems to believe they're calling the shots, just because they pay people's salaries. Chapters 9 and 10 discuss the keys to keeping people motivated. When people understand how their job supports the organization's larger goals, they have a greater sense of purpose. They see their success is part of the organization's success. They know and appreciate how they're contributing. They also understand how the work they do daily supports their career and life direction — the three-year vision or mountain that Chapter 12 discusses for career self-reliance.

Melinda's organization understands they're fueled by their people. They continually invest in them. They spend time on planning company goals, making sure people see them, and tie them with their performance.

Defining the Three Types of Goals

Sometimes referred to as an *objective*, a *goal* is a performance effort that you want to accomplish or a target that you want to reach. A goal answers these questions:

>> What result are you seeking that will help your organization?

>> What important undertaking do you want to accomplish?

>> What milestone will you reach in your development?

For the purposes of coaching and mentoring employees, three types of goals, which the following sections examine, are useful: strategic goals, performance goals, and development goals. In my (Leo) experience, every organization has their own terms and process. This is a universal approach you can tweak. The important thing to keep in mind is that the different goals serve different purposes but work together.

Strategic goals — Where the organization is going

Strategic goals are typically set by the organization and outline the organization's overall direction. They provide a road map for everyone to follow and support. Smart companies invite employees to participate in defining what success looks like. When employees participate in setting a common direction, they have more ownership of their contribution because they helped create it. The common denominator in strategic goals is that they're shared, common goals that every employee understands and works toward.

Assessing success

Companies measure success in two basic ways:

>> **Financial success:** This is the most commonly used metric for performance, including revenue growth rate, net profit, and return on investment, among others. It can also include growth in the number of units produced, clients or customers attained, or projects completed. The metrics are quantifiable and easy to see: The company made more money than last year, for instance. Financial goals are *lagging* indicators of success — they tell you what you've achieved at the end of the year. But employees don't always know what actions will lead them to the desired result.

>> **Customer success:** More companies focus on customer success. These performance metrics are increasingly seen as the most important. Some of the main customer-centered metrics include conversion rate, customer retention, and customer satisfaction (see the nearby sidebar for more about net promoter score [NPS]). The philosophy is straightforward: The company will be successful if customers are happy and keep buying from us. Customer satisfaction goals are *leading* indicators of success and place the focus on gaining a loyal customer base by producing great quality products, anticipating what customers want and value, listening to them, and emphasizing strong customer support service. When you look at some the most financially successful companies in the world, you find a commitment to exceeding customer experience.

Focusing on shared values

Companies that focus solely on financial or production metrics miss the opportunity to define a culture that's defined by how work is done and how people are treated. Companies that create strategic goals around customer satisfaction and shared values create cultures where people do their best work. Output goals don't do much to support what kind of culture you want to encourage. More employees are choosing companies that place a higher value on cultures that support diversity, innovation, and empowering employees. Younger generations, in particular, aren't motivated by money. It's more important for them to work for a company that has shared values and treats people with respect. Chapter 8 discusses some generational differences.

The idea is if the organization is on top of tracking the right behaviors, or leading indicators, and doing the right things to make the customer happy, that will lead to financial success.

Some shared behaviors can include the following:

>> Accountability

>> Clear communication

>> Creativity

>> Curiosity

>> Effective communication

>> Initiative

>> Respect

>> Teamwork

>> Trust

Performance goals — How well the employee is doing

Performance goals are goals developed in partnership between the manager and employee. Doer managers tell their employees what they expect from them. Coach managers build commitment (as Chapter 4 outlines) by working with their employees to set goals. They're interested in developing their staff and see goal setting as a time to set realistic expectations in collaboration with employees. These sections look more closely at what makes clear, relevant, and achievable performance goals that you and your employee can agree upon.

Recognizing the best performance goals

The best performance goals are as follows:

>> **Aligned with the company strategic goals:** For the employee to be successful in the organization, the employee's performance plan needs to derive from the organizational strategic goals. These goals can be based on financial performance, customer satisfaction, or values that the company has defined as important to creating a healthy strong culture. As Chapter 12 on career self-reliance covers, employees will succeed within a company if they work toward the company's goals.

One of your responsibilities as a coach and mentor is to encourage your employees to take an interest in understanding the business goals. Remind them that becoming educated on where the organization is going is in their best interest. Be available to fill in the missing holes in their own research. Some companies are very good at sharing strategic goals throughout the organization. Others don't mind if people are in the dark, as long as they're staying busy. As a coach and advocate for your employee, help them make the connection between the company's success and their success.

>> **Aligned with the goals of the team:** The team often has more specific goals than to their functional area. For instance, the marketing team may have a goal of launching a new website. The production team may have a goal of upgrading the equipment on the manufacturing floor. The employee's performance goal should reflect what role they'll play and by when.

>> **Clearly understandable to both the supervisor and employee:** Goals are worthless unless they're meaningful and understandable. Employees should draft their own performance goals as a starting point. The manager can then provide feedback.

>> **Reflects any gaps in meeting expectations:** Performance goals aren't job descriptions. People generally know what's expected of them when they're hired (though that's not always the case!). Performance goals should target areas of skills or knowledge that the employee needs to develop to meet expectations.

If you're a doer manager reading this book, maybe your manager expects you more to act like a coach. Your performance goals may be:

- Meet weekly with your team on their progress and ask what support they need.

- Mentor junior staff in computer-aided design so they can work independently.

- Coach people to do more of the work rather than doing it yourself.

>> **Reflects the aspirations of the employee:** Performance goals should reflect not just what the current position requires for meeting the company or team's goals. They should also stretch the employee by challenging them. Your goal is to keep your employees engaged and productive. Performance goals that help build their competence helps them advance in their careers.

>> **Serves as a benchmark for reviews:** A good performance goal should serve to accurately assess an employee's performance throughout the year. During an employee's formal reviews, the goals should reflect what's expected of the employee and what both the manager and employee agreed upon. The review is an opportunity to compare the goals with actual performance and address any gaps and decide on any corrective measures (see Chapter 16).

An example — Performance goals in action

Dave wanted to expand his coffee shop to several locations. He knew that the key to success was to somehow duplicate how they operated the original location. What was the recipe for success that would make the other locations just as successful? Dave brought together his employees to brainstorm and define how the employees can support the company's strategic goals of expanding operations. What can the employees do to support the company's strategic goals? These are the strategic objectives toward the larger goal. What are the strategic objectives or employee behaviors that will keep people coming back and telling their friends?

>> Enthusiastic: Greet every customer with a smile and positive attitude.

>> Accurate: Accurately record each order in the point-of-sale system, repeating it back to the customer.

>> Inquiring: Ask each customer for their preference and ask if they want something to eat.

>> Knowledgeable: Be able to describe the differences of each drink or food item.

>> Respectful: Be respectful of customers and fellow employees by not being rude or disrespectful of their appearance, attitude, or behavior.

This was a good first start. Setting standards was helpful in hiring and training new employees as well as keeping existing employees focused on meeting service expectations. But Dave also found it was important to establish performance goals for each employee. Performance goals sets clear expectation and direction for employees. He wanted to make sure the goals weren't too formal or complicated.

Sharleen, who was Dave's best employee, wanted to operate her own location. That required Dave and Sharleen sitting down and defining performance goals for her new position. Some examples they developed:

>> Software: Learn the new scheduling software to effectively schedule employees without Dave's help.

>> Community relations: Network with local businesses in the area to develop relationships that drive word of mouth business.

>> Delegate and mentor: Develop key front-line staff so she can spend more time in the back office and in the community.

Sharleen then drafted action items for the first quarter to review with Dave. Dave could not only review how she's contributing to the overall company standards but also he could review her progress on her personal goals related to her position.

The only problem was that Sharleen didn't have a plan on how to develop her skills and knowledge to meet the performance goals. That's where development goals come in.

Development goals — What skills, knowledge, and abilities are key

In the example in the previous section Sharleen is challenged in stepping back from the work and delegating responsibility to someone else. She's very good when she's in charge, but delegation and letting go is hard. Delegation, which Chapter 13 covers, is difficult for many people. Dave could work with Sharleen to define *development goals* that would develop her skills, knowledge, and abilities or what's often referred to as KSAs:

» **Knowledge:** Facts, process, background, information that's important to performing the job. For Sharleen: Knowing specifically what she needs to delegate, identifying the steps to delegation, and understanding the capabilities of the employees she wants to delegate.

» **Skills:** What you need to do the job on a very specific level, most often displayed or measured (typing, operating an espresso machine, interpersonal communication). In Sharleen's case, she needed to work on developing the skill of slowing down and being clear with employees and learning to listen and not talk.

» **Ability:** Ability is putting skills and knowledge together to perform tasks on a job. Sharleen needed to develop the ability to delegate effectively so she could devote more time to managing the office. Ability often translates to the net result you're trying to achieve.

To develop her knowledge, skills, and abilities, Sharleen needed a development plan to help her learn to delegate. Dave explained it to her this way:

"Sharleen, this position requires you to focus on other things than making coffee drinks. To be successful, you need to learn to delegate and let others do the work. I don't want you trying to do it all and working crazy hours to make up for it. That's not good for you and it's not good for the company. Learning to delegate has to be a skill you master."

Dave wasn't telling Sharleen what to do. Instead, he was coaching her by being an ally for her success. He can mentor her throughout the process by sharing his own challenges with delegating. But as someone once said, a goal without a plan is simply a wish. The best plans are those that are tied to action. They get done.

Creating SMART Goals

Making goals can be like resolutions — exciting to make, but not so much fun to actually accomplish. *I'm going to go home by 5:30 each day. I'm going to do that fishing trip with my son. I'm going to be a senior associate and have a greater say.* One of the best ways to develop actionable plans is to follow the SMART goal formula: Specific. Measurable. Achievable. Relevant. Time-bound.

The following sections explain the parts of SMART, the ways that SMART goals can be created, and some sample plans.

Examining what SMART stands for

The following breaks down SMART:

>> **Specific:** Identify steps that are specific, ones you can see and hear. Imagine if someone has a video camera and is recording your actions of your mountain-making activities. They should always include an action verb so the camera can see it. Reread those examples: *read, report, schedule, walk.* Compare that with using verbs like *think, consider, be aware.* What does it look like to *think*? Instead, use verbs that are observable. When you add detail like "capital improvement plans for Lake Oswego," you're being more specific than "research business development opportunities." You've got a specific task you can write down and check off when done.

>> **Measurable:** You should be able to measure or quantify your goals. Put your steps into numbers like above: one hour, 15 minutes, five miles. If you train for a marathon, you set measurable goals: weight train on Monday for 30 minutes; increase from five miles to six miles. It's no different in setting SMART goals. You could have said that you would read about integrated design, but making it 20 minutes helps you in estimating how long you can take on a task and helps make it more concrete in your mind.

>> **Achievable:** With all the demands on your time, the only way to carve out time for tasks that you feel take you away from other obligations is to make them small enough to achieve them. My rule is the smaller the block of time, the better. Note the action item: "Schedule monthly lunch meetings with Beth to support each other by the end of the week." That probably takes less than a minute to do and is something you can fit into your week. You could have easily said, "Schedule five lunch meetings with peers for support." That might have felt good to make a big resolution, but you don't have time for all those meetings. Choose one thing you can do. Think 15 minutes here and there. Still too much time? Try ten, five, even one minute is better than nothing!

>> **Relevant:** This is the only test: Will this step take me closer or farther from my mountain? When you look at your to-do list for the week, how many of your tasks are relevant to where you want to go? If you have your mountain clearly defined in front of you, it helps you see if tasks can get you there. The new leader who identified "take an hour and read capital improvement plans for Lake Oswego and report future opportunities to the team by next Wednesday" had been told in his recent review that if he wanted to become department head, he needed to bring in more of his own clients. Becoming department head was part of his mountain and taking an hour to do specific research was definitely relevant to getting to his mountain.

>> **Time-bound:** The best way to ensure you'll do a task is to give yourself a timeline when it will get done: by next Wednesday, by Friday, and so on. Ideally, get as specific as possible. Remember the example: "Read for 20 minutes about integrated design delivery Tuesday morning at 7:30."

Connecting SMART goals

Revisit the example about Dave and Sharleen in the section "An example — Performance goals in action," earlier in this chapter. They brainstormed for 15 minutes on the different ways she could develop the ability to delegate, which included the following:

>> Reading a book about delegation

>> Watching Dave as he delegates to someone and talking afterwards

>> Looking at some instructional videos online about delegation

>> Getting feedback from employees on delegation

>> Working on asking questions and not talking as a skill

>> Attending a management webinar

>> Networking with peers at her level for support

Dave then asked Sharleen to make just two of the ideas into SMART goals. He knew from experience that it was better to start small and not have too many goals. Here's what she came up with:

>> Buy *Coaching & Mentoring For Dummies* and read Chapter 13 by March 15.

>> Go out to lunch with Ben, a college friend who was new to managing people, and specifically talk about delegation by March 25.

Dave looked them over and assessed the first one. Was it a SMART goal?

>> Specific: Yes, "buy" and "read" are action words. She even had a great idea for a specific book and chapter!

>> Measurable: Yes, reading 24 pages of one book is quantifiable measurement. She could have added "take a quiz after" or "summarize the key points to Dave after."

>> Achievable: Yes, she gave herself three weeks to buy and read one chapter. Not the whole book. This is a good stretch for her. Employees often set goals and don't get them done. The key to achieving more goals is shrinking the size of them.

>> Relevant: Yes, learning about how to delegate is in line with Dave's goals for the company and Sharleen's mountain for her career.

>> Time-bound: Yes, she set a reasonable date to complete it. To help her hit the completion date, she should schedule reading time — and not late at night as she drifts off to sleep. Blocking off time in your calendar is a great way to ensure your SMART goals get done.

Before Dave lets Sharleen loose to pursue her goals, he asks what kind of support she needs from him. They decide to check in every two weeks to talk about how delegation is working. Dave mentions that he'll periodically check with the team to see how Sharleen is doing and give her feedback.

Your job as a manager is not just to help set goals for your employees but also to coach and mentor them along the way. Pay attention to setting a check-in time. Make sure the employee knows they are responsible to schedule and follow through on check-ins.

Sampling SMART performance plans

Here are a few performance plans that give you examples of goals, along with their appropriate action plans. Keep in mind that your metrics may change as you proceed because of things out of your control. In terms of action items, focus on the action items for Q1. It's too difficult to schedule beyond a quarter — too many changes. Also keep in mind that the goals are set *with* your staff members, not *for* them.

Sample #1

>> **Goal:** Create and implement process improvements that reduce the current cycle time for month-end-closing activities with the general ledger from four days to three (25 percent).

>> **Q1 action plans:**

- By January 20, document current processes for handling month-end-closing activities and the average time for each process.

- By February 15, gather input from other staff in the department and draft a plan for a streamlined process.

Sample #2

>> **Goal:** Develop a marketing program that provides the field sales force with tools that they find useful in increasing their effectiveness in selling our company's product.

>> **Q1 action plans:**

- By January 31, survey the sales force to assess their needs for marketing tools, product samples, and other items that will help their sales efforts.

- By February 22, draft key messages and case studies and get initial feedback from sales staff.

Mutually Setting Goals

Getting the most success out plans means that you set plans *with* your employees, as opposed to *for* them. It's a mutual process — something that you do together. Your role as a manager in this two-way process is to provide the employees with direction. Tell them where the business and the group are going, what the high-level targets or objectives are, and what key issues to tackle. The role of the employees is to set challenging yet attainable goals and standards that align with this direction and to outline the key steps or road maps (the action plans) on how to achieve the goals.

Because many employees initially may not be familiar with how to set results-based employee plans, follow this process to mutually set plans:

1. **Prepare your employees for the meeting to set their plans.**

   Provide direction on the priorities and targets for the coming period. To help your staff understand this direction, give them a copy of your own plans. Doing this also helps them understand the key ingredients that go into an employee plan. Ask them to come ready with a list of ideas for their own goals. Here are a few questions that stimulate thinking:

- What should you accomplish to help the group achieve what it needs to accomplish?

- What changes or improvements need to be made to help the group work more efficiently?

- What key behaviors or responsibilities need to be reinforced or maintained to achieve high levels of performance?

2. **Facilitate the planning meeting.**

At the one-on-one planning meeting, incorporating the employee's ideas, draft each plan one at a time. Maintain a two-way conversation and have the employee do the writing as together you shape the plans. Go in this order for each plan:

- Review the corporate strategic goals.

- Identify three solid performance goals, using SMART goals.

- Develop Q1 action plans.

- Identify three development goals, using SMART goals.

Have the employee take the lead in developing the action plans portion. Telling people how to do their jobs invites compliance, not commitment. If differences in points of view come up while setting the goals or standards, discuss them thoroughly and hear each other out. If you have concerns about what an employee wants to do, express them constructively and have the employee address them — and vice versa if the employee has concerns about your ideas. Then collaboratively propose ideas that settle the differences.

The corporate strategic goals as a foundation. Use them as the focus for the solutions you work out.

REMEMBER

3. **Finalize the plans.**

Have the employee recap what has been written and agreed upon and then type up the plans and provide you with a copy. Have the employee keep their performance plans visible while going forward. Set a check-in date to review the plan (see Figure 15-1).

Strategic Goals
(set by the company, defined by outputs or behaviors)

Performance goals (developed individually with manager):

1

2

3

Q1 action items:

1

2

3

Development goals (developed using SMART system with manager):

1

2

3

Progress check-in date (between employee and manager):

FIGURE 15-1:
A worksheet
for setting
performance and
development
goals.

© John Wiley & Sons, Inc.

Planning Goals — The Keys to Success

There are countless ways to set goals and establish plans. Here are some fundamental elements that distinguish a successful plan:

>> **Keep it short.** Too many goals simply don't get done. And loading a plan down with too many obscures the really important ones. Focus on the goals that will have the biggest impact. No more than three, as a rule.

>> **Do it together.** The planning process is just as important as the final document. Planning should be an opportunity to sit work aside and reflect on where you're going and what you need to focus on.

>> **Put it to work.** A plan is only as useful as any tool. It needs to be used regularly for it to be valuable. Refer to it often. Keep it visible. Research Gemba boards, an interesting way to visually track real time progress on meeting goals. Gemba is a Japanese term that translates as "actual place." A Gemba board is a visual management tool that works cohesively with your existing set of solutions and keeps everyone on the same page. Search online for more about Gemba boards.

>> **Use your calendar.** You can easily get distracted and too busy from completing important work. Incorporate sound time management techniques to set deadlines to complete your SMART goals and block off time for professional development (see Chapter 3 on time management).

- >> **Revisit the plan quarterly.** Goals and plans are meant to change as issues and opportunities come up. A major project comes out of nowhere. You lose a valuable team member. Your database is breached by hackers. The plan you had isn't working out. Annual planning is a good start, but you'll need to revisit quarterly to check on progress and discuss if the goals are still relevant.

- >> **Talk about it.** Coaching employees to stay focused and engaged is more effective if you're continually revisiting goals. Are your goals still the same? Is this the best direction? What progress are you making toward your goals? What are your challenges?

- >> **Support the employee.** As a coach manager, you can support your employee in meeting their goals in a number of ways: Give them the tools and resources to do their work; give them the time needed for focusing on their development goals; advocate and protect them from colleagues who may to pull them into their projects and away from the employee's goals.

- >> **Prioritize development goals.** Too often, companies are focused on what needs to get done. That's fine, but if employees don't take time to grow and develop their KSAs (knowledge, skills, and abilities), very little progress will be made in meeting their performance goals. Make development a priority at every opportunity. When you take the time to mentor and coach employees, they grow as motivated and productive employees.

Now that the plan is in place, follow it! Too many times goals are set without frequent follow-up. As a last step to your planning, set a time in your calendars to meet and discuss progress. Chapter 16 walks you through how to continually revisit the plan throughout the year. Chapter 14 provides guidance on how to give regular and timely constructive feedback.

Helping Build the Pillars of Commitment

Take a look at how setting employee plans, when done as a regular coaching practice — collaboratively and SMARTly — affect the pillars of commitment (see Chapter 4). Which ones are impacted and how so?

- >> **Focus:** Planning greatly influence focus, helping employees determine what their priorities are and what needs to be accomplished. Be sure that your goals and standards follow the SMART guidelines, keeping them results-focused (see the section, "Creating SMART Goals," earlier in this chapter).

>> **Involvement:** The mutual effort of setting plans impacts the employees' involvement. Because the plans are set with the employees, they have direct input in shaping their own goals. In setting the action plans, employees take the lead in defining the steps to take to accomplish the goals and standards — which achieves a high degree of involvement. The key to using the process of setting plans as an effective coaching tool is to set them collaboratively.

>> **Accountability:** Keeping the plans visible and as part of conversations between you and your employees helps drive accountability. Employees are able to measure their own progress and also gain their own sense of accomplishment when they achieve their goals. And they certainly know what results you expect from them.

>> **Development:** When performance plans also address areas for professional development or have employees working on areas where they expand their knowledge and skill, employee development is enhanced. Employees are learning and growing as they produce important results.

>> **Gratitude:** Most employees appreciate and value when they're listened to and supported. Planning is an outward expression that you value what they bring and are genuine about helping them grow.

IN THIS CHAPTER

» **Driving accountability with regular performance reviews**

» **Integrating status reviews for managing projects and big assignments.**

» **Conducting mini performance reviews**

» **Applying the postmortem tool**

» **Building employee commitment with periodic review tools**

Chapter **16**

Taking the Pain Out of Employee Reviews

The practice of doing a formal performance review is common in many organizations regardless if they're in the private, public or nonprofit sectors. In terms of frequency, managers generally write reviews on an annual basis. Occasionally, some organizations carry out performance evaluations quarterly or every six months.

The review is the designated time when employees are told how they're performing. But a lot happens during the 12 months between reviews. How do managers who function as coaches monitor progress and let employees know how they are performing *between* reviews?

Many managers, especially the doer types (see Chapter 2 for more on doer managers), use one of two methods:

>> **Micromanaged:** The manager knows every detail and frequently checks on what the employees are doing, sometimes to the point that the employees feel smothered.

>> **Hands-off:** The manager goes the other direction and practices a *laissez-faire* approach, assigning work and taking a "no news is good news" approach. The manager is too busy with their own work to pay much attention to how their employees are doing until something goes wrong.

In either case, employees often aren't getting direct and timely feedback as to how they're performing. Managers, who complete the annual performance, often wait to the last minute and stress out about how to write meaningful evaluations that don't hurt the employees' feelings.

This chapter tells you how to put an end to that anxiety and how to use three coaching tools — the status review, the checkup, and the postmortem review — to improve your performance review process.

Relaxing about Performance Reviews

Managers who actively coach their employees believe that performance reviews are part of an ongoing process of performance management. These managers don't wait for once-a-year reviews to finally tell employees how they're performing (too much is continually happening to talk about it just once a year) or to tell them that something has gone wrong.

Instead, coaching managers give ongoing positive and negative feedback (see Chapter 14) on staff members' performance as events occur. They also use periodic performance reviews — an ongoing process that promotes success and maintains their sanity! These sections explain what you need to know to reduce any anxiety about reviews.

Looking at the process of reviews

Using the coaching approach, managers see performance review as a process that falls into three stages in an annual cycle:

>> **Stage 1 — planning:** In this stage, manager and employee in a collaborative effort set the performance and development goals that focus the employee on the important results to be accomplished. *Performance goals* are aligned with job expectations, and *development goals* are the knowledge, skills, and abilities that help the employee meet the performance goals. (See Chapter 15 for the details of the process.) This typically happens in the beginning of the year or every six months. Action items are created and reviewed quarterly.

>> **Stage 2 — feedback, periodic review, and documentation:** The second stage involves ongoing two-way coaching discussions about performance with positive and negative feedback given informally along the way. You also hold periodic performance-review meetings — organized, yet informal in nature — to assess progress with projects, key assignments, and overall performance plans, and to do necessary replanning in order to stay current with changing priorities. Although feedback should be timely and frequent, a more structured check-in every three months helps monitor progress on the action items and set new ones. As the manager, you record the feedback you've given and the important review meetings held so that you don't have to rely on your memory for this information.

>> **Stage 3 — wrap-up:** In this stage, you bring the year-long discussions and feedback about performance to a close, and you write the performance review and discuss it with the employee. The performance review serves as a summary of these discussions. The review tells you how well the employee delivered the results expected as set in the performance plans in Stage 1.

The meeting to go over the performance review not only discusses how performance turned out for the past period but also looks to the future as ideas for new goals and professional development are discussed, leading the way for the next period's performance plans to be set (and finalized shortly after). Thus, the cycle gets restarted and on you go. This meeting is also an opportunity to evaluate how your coaching efforts and working relationship with the employee went during the performance review process — with the chance to then adjust going forward.

Understanding why you're anxious

When managers treat performance reviews as an ongoing part of coaching and performance management, Stage 3 of the process (see the stages in the preceding section) is no big deal. Because of the efforts to set performance criteria upfront and to informally assess progress along the way with the employee (in Stages 1 and 2), writing the annual or semiannual review is easy. You know what has happened in regard to your employees' performance, and they know you know. Most important, they know where they stand. No surprises come at review time, and honest evaluations occur as well.

As a result of these efforts, your employees can read their appraisals and say, "That's pretty much what I expected." Comments like this are recognition to you that you've done your job as a manager well. Of course, such a compliment is part of the good results that happen when you make Stages 1 and 2 part of the review process.

Waiting until the end of the year to finally focus on employee performance and write the review can be an onerous task. And for many people, the more onerous the job, the more they procrastinate. When you put off doing your reviews in a timely way, you risk sending your employees the wrong message — that their performance isn't important to you. (That's one sure way to demotivate employee performance.) In addition, the following can happen:

WARNING

>> A lack of effort in Stages 1 and 2 can leave managers not knowing what to write about negative performance, and this situation can, in turn, lead to high stress. As a result of not discussing problems previously, managers may gloss over them. Or the opposite occurs: The manager uses the review as a vehicle for finally spelling out the problems — and the employee experiences what's called the *surprise syndrome* (feeling hammered or shocked). The shock from the surprise syndrome generally leads to counterproductive behaviors — feeling bitter or anger, resisting subtly or even overtly, being demoralized, or resigning.

>> The irregular discussions and feedback about performance and the lack of documentation on what has been happening leave managers with a heavy reliance on their memories at review time. Managers in this situation have to write what they remember best — the last couple of months of performance. The rest of the year may get largely bypassed.

To say that people have short-term memories is an understatement. For example, can you remember what you were doing at 10 a.m. on Monday three weeks ago? How about the same hour and day nine weeks or nine months ago? Now, try to remember what or how one of your employees was doing at these times.

WARNING

A few employees pick up on their managers' overreliance on memory in place of regular communication and documentation. So a month or two before their reviews are to be done, their performance really excels. After receiving very good reviews from their managers, and often pay raises to match, they go back into cruise mode for a while. Umm . . . would you call this a timely strategy?

>> You run out of time to cover everything. Commonly, managers schedule an hour to conduct an employee review. If they haven't had periodic reviews and ongoing feedback about the employee's performance, managers quickly run out of time trying to cover everything, which can include hearing from the employee about their acknowledgements, challenges and long-term career goals. Much of the time, the review process is rushed, inadequate, and unproductive for both the manager and the employee.

>> Managers may also experience anxiety attacks at review time if they don't set and develop results-focused performance plans with their employees; that is, if they skipped Stage 1 and are stuck trying to fill out a generic trait-based appraisal form. A *trait-based appraisal* usually has a list of characteristics or traits that the manager is expected to evaluate. For example, quality,

organization, planning, communications, productivity, and attitude are commonly found in trait-based evaluation formats.

These attributes come with general definitions and usually a five-level rating (evaluation) system, much like a school report card. Managers may be tempted to give out good grades to most of their employees, thereby creating rating inflation and writing general and subjective comments, such as, "Georgina produces lots of quality work. She is a quality-driven employee whom you can count on to deliver quality work. Outstanding rating for quality." When this one-size-fits-all appraisal format is used, the focus on performance often gets lost.

REMEMBER

Managing by coaching, on the other hand, emphasizes evaluating employees on whether they're delivering the results needed for the needs of the company and team, as well as for the employee's career and long-term satisfaction.

Starting with Status-Review Meetings

If you're like many busy managers, trying to keep track of what's going on with your own work is tough enough, let alone keeping up with your employees' projects and assignments. Yet, you're responsible for what they produce.

REMEMBER

A *status-review meeting*, which the following sections discuss more, is an effective coaching-assessment tool aimed at driving responsibility and results, without driving you or your employees crazy. (Of course, some employees don't appreciate your asking them to take responsibility. Some like to have you take all the responsibility so that they can blame you when things go wrong. But you don't want to let this stop you because, in time and with good coaching, an employee like this will become capable of handling responsibility.)

TIP

You conduct a status review as a one-on-one meeting between you and your employee. If the project is a team-oriented one, you can do a one-on-group review. When the meeting is a group meeting, however, each member's report needs to be relevant to the other members' reports; otherwise, chins tend to drop and yawns increase as the people find the meeting a bore and a waste of time.

Running a status-review meeting

The purpose of a status-review meeting is to review and plan ahead for an employee's progress on current projects or key assignments. I suggest that you use a *tracking sheet*, such as the one shown in Figure 16-1, to set the agenda for the meeting.

Status-Review Tracking Sheet

Name _____   Meeting date _____

Deliverables	Due date	Status

FIGURE 16-1:
Status-review tracking sheet.

The one-on-one status-review meeting usually is brief and can be done in 30 minutes or so. The employee knows going in what to report progress on, as outlined on their tracking sheet, such as the one shown in the column named "Deliverables" (a *deliverable* is sometimes referred to as an action item). The employee reports progress on each deliverable on the list, one at a time ("Here's what is done or not done"), and the evidence for it is shown as needed on the tracking sheet. The deliverable is the task that the employee committed to accomplish during a given, short-term period. The "Due Date" column is usually the meeting date, though it can be a later date, such as a project milestone. In the latter case, for each item, the employee reports their progress toward meeting the milestone.

As the employee goes down the list reporting their progress, both you and the employee fill out the "Status" column about the progress to date. Your role in this meeting is to listen, ask questions for more specifics as needed, and provide the appropriate constructive feedback. The employee does the majority of the talking. Responsibility for the employee's performance is shifting to where it belongs, with the employee.

After the employee has given the status on each item, the two of you set the deliverables for the next status-review meeting. The employee records the action item list and sends you a copy of the list.

Should problems arise as the employee reports progress, the two of you can take time to problem-solve together and to set a course of action for going forward. If a major problem exists and time permits, you can deal with it at that moment. Otherwise, you can plan a separate meeting in the near future to deal with that single issue.

TIP

Status-review meetings help you and your employees stay on top of current projects and key assignments. Because of this, they work best if the frequency of the meetings is fairly regular. I recommend holding them once every one to two weeks. Keep in mind that if some of your employees do work that is more routine in nature and less project-oriented, you won't need to use this coaching tool with them very often.

REMEMBER

Status-review meetings are most effective for helping to manage projects and key assignments. They're designed to be quick and are organized to focus on the following:

>> Status on each deliverable

>> Brief problem-solving, as needed

>> New deliverables set for next meeting

TIP

At the end of each meeting — after defining the next set of deliverables — make sure to set the date for the next meeting with your employee. Communicate the expectation that they're responsible for ensuring that the meeting with you happens, not vice versa. In this way, you keep the momentum of status review rolling while driving the responsibility for the meeting to your staff person.

Realizing the benefits of the status-review meeting

When done as a regular coaching practice, the status-review meeting provides you and your employees with some strong benefits, such as the following:

>> Breaks long-term projects into manageable bites for the employee.

>> Gives employees a tool (the tracking sheet in Figure 16-1) by which to come prepared to report their progress on the important tasks.

>> Eliminates frustration about grilling employees in order to find out what they're accomplishing.

>> Helps you and the employee track important output activities, such as in sales, production, or customer service functions.

>> Allows you the opportunity to focus your employees' attention on the aspect of their work that needs attention. You're able to challenge them if they're being too lax in their expectations about what they can get done, or, on the

other hand, you can steer them away from taking on more than they can reasonably get done during a given period.

>> **Builds quality time.** The efficient nature of the meeting makes good use of time for you and your employees. You stay more aware of how your employees are progressing and what they're producing. You no longer have to chase them down to get information, and they no longer have to waste their time writing weekly reports on what they've been doing — which they wonder if you ever read anyway.

>> **Promotes accountability** — employees can't just look busy; they have to come ready to report results. They commit to the tasks they'll get done, and they take the responsibility for delivering on them. Status reviews allow you to help employees stay successful. If problems arise, you can help resolve them in the early stages instead of finding out about them after they're out of hand.

>> Lets employees walk away from the meeting knowing what's expected and what their priorities are.

REMEMBER

The status-review meeting helps you avoid acting like a micromanager. No need to constantly chase after your employees to see whether they're handling every task: Did you get that done, or did you check with so and so? If you want to be informed about a particular task or issue, just have your employees put it on the tracking sheet. Then set the frequency of the meetings based on how often you need to stay in the loop, perhaps once every week or two. This way, you can let your employees do their jobs.

Following up with Checkups

The second periodic performance assessment tool for effective coaching, the *checkup meeting*, operates much the same way as your annual visit to the doctor does. You want to take the pulse of how the employee is doing in both meeting performance goals (executing) and development goals (learning).

The purposes of checkup meetings are to review an employee's overall performance and to reset performance and development goals as needed in order to focus attention on the right priorities as you go forward. In simple terms, this meeting is a mini performance review that's done without written formality and final judgments. These sections explain more about what you need to know about checkup meetings so you can have productive ones with your employees.

REMEMBER

This coaching tool is quite different from the status-review tool. Status-review meetings are done when you need to stay on top of projects or critical assignments that are currently going on. The checkup meeting takes you to the big-picture level. It has you reflecting with your staff members on how they're doing with their *total performance* in working to achieve their goals. Therefore, its frequency is much less than status-review meetings — once per quarter is what I recommend. While the status-review tool is less applicable when employees are less involved in project-type work, the checkup is a must for all managers to use if they want to make their lives easier.

Managing a checkup meeting

The checkup meeting is an informal, one-on-one conversation between you and your staff member, divided into three steps:

1. **You and the employee review their progress toward meeting each goal included in the employee's plan.**

   Have both the employee and the manager devote some mental space to consider how things are going and what you want out of the meeting. Too often, these meetings are scheduled without any preparation or planning. They can start with the employee and manager rushing from another meeting, sitting down to catch their breath and just looking at each other. Instead, block some time before the meeting — even if it's just 15 minutes — to review any notes from your last meeting, jot down some goals you have for the meeting, and consider maybe some key questions.

   Start by pulling out the action steps you both established. What was completed, what's in progress, and what's undone? Using the SMART goals from Chapter 15, your discussion will be much more focused, productive, and efficient than if it's just, "How are things going?"

   TIP

   It's not uncommon for employees to be hard on themselves about the lack of progress they've made toward their goals. As Chapter 17 discusses, your job is to encourage and promote progress. When you take the time for these quarterly checkups, you help the employee stay focused on their action plans — the recipe for success.

   If there are performance issues, particularly around underperformance (see Chapter 17), this is the time to give direct and honest feedback on the lack of progress. Reminding someone of the goals you both established to help them improve their performance now is much less threatening than sitting on it and delivering bad news at the end of the year — which is too late to be actionable.

2. **Collaboratively discuss whether you need to modify the goals and action plans.**

   If new priorities have come into the mix, you and the employee develop goals to include the new priorities. The objective here is to ensure that the plans stay current and continue to encompass total performance and development.

Remember to use SMART goals and focus on development goals to enhance the performance goals. Your job as a coach is to develop your employees to perform — development goals support performance goals.

3. **Recap the agreed-upon modifications and close with the employee setting the date for when they'll give you a copy of the next action steps.**

   The employee creates the revisions because the performance plans are theirs not yours. You document the highlights of the checkup meeting for your own notes.

TIP

You may also find it helpful to summarize this documentation in a memo and copy the employee on it; be sure to let the individual know you'll be doing that. If you write more than one page, you're writing too much.

TIP

To gain the most value, I recommend holding checkup meetings on a quarterly schedule, and book them in advance. This one-on-one meeting can generally be done in an hour. In an annual performance evaluation cycle, you meet with each staff member three times during the year to look at overall performance. In the fourth-quarter meeting, you conduct the formal review.

EXAMPLE

Janice wanted to become an associate principal in her civil engineering firm. Her boss, Fernando, said it was important for her to get her license so she could approve the work of people on her team. She identified a study schedule to take the exam in four months.

Fernando knew from his own experience that it was difficult to find the time and discipline to do the studying. He didn't wait until her quarterly review to casually check in on Janice. "How's that studying going? He winked, making light of a hard task. Janice laughed and said, "I know. I know. I'll do it!" It only took two times before she applied herself and started into a routine of studying.

When Fernando saw she was working on it, he supported her by giving her time to go home early or come in late to work on it. As a result, Janice ended up acing the test a month ahead of schedule, thanks to Fernando's checkups.

Understanding the benefits of the checkup

Here's why you want make checkups a priority:

>> **Enhances quality time.** This one-on-one meeting for an hour or so puts you in touch with your employees' overall performances, while at the same time lets them know where they stand with their performance.

- **Enables employees to stay on track in terms of their performance plans.** The discussions focus on the results that are taking place and push employees to take responsibility and minimize excuses.

- **Builds flexibility into your performance management process because it allows you to keep performance plans up to date.** There's nothing worse than coming to the end of the review cycle and trying to evaluate an employee's performance on a goal that's no longer relevant — and not having a replacement goal on this list of priorities.

- **Helps you eliminate the surprise syndrome for employees and review-writing anxiety for you.** When the formal review is given, coupled with informal constructive feedback along the way including necessary status reviews, employees know where they stand in their performance. No surprises. Your annual review simply summarizes your quarterly checkups.

- **Helps you eliminate possible discrepancies in how you and your employees see their performance.** As one manager who uses this coaching tool described, "If the two of us see issues differently on how the employee is performing on a goal or an overall level, that discrepancy is gone before the end of the year. The employee knows where I stand, and the onus is on that person to show evidence of results to change my view." Employees quickly learn to adapt and produce. This communication eliminates surprises occurring with the final evaluation.

- **Builds a support system.** By plugging in the self-evaluation approach to this meeting, you end up listening more than half the time. This shows that you care and are in touch with your employees' challenges and successes. And by updating the performance plans together, employees walk away with renewed focus. Communication and understanding are enhanced, which is support at its best, and makes this one-hour meeting once a quarter a worthwhile investment for you.

Conducting a Project Postmortem

The term *postmortem* may bring to mind cadavers and scalpels. The only thing a dead body and a past project have in common is that in both cases you're curious what you can learn from the past through careful analysis of what happened.

TIP

So often in business, major events occur, and as soon as they're over, everyone involved takes a deep breath and moves on to other issues. The next event, similar to the one before it, comes up, and everyone scrambles around and ends up repeating the same mistakes they made in the previous event. This pattern occurs with trade shows, product development and launch efforts, and numerous other special projects and events. It's amazing, sometimes, how managers and employees can let bad history repeat itself. The performance assessment tool, the *postmortem meeting*, aims to foster continual learning. The following sections take a closer look at this meeting.

The main purpose of the postmortem meeting is to evaluate results from projects and other key performance events and to apply lessons learned from them to similar situations in the future. The meeting can even be used as a method of debriefing and learning from sales calls, formal presentations, and other important or public displays of employee performance.

"Operating" a postmortem meeting

As a coaching tool, the postmortem is done on a one-to-one basis or on a manager-to-group basis when the event is a team situation. (Generally, most one-on-one postmortem meetings can be done in 30 minutes to an hour. For large team-like projects, the time may be longer.)

Although you're one of the participants in this meeting, your primary role, as manager, is to be the facilitator. The meeting is divided into four steps:

1. **Draw key conclusions from the work done on the project or performance event.**

   Two questions are answered:

   - What worked well in the project; what were the successes?

   - What didn't work as well as needed or desired?

   Have the employee respond to the questions first, then you go second — without any comment or discussion so that the initial input comes out unbiased. (If a team is involved in the postmortem, follow the same process by allowing one person at a time to respond, with no discussion.) Have the inputs recorded on a board or flip chart so that they are visible. Then start the collective discussion and focus on determining the key conclusions being reported.

TIP

   Thanks to the postmortem assessment meeting, your staff members obtain valuable lessons from the past that help them perform more effectively in the future. In this way, you drive employee responsibility because they are the ones expected to apply the lessons learned.

2. **Shift the meeting focus to future steps or actions.**

   Start with your employee giving ideas and then add your own. Often, you can hold a brainstorming session in which you each throw ideas back and forth, one at a time. Refrain from discussion so that the ideas can flow, and have the ideas recorded so that they are visible. Focus the ideas on two endeavors:

- Actions to maintain for continued success
- Improvements to enhance effectiveness in the future

3. **Discuss and evaluate the ideas shared and collectively decide which ones to go forward with for the next event.**

    Have the agreed-upon actions documented along with the key conclusions determined in the first part. Guess who should do most of this documentation? Hint, it's not you.

4. **Pull out the information documented during the postmortem meeting and use it in the planning phase of the new project or special event.**

    (This step occurs in the future!) You can evaluate past experiences instead of being doomed to repeating them.

Adding up the benefits of the postmortem

The postmortem meeting works best when held at the conclusion of every important project or special event. Have it be a regular part of the process so that it isn't overlooked. When the postmortem is used for learning and training purposes or for other projects of small scope — such as handling a sales call, making a special presentation, or demonstrating new job skills — you may not need to schedule it on a continuous basis. But do use this debriefing coaching tool whenever needed. Just be sure to announce up front, before the performance efforts take place, that you will do a postmortem right afterwards.

Conducting regular postmortems has several benefits:

» **Employees gain analytical skills as they evaluate what happened.** Dwelling long and hard on the problem, blaming, and finding fault are not part of the process. They then gain a solutions orientation because the postmortem meeting is not complete until solutions or steps for next time are worked out. The emphasis is on performance, which helps build trust and motivation, not blame.

» **You get to listen and teach.** The employee gives input and ideas first; you play the role of listener, supporter, and, of course, teacher, because you're providing lessons based on past mistakes and successes.

» **You gain quality time with your staff.** The postmortem helps you spend quality time with your employees, during which you reflect, learn lessons, and set actions going forward. Thus, you're having productive meetings with your employees to help good results roll on for the future.

>> **You build a culture of collaboration and continual learning.** Organizations that aren't afraid of openly discussing failures and lessons learned grow and evolve from past experience. They innovate, streamline, and improve what's produced and, in turn, build customer satisfaction, company growth, and employee satisfaction. Everyone wins.

Building the Pillars of Commitment

When used as periodic performance assessment coaching tools, the status-review, checkup, and postmortem meetings affect the five pillars of commitment that I discuss in Chapter 4. Take a look at each pillar within the context of these meetings:

>> **Focus:** All three of these coaching tools help drive focus. Employees come out of these meetings clearly knowing the goals, plans, and priorities on which to focus. No guessing games as to what they should spend time on in order to produce results.

>> **Involvement:** All three of these periodic performance review meetings are conducted as two-way conversations with the employees doing more than half the talking. The employees' input shapes the action item list in status reviews, their ideas are used to help modify performance plans in the checkup meetings, and their experiences help determine the lessons to be learned and better ways to do things covered in the postmortem meetings. Active participation is encouraged and solicited in these meetings.

>> **Development:** Employees receive coaching on areas that they can apply in future performance endeavors and thus grow from their experiences. During the status review and the checkup, opportunities often come to light in which employees can gain experience, skills, and knowledge that will help them in the future. Most importantly, they develop self-sufficiency as they begin to take control and drive the results of their own performance.

>> **Gratitude:** Employees are grateful for the attention and mentoring when you take time to have meaningful dialog with them.

>> **Accountability:** A major emphasis of these review meetings is reviewing results. As long as you follow through, holding the meetings and maintaining their organized and collaborative structure, the employees are the ones who carry the primary responsibility to evaluate and report the results of their performance. They also can track their performance and see the progress they make with it — and thus experience a sense of achievement from their own efforts.

Chapter 17

Coaching for Development and Improvement

Developing your employees is central to managing as a coach. Doer managers (refer to Chapter 2) tend not to put much emphasis in this area — you do your job; I'll do mine.

Under the coach approach, developing employees is an important part of how time is spent at work. It's about strengthening and growing employees' skills, knowledge, and abilities so they're engaged, committed, and motivated to their own success. You're emphasizing how job performance and career development complement each other. If the employee is developed to perform at greater levels of skill and capacity, then they're better positioned to advance in their career.

Chapter 15 describes a process to work alongside the employee to create a plan that integrates both performance and development goals that support the organization's strategic goals. This chapter looks more closely at how to collaboratively design development goals with your employees, how to support their growth through coaching, and how to navigate employees who face challenges in building their skills and abilities to meet expectations and find a useful role in the company.

Knowing What to Develop

Creating a development plan is done as a collaborative effort with you and your employees. You don't write the plan for your employees. If you do, it becomes your plan, not theirs. This point becomes even more critical when the target of your development effort is on improvement in performance that is deficient rather than being on an area for growth (see the "Coaching Underperformance" section, later in this chapter, for further details).

REMEMBER

People support what they help create. For development plans to be effective, they must belong to the individuals for whom they're created. Thus, employees need to be part of the collaborative effort to create development plans if they are to own and drive them. You help by assessing performance, giving direction about the business, and providing input to assist in shaping the development plan. Your role in the overall development process is to support, which includes helping to reinforce accountability along the way.

These sections help you identify potential areas that may go into an employee's development plan with examples of critical areas tied to job performance. You can find out what makes a good development plan and discover a five-step process that ensures the plan is done in collaboration with the employee.

Focusing on growth

I (Marty) have seen managers who think they're creating development plans when writing annual performance reviews. In such attempts, what usually happens is the manager writes something — usually a suggestion or two for areas to get training in the coming year — in the development section of the appraisal form so that nothing on the form is left blank. This often happens without any discussion with the employee.

Although the performance-review meeting is a good opportunity to work on development because performance is being evaluated, making a few suggestions on an appraisal form isn't a development plan. In addition, a list of a few areas in which to get training isn't development. Training is one of many strategies for helping to make development efforts happen but learning for learning's sake is not career or performance development.

TIP

The key, then, is to create development plans *with* your staff members (not *for* them) and to include the ingredients that a good plan has (as I describe in the "Crafting the plan" section later in the chapter). You also want to know what areas to target. When the development emphasis is on growth, the focus of the development plan should be on the outcomes or level of performance you're helping the employee to reach. You want to target the levels of expectation for competent performance.

Here are some areas to target for growth in a development plan:

>> **Strengthening or building skills to deliver greater levels of performance.**

Example: Helping a junior engineer grow in skills to play a more independent role in projects.

Example: Helping a product manager develop formal presentation skills for delivering effective presentations to customers at marketing seminars and trade shows.

>> **Developing certain behaviors to increase performance effectiveness.**

Example: Targeting efforts to help a customer-service representative understand how to greet and service customers in a way that makes them want to come back for more business.

Example: Developing an inexperienced sales representative to listen and present themselves so that customers' key decision-makers see this individual as their main contact for business.

>> **Developing certain skills and behaviors to handle new or changing situations.**

Example: Helping everyone in the warehouse, which needs to have more coverage, become able to handle all shipping, receiving, and traffic functions.

Example: Ensuring that one of the technical support specialists, who has transferred into your inside sales group, masters the skills and duties to handle a sales role.

>> **Building competencies to handle greater level of responsibilities.**

Example: Delegating to one of your staff the responsibility to handle all technical support and maintenance activities for the department's new inventory management system.

Example: Delegating to one of the junior recruiters in the human resources department the responsibility to coordinate all hiring of temporary and contract staff for the company.

>> **Improving underperformance.**

Example: Helping the controller improve accuracy in financial reports.

Example: Coaching a team member who has no filter and alienates both customers and colleagues to improve their interpersonal skills.

Example: Working with a sales associate who often falls below quota to meet their quota.

>> **Grooming someone to handle a new role now or in the near future.**

Example: Developing your successor to handle management of your group so that you're able to move on in the near future to a larger role in the organization.

Example: Creating the role of project manager to coordinate the growing volume and demands of the customer accounts you oversee in your group, and developing one of your staff members to handle the new role.

>> **Grooming someone to take on a new role sometime in the distant future.**

Example: Developing a recruiter in your contract staffing branch, who desires to one day move into a sales role, to understand and support sales operations while still maintaining his current job.

Example: Grooming one of your staff, based on their interests and the anticipated growth of the business, to handle a first level management role should the opportunity come to pass, as you think it may.

The target you and the employee want to achieve is what's most important. Coaching for development means putting focused attention on increasing employees' levels of performance and capability, which often includes career growth. It's outcomes-based (as opposed to signing an employee up for a training class and thinking that will cover the development effort).

Starting the process — Five steps to follow

Unfortunately, what generally happens in discussions about development issues between managers and their staff members is, well, not much. Look at these examples to see if they sound familiar:

>> Development issues are discussed every now and then, but often little results.

>> Behaviors or other areas of performance that the employee should pay attention to aren't talked about.

>> Attention is given to areas that aren't relevant to the employee's performance.

These are all misguided and unfocused efforts.

TIP

To attend to and guide employee development, look at the coaching effort as a process. In a process, key elements or steps occur, and the process is ongoing and evolving. This five-step process provides you a focused approach for coaching for career and performance development with your employees. It takes threads of discussions about performance needs and career interests from scattered conversations into a guided tour so you know how to move down the road. It also defines how both parties play a role in helping to make employee growth happen — the employee is the driver, and you are the supporter.

Step 1: Assess competencies and explore needs and interests

These questions represent the issues you want to explore with your employees when assessing their competencies and exploring their needs and interests:

>> What job-related skills, knowledge, and abilities does the employee have — from the ones of strength to the areas of weakness?

>> What does the employee need for future growth?

>> What are the employee's interests for performance and in career development?

Chapter 9 can help you understand an employee's motivation. Chapter 12 discusses how you can support them in building their own career. And Chapter 15 talks more in depth about how to set employee goals, which is the foundation for a useful dialog between what the organization needs now and may need in the future and how the employee can play a critical role.

TIP

When you take the time to work with your employee to develop specific and actionable development goals, you lay the standards for providing constructive feedback throughout the year. You have a starting place for your reviews: How are they doing on their own plan? This puts the accountability where it really belongs — with the employee.

Step 2: Clarify the organizational needs and competencies required

As Chapter 15 mentions, encourage employees to take an interest in learning about the company's goals and opportunities. You want employees to be self-directed and engaged in their careers. That doesn't mean you can't be helpful in clarifying the organizational goals and needs, now and in the future. Consider the following:

>> What are the challenges and needs of your department, currently and in the future?

>> What are the needs of the business overall, currently and in the future?

Step 3: Analyze and prioritize career issues and needs

Determine what to work on for employee development to meet business needs — create a match between employee and organization needs that makes the development effort relevant. If employees have other interests unrelated to their current job situations or future growth in the organization, redirect the focus to what is relevant and needed.

EXAMPLE

Here's an example: "I understand you have a passion for sustainability and climate change, and I'm sure we can find a way for you to contribute, but we are severely understaffed, as you know. We have a three-month backlog of projects we promised clients. Developing your time-management skills will help you focus on important deliverables, instead of getting distracted by other demands."

TIP

If improvement is needed in an area of performance, start there before worrying about working on growth. (See the "Coaching Underperformance" section later in this chapter.) In essence, get the foundation of the house in order before you work on adding new floors to it.

Step 4: Mutually construct a development plan

Make sure this plan targets the selected needs and involves building a road map together to formalize and focus the development efforts. The plan allows both you and the employee to manage the development effort. You're building involvement and accountability from the get-go. What to write into the plan is detailed in the "Crafting the plan" section later in this chapter.

TIP

Don't be overly ambitious and target a bundle of areas for development. Usually one or two is enough and is all that you support with each staff member. You want to take a long-term view with your development efforts. It's not about what assignments or tasks you need to learn to do for next week. It's about growing employee skills and capacity levels for bigger and better performance.

Step 5: Follow up to review progress and offer support

This step makes the process continuous and focuses on getting results that benefit both the employee and the organization. It ties development to a regular part of employee performance — not an extracurricular activity that everyone forgets about when they go back to work.

TIP

Set the frequencies for checkpoints at a reasonable level. Weekly check-ins for a long-term effort usually aren't relevant. Tying into the checkup review you have each quarter may work just as well. Tailor to what best fits the development plan.

Crafting the plan

You can spend time developing a specific development plan or you can just identify two or three goals for the employee to work on. (Chapter 15 illustrates a simple process that ties organizational goals with performance and development goals.) Don't make it too ambitious. People are busy, and you'll stress your employee out if you identify a long list of skills to develop. Go slow and have them identify one they'll work on for a month, for instance, and then touch base with them to see how they're doing.

REMEMBER

Action plans drive the entire development plan. They're the activities and efforts to be carried out that move the employee towards reaching the development goal. What are some strategies that are helpful to have in development plans? Here is a list to consider that covers training and educational efforts, work activities and experiences, and working with mentor-types who can help — including you:

>> **Formal training classes:** This strategy can be fulfilled through college courses, outside seminars with training companies or professional associations, in-house offerings, or training sessions for your group that you organize with an outside professional or internal staff to teach. In order for formal training to be a true success, the employee should be required to return from training to immediately apply at least one skill/principle to their job or they should train others on what they learned. Otherwise, formal training is just passive learning and managers check the box for "developing" the employee with little return on investment.

>> **Cross training:** Sometimes, the employee is taught by others on how to do their job functions — referred to as *cross training*. Sometimes, an employee's development plan may include being the cross trainer, allowing that person to train someone else, thereby freeing up time to get into other areas of work. Cross training is a form of mentorship, whereby more experienced employees share their knowledge and help guide the development of a junior employee.

Not only is the next generation of staff being developed, but older employees are also sharing critical institutional knowledge that would be otherwise lost.

>> **Job rotation:** Some companies encourage and promote employees to rotate positions within the organization. Job rotation has several benefits:

- Employees are challenged and engaged by learning new skills and processes.

- Employees gain an understanding of the responsibilities of other positions and how they contribute to other positions.

- Organizations develop a more diverse and deeper bench of talent, which allows greater flexibility and adaptability as changes happen.

>> **Readings:** Reading articles, books, or online information helps with employee learning and development.

Reading alone without any connection to a task is a passive development activity. To make the most out of this strategy, have the employee share with you or others what they're learning from these sources.

>> **Spending time outside the group:** Another helpful development activity is to allow an employee to pick up skills by spending time away from the work group. This may mean visiting another organization or working with another department or office location within the organization. The idea is to see and grow from what others do. Outside exposure often broadens horizons of thinking.

>> **Special projects or work assignments:** This strategy is about learning by building experience. It's being given responsibility to handle a project or important assignment that helps grow skills and knowledge. You have to provide the right level of guidance that the employee needs, but let the person run with the job and gain success from it.

>> **Special committees or project teams:** These activities usually involve participating in inter-departmental or organizational-wide teams to work on special events or tackle important business issues. These teams are helpful in giving a person exposure to other people and functions in the organization and in gaining a broader-level understanding of the business.

>> **Activities for higher-level exposure:** This strategy involves giving the employee more management-level exposure and visibility. It may mean including the individual in management meetings you attend, having the employee make presentations to management groups, or having the person represent the group at outside functions.

>> **Manager-employee mentoring discussions:** This activity works best when scheduled. It's carried out through periodic meetings during which you teach

or informally tutor skills or knowledge areas that are important for that person's development. Quite often, such efforts help in your own development, too.

>> **Providing a coach:** Sometimes the best way for a staff person to develop new skills or meet new challenges is to get one-on-one coaching with an outside expert or consultant. You support the effort budget-wise and stay tuned in to see how the employee is progressing. Sanctioning the investment to work with a special resource often serves as a great boost and motivator for that person's development.

Case study: Development plan in action

Here's the scenario of a sample plan: Work gets done in your group through project teams. You've served the role of project leader because usually no more than three teams were functioning at one time with a total of ten employees involved. Due to the pending growth in the business, you know that in the near future you'll be asked to oversee more projects. You see the need put someone in the role of project leader, as larger groups have done elsewhere in the company. The role isn't supervisory, but one that carries project management and leadership-by-influence responsibilities. Paula, a member of your group, has shown some initiative and leadership abilities in working with fellow team members on projects and has expressed an interest in growing in this direction in her career with the company. You both agree to target this area for growth and to put together a development plan to help the effort.

Employee: Paula

Development goal: Develop Paula to proficiently handle project leader responsibilities so that the project teams she manages meet their schedules, deliver the work products that their customers need, and work together in a positive and productive manner.

Q1 action plans:

1. Paula will take up to two classes or seminars in project management and team leadership over the next three months. As her supervisor, you'll allow her the time to attend.

    When: Complete by March 31. Immediate step: Identify and sign up for one class in the next two weeks.

2. Paula will spend time with Sari, the project leader in the engineering group, to pick up skills in project scheduling, resource allocation, and team facilitation. An average of three hours per week will be allotted for this effort over the next month or so.

When: Start immediately. Immediate step: Coordinate schedules with Sari to work together in the next week.

3. Paula will assist Dante with the three current projects that the group is handling by taking on all status-review tracking and overseeing all product-documentation functions.

   When: Start immediately. Immediate step: Meet with Dante in the next week to review the current process and status of tracking and product documentation functions.

Checkpoints: Meetings to review the overall progress with this development plan will be held on a monthly basis, starting at the end of February, for the first three months of this plan. Further checkpoints will be determined from there based on Paula's progress and the needs of the business.

How to measure:

1. Completion of Steps 1 through 3 of the action plans by Paula.

2. Your observation and feedback to Paula on her performance in the monthly review meetings.

3. Paula will provide you with a brief oral summary of key learnings each month.

4. Paula can blind copy you on emails marking her completion of tasks.

This sample development plan represents what you want to do when creating development plans, including the following:

» The goal defines an objective that the employee is working toward achieving.

» The action plans map out strategies in clear and specific terms — who is to do what and by when.

» The action plans spell out key steps, not a slew of detailed tasks.

» The manager's name is in the action plans at least once, with some effort to support the cause.

» Follow-up review on the whole plan and ways to measure progress are defined.

» The plan is written with the employee, not the manager, as its focal point and its driver.

» The plan ties individual interests with business needs. It's development- and performance-based.

You can tell that this sample plan will be evolving. If Paula progresses as hoped and the business needs grow as anticipated, she'll take on the project-leader role. It's likely then, after Q1, that the plan will be updated to focus on Paula's development in her new role. Coaching for development is an ongoing and evolving process.

REMEMBER

The development plan, created collaboratively, provides a road map to help make growth happen, which is much better than having scattered and occasional conversations with little focus or clear steps for action. It's also meant to be a living document, not something cast in stone that you can't change. You're making best estimates on strategies and time frames when you start and are adjusting along the way. Make your follow-up efforts so that the plan stays relevant and so that both you and the employee stay accountable for its success.

Figure 17-1 shows you a format for a development plan with the key ingredients in Paula's plan: Goal, action plan, checkpoints, and how to measure.

Development Plan

Employee _____   Date _____

Development goal:

Action plans:
(What steps the employee will take and what the manager will do to support to make the development goal happen. Include applicable target dates.)

Checkpoints:

How to measure (as applicable):

© John Wiley & Sons, Inc.

FIGURE 17-1:
A worksheet for development planning.

Coaching for Development

Continually coaching your employee leads to higher employee accountability and commitment to development. Performance reviews are more focused on skill development — how is the employee progressing and what's the next step in developing — not just how they're executing on performance. The discussions tend to be more fruitful and positive rather than a discussion only on performance, which can be stressful and hard to manage. To encourage the employee to continue to do the hard work of developing themselves, make sure to give the employee lots of positive reinforcement. The following sections look closer at what it means to coach for development by taking more of a glass half full approach than a glass half empty.

Encouraging progress

Much of my (Leo) coaching work is developing a specific skill in an employee. The employee may be strong in one area but needs help in another area, such as presenting, delegating, or resolving conflict. My goal is to identify one specific behavior that the employee wants to develop and help them build that skill over time by positive reinforcement. Here's my successful formula:

>> **Understand the supervisor's expectations.** I first establish the goals of the coaching engagement with the manager hiring me to work with their employee. "What change in attitude, behavior, or performance do you want to see in this employee in three months?"

>> **Make sure the employee is on board.** Interview the employee to see if they self-identify that a skill needs to be developed. It's not effective if the manager mandates it, but the employee doesn't see the need to improve. I ask the employee why it's important for them to develop for their career (see Chapter 12 for helping to develop a vision for your employees). I've found it effective when I coach a skill that contributes to career or life goals that the employee has identified.

>> **Give them tools and instruction.** If it's delegation, for instance, I give them a copy of my management book for emerging leaders, *From the Ground Up*, or I give them access to my online course on delegation. I might suggest they observe someone who models the right behavior.

>> **Ask them to set a reasonable goal.** I help them set a reasonable assignment to try using the tool in the next couple of weeks. I remind them of the assignment two weeks in an email. I meet with them a month later to review progress.

>> **Encourage progress.** In my coaching sessions, I'm always looking for ways to give them positive feedback on any progress. Many times, the employee is apologetic about not making enough progress. Even if they say, "I was more aware of doing work I should have delegated," I applaud it as an important first step. The key is to encourage forward motion. People are commonly their worst enemy when it comes to skill development. As a coach, build their confidence by being positive and encouraging.

Measuring progress

If someone needs software or a technical process, they can get mentored from someone more experienced or take a course, read a book, or watch a video or webinar. It's relatively straightforward to measure if someone knows how to format a document or input an order into a POS system after a training. You can give them a written test or have them demonstrate performing the required task. Measuring progress in life skills like interpersonal communication skills, however, isn't as easy. Here are some ways to measure progress in emotional intelligence skills:

>> **Self-report.** Change will happen when employees are invested in wanting to change. That takes time to regularly reflect, try new strategies, and be honest with your challenges. I coach my clients to keep track of any progress by journaling and making a record. I've found that when clients see they're making progress, they're motivated to continue. When I sit down with clients, I always start by asking what progress they've made toward their goals. They often make excuses and downplay any steps they've made. My job as a coach is to dig to find any signs of progress and celebrate it.

>> **Observe.** My number one measurement is to check with the manager on the employee's performance. Are they delegating more? Are they meeting more with their team? Have they noticed any progress or changes? This requires the manager having the direct experience of seeing the employee in action. With more people working remotely, this is harder.

>> **Report.** The manager can regularly check with people on the employee's team to see if there have been noticeable changes. Checking in with the people that the employee interacts with most often helps give you a better picture of progress.

>> **Enlist stakeholders.** There is an entire approach to coaching based on the employee taking ownership of their growth. Stakeholder coaching starts with the employee identifying key stakeholders who are key to their success — direct reports, peers, and manager. The employee meets individually with each of them and shares their development goals with them. The employee

invites real-time feedback from the stakeholders on how they're doing and meets with them monthly for a more formal check in. Being mentored by people at all levels is a great opportunity to make real progress to the people; it allows the people who are in the best position to help the employee grow as a leader.

>> **Conduct surveys.** I've used emotional intelligence surveys to gather data to help my clients see what areas of development they need to focus on to work more effectively with people and build trust. These surveys are 360-degree assessments, meaning the employee is getting feedback from every important person they interact with: staff they manage, peers they work with, senior people they report to, and customers they take care of. It's not uncommon for an employee to get strong marks from one group — customers, for instance — and get low marks from another group — staff or peers. A 360-survey is a great foundation for kick-starting coaching and setting goals. I've also used follow-up surveys after a year of coaching to see if there have been changes. In one case, a coaching client was amazed to see how much their ratings improved from their peers. It gave him a real boost of confidence.

>> **Use outside coaches.** An executive coach is an effective strategy for helping employees develop emotional intelligence. An outside coach is solely focused on coaching for specific development goals and doesn't have any other agenda. An outside coach can provide a safe sounding board for employees who don't want to admit or share personal challenges with their manager. Coaches can also provide independent, unbiased feedback on an employee's performance: An employee who challenged by their schedule starts to show up on time for coaching appointments; an employee who is stressed out in the first coaching session is noticeably more relaxed in the second; an employee who has difficulty getting to the point now pauses to think before speaking and gets to the point more consistently.

Don't promote promotions in your development efforts

Don't fall into this trap of tying promotions into developing employees. Promotions aren't prizes to be claimed after successfully completing a course of action. They aren't like some class in school in which the teacher spelled out what efforts and assignments to do to earn an A. If you respond to questions about what one has to do to get promoted as if you have a simple formula to follow, you set yourself up for making promises you often can't or don't want to keep.

As part of your ongoing efforts of coaching for career self-management and development, help your employees understand promotions. Here are a few tips to help build this understanding:

» **Ask them to take a manager's perspective.** In your coaching discussions with staff, ask them this question: "If you were a department manager who had the opportunity to promote someone in your group, what would be the reasons for granting the promotion?" This question usually sparks an interesting discussion. Answers certainly can vary, but staff members most likely will say that those who deliver quality results are reliable, work well with others on the team, and show the capability to take on greater responsibility are the ones who should be promoted.

The sum of these thoughts answers the question, "Who gets promoted?" The biggest factors on who gets selected to move up in an organization involve merit, not time on the job; performance, not who talks a good game. Promotions are earned well after the performance is documented or observed. I've often heard that younger employees want a promotion because they think they deserve it, not that they've earned it. Sit down with them to show them what skills they consistently need to show to earn a promotion. Promotions aren't a promissory note of future expectations. They're recognition of past and current performance.

» **Tell them what creates promotions.** Promotions most often come about because a business need exists and, therefore, an opportunity is given to meet that need. The same goes for why managers get the approval to recruit and hire someone when new or open positions exist. Sometimes, opportunities that could be promotions are filled by hiring people from outside the organization because no one internally has shown the quality performance and readiness to take on the role.

REMEMBER

Let your employees know that promotions don't usually operate by a schedule. The opportunities for them happen as business needs present themselves to be filled, which happens any time and all the time.

» **Advise them to do the job they want to have.** With a few exceptions, the loudest whiner isn't at the top of managers' list as the person to promote. Tell the individuals on your team that letting their desires for career advancement be known is fine, but they should go out and let their performance do the talking for them.

Following this advice also means the following:

- Tuning in to the needs of the group or other areas of the organization
- Taking initiative
- Taking on responsibility to help
- Offering and acting on good ideas that help meet needs
- Building positive working relationships

For example, why should you be promoted to team leader when the team members don't see you working hard and often see you getting in conflicts with them? On the other hand, if you consistently produce results, go above what is asked for to help the group do even better, and are well respected by the team, sooner or later, promoting you to team leader is an easy decision to make.

What occurs today in the fluid nature of business organizations is that opportunities for advancement occur because people take initiative and carry out responsibilities that fill voids. This sometimes leads to upgrades in current positions and sometimes to the creation of new positions.

>> **Create development plans that help prepare your employees.** Although there's no telling when opportunity for advancement is going to knock, nor are there any guarantees that when it does that the employee will be given it, you can work with employees to prepare themselves for opportunities, should they come knocking. The worst thing is to have it pass the employee by because they weren't ready to handle it.

Remind your staff members of this message and then, as you work with them to construct their development plans, focus on areas that will help prepare them for the future opportunities that they desire within the organization. As part of this planning effort, keep in mind that career advancement sometimes involves taking steps in sideways directions (instead of upward) that eventually lead to people moving upward. Therefore, work with your staff to help them to grow in depth and breadth.

Coaching Underperformance

Coaching for development can be fun and rewarding. Through your support, your employee has mapped out a plan, and now you get to see employees grow and achieve success. They gain satisfaction and you get stronger levels of performance.

However, when you're developing for improvement, you aren't working on growth and building someone to be a bigger and better performer. Instead, you're dealing with issues in which performance is unacceptable and is having a negative impact on the team and the organization. Some of the common performance issues are examples such as the following:

>> Attendance is sporadic with increased absences.

>> They have punctuality problems and difficulty in consistently being to work when scheduled.

>> Thoroughness and accuracy of work are lacking or inconsistent.

>> Output produced is of lower quantity than needed.

>> Timeliness in getting work done is inconsistent or behind schedule.

>> Lack of follow-through or initiative slows accomplishment.

>> Periodic clashes or outbursts make working with others difficult.

>> Abrasive or challenging behavior rubs people the wrong way.

How do you approach problems in a productive way, so you can move forward and not get derailed by dealing with issues of underperformance? That's what the next section addresses.

Approaching it the right way

To solve a problem, you have to first recognize that one exists. Seldom in these performance-problem situations is the employee in question totally incompetent or all bad. In fact, in many cases, while less-than-satisfactory performance occurs in one area, the person does very well in other parts of the job. Here are a few examples:

>> Kelsey has the strongest computer skills of anyone in the group and she produces top quality work. However, she seldom meets deadlines with her reports.

>> Lyle is the most capable performer in the group and helps everyone on the team learn to do their jobs better. He shows up to work late half the time, however, and that holds up the production process from starting on time.

>> Nia is well liked by everyone on her team but produces work that is sloppy — full of errors and mistakes that have to be corrected. Even though she is good natured and easy to work with, her lack of attention to detail is a problem.

>> Bill is a brilliant engineer. He can solve any technical problem thrown his way. But when he needs to work in team-like situations, he clashes with other team members who no longer want to work with him.

>> Tamara knows the business so well and has done a good job at growing her group and the volume of business it produces. At the same time, her verbal attacks on staff have alienated them to the point that turnover is high and many employees want transfers.

These examples represent situations you often see. You have an employee who has a lot of strengths and is a valuable contributor in your group, but that person's weaknesses are causing a problem. Unfortunately, many managers actively avoid taking action to correct the issues. Instead, they

>> **Do work-arounds.** Structure assignments or other situations so that you or others cover for what should be the responsibility of the individual to handle.

>> Complain about the person to peers but say nothing directly to the employee.

>> Make excuses for the employee. "Oh, that's just Bob," or "Yes, but Bob really knows his stuff."

>> Give occasional, vague, unclear criticism.

>> Act as if the performance problem doesn't exist at all.

>> Put off raising the issue to the employee with the idea of addressing it at a better time sometime in the near future.

These actions, or I should say inactions, are means of avoidance. Managers who take this approach aren't dealing directly with the problem. What happens to the performance issues you avoid dealing with? They continue, and often grow into worse problems. Behavior that is rewarded is repeated.

Other times, managers take the *hammer approach:* Yelling at the employee, threatening the individual's job, or putting the person on warning, usually as the first real attempt to address a performance problem. Most employees respond to this harsh approach with bitterness, covert to overt resistance, fearfulness to perform, boisterous confrontation, or just don't show up the next day.

Neither the hammer nor avoidance approaches do much to advance employee performance. The better path is coaching with the focus on improvement:

>> **Understand the root.** Take the time to talk to the employee about the issue, starting by asking if they're aware an issue exists. Then stay open and curious to understand the root or cause of the issue. Frequently missing deadlines may be a combination of poor communication on when a project is due and an employee being overwhelmed with other responsibilities. As the employee's manager you may be able to help solve the issue. Don't assume the issue is simply underperformance. There may be other issues contributing to the problem.

>> **Focus on solutions.** Employees who are good technical problem solvers are often the most challenged when solving behavioral issues. Ask them to engineer a process to streamline manufacturing and they jump into problem-solving mode. They analyze the problem for a firm understanding and then

get creative in proposing alternatives for a solution, generating a lot of positive energy and some good solutions.

But when it comes to emotional intelligence or interpersonal issues, they're clueless (see Chapter 5). Appeal to their ability to solve other kinds of problems to engage them in people-related performance issues.

>> **Remain in control.** When an employee isn't performing well, a lot of emotions come into play. You're disappointed, angry, or frustrated. Be aware of the emotions you feel and focus your attention where it needs to go — on defining a course for correction with the employee. Like driving on the roads, you need to have this frame of mind to be able to stay out of accidents and reach the intended destination.

>> **Be helpful.** Work with an employee to map out a course of action for improvement in performance. To make it work, the employee must hear sincerity in your tone of voice and use of language. Employees generally work better when they see that a manager cares and is trying to help them resolve a problem rather than blaming, dictating, or ignoring the situation. Keeping things future-focused helps reduce shame, anger, or other emotions the employee may experience and shows the manager is genuinely committed to the employee's success and a positive outcome.

>> **Stay firm.** Staying firm is letting people know the importance of an issue. It means not shying away from working out a solution. Be positive and respectful but insistent on seeing positive changes made. Some managers may think they either have to be mean and firm or kind and soft. The art of keeping people accountable is being kind and firm. Being a good coach is not unlike being a good parent. Stick to your position, knowing it's the best interest of everyone, including the employee.

>> **Act immediately.** You can get the best improvement if you take action when the issues start to surface. The longer you wait, the harder the problems become to deal with and resolve successfully.

>> **Accept discomfort.** Many managers avoid conflict because dealing with personnel problem-related situations aren't comfortable. Ironically, difficult conversations are rarely as disastrous as you imagine them. It's more common to waste time and productivity worrying than dealing with the aftermath of a hard conversation. Just roll up your sleeves and do it!

>> **Collaborate.** The more you coach rather than manage employees, the more they'll come to trust and collaborate with you. You're just trying to coach them to what's in their best interest at the company. You aren't telling them what to do. It's directly relating a performance issue that's standing in the way of their own success and working with them toward a solution. Make employees aware that you aren't trying to impose solutions. You're firm about wanting a

solution worked out, but you're involving the employee. In fact, managers I have taught to coach for improvement often report that by working collaboratively in their approach, the employees come up with better ideas than the managers would have. This isn't surprising because those closest to a problem can work often out solutions if given opportunity and support to do so.

Following these characteristics puts you in a coaching frame of mind and makes you ready to tackle performance issues with your staff members.

Having the hard conversation

As I discuss in Chapter 14, when given in a timely fashion and on an ongoing basis, constructive feedback — that is, positive and negative feedback, not praise and criticism — helps employees know where they stand in their performance. Using this coaching tool correctly means that when someone slips a bit in performance or gives you less than the standards you need, you have a situation that calls for negative feedback. And after the negative feedback is given, you have a discussion with the individual and work out steps for correction or better performance going forward.

In most cases, this simple, straightforward coaching with constructive feedback corrects problems on the spot and prevents performance problems from forming into patterns — continuous signs of similar, less-than desirable performance. When you find yourself giving negative feedback over and over again on the same types of issues, however, a pattern exists with your employee. When you see these patterns, you need to coach for improvement just like you coach for development.

Following up with your employee in four easy steps

Here are the steps to follow in your coaching for improvement effort with your employee:

1. **Define the performance problem.**

Summarize the pattern of performance that needs improvement. Follow the guidelines in Chapter 14 for giving constructive feedback: Be specific, direct, sincere, and offer observations, not interpretations. Stay away from stating why you think the problem is occurring; instead, avoid the assumptions and tell what you see happening in concrete, observable terms.

2. **Invite the employee into the discussion.**

Listen closely so that you can understand the employee's perspective on the situation. As needed, explore possible causes for the problem. Discovering root causes helps you pinpoint solutions that help improvement happen.

Don't debate, listen. Neither of you have to see exactly eye-to-eye on the problem. What you need instead is for both of you to understand what each other has to say. Quite often, by avoiding the blaming or other problem-dwelling focuses, the dynamic of the interaction has opportunity for openness, and you can both gain insight. Remember, you're here to be helpful; otherwise, why should anyone want to work with you for improvement?

3. **Collaboratively create the plan for improvement.**

Follow the same format for creating development plans — refer to Figure 17-1. List the target as the "Goal" versus the "Development goal." The goal here is the expected level of performance you want to see from the staff person — come ready to spell that out and let the employee help define it with you for clarity. Work on the action plans, the substance of where the solution comes from, which should define which steps the employee will take to reach the goal, and what steps you will take to support the effort. Ask the individual for ideas — brainstorm together, if needed, so that this planning and solution-building is a two-way effort.

4. **Manage by plan and do your follow-ups.**

The checkpoints to review progress are best if relatively short-term initially — say, two to four weeks out. As you complete each progress review with the employee, exchange feedback on what has occurred relative to what the plan defined and update the plan accordingly. Set your next checkpoint from there.

Plan on doing at least three follow-ups over a period of time with your employee when you create a plan for improvement. Quite often, because focused attention has helped set a course for correction, you see immediate improvement. Holding follow-up meetings ensures sustained improvement (as opposed to short-term improvement) and keeps old habits from returning after the initial try.

Continuous follow-ups over time help keep positive momentum going and lay a groundwork for accountability to make the plan work. As progress is made, set the next checkpoint out further; for example, 30 days the first time, 60 days the next time, and then 90 days. Make your goal to get this person's issue improved upon, sustained, and then maintained through the quarterly checkup meetings that you do with each of your staff (see Chapter 16).

Case study: A development plan focused on improvement

Here is a sample development plan targeting improvement for an employee who has had difficulty in working with team members positively and productively. This is created by the employee and manager — it isn't created for the employee.

Employee: Joe   **Date:**

Goal: Consistently maintain working relationships with team members that demonstrate constructive assistance and respect, especially in situations when differences or conflict arise.

Q3 action plans:

1. Joe will maintain a sincere tone of voice and constructive use of words in interactions with team members. If angered by someone else, he'll walk away and gather thoughts first so he can return, if needed, and express himself constructively.

   When: Start immediately.

2. Issues of concern that Joe has with any team member will be addressed one-on-one with the emphasis on developing solutions together.

   When: Start immediately.

3. Siri (Joe's manager) will serve as a resource Joe can go to when he needs to plan how he will handle challenging situations constructively.

   When: Start immediately.

4. Siri will organize a conflict-resolution seminar for the whole team to participate in, and Joe will set learning goals from it and discuss them with Siri.

   When: Seminar to happen by August.

5. In project team meetings, Joe will speak up if he has a need to clarify his role and will offer ideas or help that aid team members in getting the project done.

   When: Starting at the June team meeting.

Checkpoints: Siri and Joe will meet every two weeks for the first month, starting May 22, to do progress review on the plan, and will set further follow-up meetings from there.

How to measure: Siri will solicit feedback from team members periodically as well as share feedback from her own observations. Joe will share feedback on his own efforts, especially in making his learning goals from the conflict-resolution seminar happen.

Dealing with difficult obstacles in getting improvement

When managers collaborate with their staff members to set plans and then do the follow-ups with them, it often leads to improvement. Two circumstances that managers often find difficult to deal with, however, occur when performance issues are behavior-related and when personal problems are impacting the performance. Coaching for any kind of development is certainly not easy under these circumstances.

Hold onto the wheel — time to change behavior

Sometimes people can be quite capable in their work performance, but the behaviors they display spur clashes, turn off customers, intimidate others, or just greatly annoy you. Whatever the case, this *toxic behavior* detracts from their performance and is a hindrance for future development or success. Toxic behavior also harms company/department culture and/or threatens employee retention of others who don't want to work in toxic environments. The consequences go far beyond the individual's performance.

TIP

Follow these steps to coach and develop the right behaviors for good performance (refer to the development plan in Figure 17-1):

>> **State observations, not interpretations.** You want to give specific, observations-based feedback about the person's behavior. Tell what you see, not your characterizations of how that person is. Demonstrate the behaviors of concern so that the employee can truly see what you're talking about.

EXAMPLE

Instead of saying, "You're nasty with your team members," give constructive feedback such as, "What I've noticed and heard from some of your team members is when disagreements occur, your tendency is to raise your voice loudly, talk over when others are trying to speak, make comments about how stupid people are, and not address the issues being raised."

>> **Set the goal to define the behavior you want to see.** The level of performance you expect related to the behavior desired is the basis for the goal written in the plan. State the behavior in positive terms — what to do versus what not to do — and in specific and observable terms that define the picture of the behavior expected for good performance. Don't yet talk about desired behaviors; save that for the action plans.

EXAMPLE

For example, a goal can be as follows: "Maintain interactions — writing, speaking, and listening — with fellow team members that show respect and are constructive." The target has now been defined for what the employee is to aim for in his behavior.

>> **Survey others.** To help measure progress, state up front when you set the plan that you'll gather feedback from the sources involved with this person as a way to measure progress in meeting the goal. Sometimes, you may also want to survey these people, or even have the employee do it, to help give a specific picture of the difficult behaviors as a way to help understand the problem.

TIP

When you gather feedback for these purposes, try to obtain information through conversation instead of in a written survey, so you get more depth and clarity of information. Ask specific questions so you get specific feedback.

>> **Define the new behaviors in the action plans.** With the employee, develop the solution of how the goal is to be met. Together, make sure the action plans clearly spell out what the employee is to do differently and better to make the goal happen. Stick with it until you've defined clear behaviors. The action plans serve as a reference guide for the employee on how to handle situations differently going forward. By developing them together, you both know whether training of any kind is needed or desired.

>> **Grow from successes.** As you review progress with the plan going forward, and good behavior towards the goal is exhibited, analyze with the person what was done. Help the employee see progress and success.

>> **Maintain accountability.** Follow through with checkpoints and ongoing constructive feedback on the behavior issue. People can change behavior and make it more positive, especially when attention and a sense of importance are attached to it.

The problem outside of work is affecting performance at work

Sometimes the cause for employee underperformance stems from personal problems. Personal problems can be a number of different things: marital problems, problems with children, financial woes, drug and alcohol abuse, depression, or other emotional difficulties. Whatever the case, the employee's attention is on outside distractions, and performance at work is suffering.

Here are some tips to help deal with this sometimes-sticky situation:

TIP

>> **Manage performance.** Your role is to be a manager, not a doctor or therapist who diagnoses physical or mental health problems. Therefore, keep your focus on the person's job performance and not on what you think may be happening in the personal life.

Follow through and work with the employee to put the plan for improvement together. Monitor progress and maintain accountability for good performance to happen.

>> **Direct to resources that can help.** Many organizations have *employee assistance programs (EAPs)*. These programs allow employees to work with a professional who can provide counseling or other assistance to deal with

personal problems or give referrals to resources that can. These types of situations are usually handled confidentially so what the employee does can be kept private. If you aren't aware of what your organization has to offer or of resources in your community, contact HR for assistance.

TIP

Don't start playing therapist, engaging in trying to help employees work through personal problems. The best way you can show concern is to let them know you want them to get the help needed and that you want to see them performing well on the job again. Unless you have suddenly become a licensed counseling professional, trying to counsel is like walking through a minefield. Listen enough to be aware, but don't play pop psychologist through which you may emotionally (if not legally) get yourself tangled in employees' personal affairs. When you keep your focus on demanding good performance, you prevent what is called enabling — excusing and allowing the problem to continue. If you're not sure how to help your employee, ask HR for guidance and support.

>> **Accommodate as appropriate.** Sometimes, to sort through the personal problems, employees need time off or adjustments in their work schedules. In some cases, the law will dictate what the employee's right is when it comes to medical/family/personal needs. In other cases, be willing to accommodate, under these two conditions:

- The person is getting professional help or taking some other action to resolve the personal problems. Do *not* write that in the performance or development plan. If an employee is on protective leave or seeking help with a personal problem — and HR has been involved — this information is already confidentially documented in the employee's file. The manager will want to focus on the desired performance for when the employee is at work or returns to work.

- While on the job, the employee is committed to giving full effort to perform well. Steps to make the good performance happen should be the crux of what's contained in the plan for improvement.

Realizing when the exit door is needed

No matter what the performance issue is, if the improvement needed isn't happening despite your best coaching efforts, terminating or coming to a mutually agreeable exit for someone is sometimes the best course of action. Coaching doesn't involve employing people who don't take full responsibility for nor demonstrate the capability to deliver the level of performance needed.

TIP

The plan you set with the employee is the key to managing and influencing the change you need in performance. Following through on your checkpoints helps you and the employee measure progress. In your follow-up efforts, if you aren't seeing signs of improvement and the performance is having a negative impact that can't be tolerated, set disciplinary consequences so the employee won't be surprised if you have to enforce those consequences. Carry out the consequences when you do your follow-ups if improvement isn't shown, but still develop a plan outlining a solution for better performance. Stay corrective in your approach. Other than severe incidents, use termination or an agreed-upon exit as a last resort.

Building on the Pillars of Commitment

In coaching for development in growth or improvement in performance, the five pillars for building employee commitment, discussed in detail in Chapter 4, are positively influenced. Here's how:

>> **Focus:** The plans provide a clear target, direction, and road map to help make development happen. The effort replaces scattered and occasional conversation with concrete plans that are designed to help make good things happen. Clarity replaces ambiguity in the process.

>> **Involvement:** This pillar is at the heart of the development effort. No plan of action or adjustment is done without the employee. That person first shapes what goes into the development plan and then becomes the driver to help make it happen.

>> **Development:** The entire focus is on developing employees. The guided path of a development plan helps people see and measure their own improvement or development.

>> **Gratitude:** Employees appreciate when their manager takes enough of an interest in their career to help them set goals to grow and provide feedback to stay focused on success. Over time, the employee enjoys the fruits of their hard work: new and better assignments, recognition for a job done well, and promotions.

>> **Accountability:** The coaching process for development has the employees owning the plan: Their success or failure comes as a consequence of their actions. When they're successful, the sense of accomplishment they experience from their own development is a great incentive for people to push their own performance. You support their growth by giving frequent constructive feedback, which encourages them to take more ownership of their growth.

5
Mentoring for Life

Expand traditional ways of defining mentor relationships to include all the ways that people need and want support.

Discover how to mentor your employees and how mentoring is different from coaching.

Encourage employees to seek and build a support team for their career and life, which can provide a sounding board and inspiration to meet the many challenges of work and life.

Chapter **18**

Mastering Mentoring

How often have you heard that employees are desperate to find a mentor? Or your organization's management has instructed you to be more of a mentor? What does it mean to mentor and how is it different from coaching and tutoring?

This chapter explores the concept of mentoring, how it's different from coaching, why it's important, what the pitfalls are, how as a manager you can mentor employees, and what two tools you can use for engaging employees.

Chapter 19 expands on the concept of mentors to include other people who can help support the employee in addition to you, their manager. Because the needs of each employee is different, mentorship can also look different.

Understanding How Coaching Differs from Mentoring

You may have been told you need to be a mentor to younger employees, but you may not be clear what mentoring is and how it differs from coaching. *Coaching* is more focused on performance, execution, and skill development toward a specific goal whereas *mentoring* is more focused on the employee's career and personal goals. Mentors have the employee's best interest in mind. Their allegiance leans toward the person, not as much the organization. The following sections look at an example to illustrate how coaching differs from mentoring, discuss what the two have in common and explain how choosing mentoring for your employees can help them.

Distinguishing between mentoring and coaching — An example

Here's a sports analogy to make the distinction between mentoring and coaching.

Sheri wanted to be a goalkeeper on her high school soccer team. Her coach Darrell instructed her on her skills and technique and set up drills to improve her footwork and reflexes. He recorded her and watched the videos with her and asked her what she saw that she needed to work on. After practices and games, he'd ask her what she felt good about and what she wanted to focus on next. He gave her praise and pointers of what she needed to work on. He could see her improvement and continually challenged her to do better.

Sheri wanted to be as good as her older sister, Beth, but she always felt like she'd never measure up to her. Beth was now in college and wasn't playing soccer because she had torn her ACL. Even though Beth was far away, she always called to talk to Sheri at the end of practice or a game. Beth shared her own challenges of not feeling good enough. "There's always someone you're going to prepare yourself against and not feel inferior," Beth told her. Sheri always felt better after the calls because Beth mostly listened and occasionally shared her own stories, but mostly she made Beth feel like she wasn't alone. As Sheri moved from coach to coach throughout her career, she had Beth as a mentor all along the way to bounce ideas off, share frustrations, learn from her experience, and feel supported and inspired.

Coaching for performance

Sheri's coach had very specific goals for her: to improve her playing so she could help the team win games. Look what Darrell did for her as a coach:

- » Set up specific drills and exercises to improve her skills

- » Recorded her performance and asked for her feedback

- » Asked after a game what she observed and wanted to work on

- » Gave her praise and constructive feedback to motivate her to push harder

All of Darrell's efforts were goal-oriented toward what he wanted to achieve. It's not unlike a manager coaching an employee to manage other employees so the organization can grow and be successful. Coaching is tied to results, often the company's goals. And coaching is often short term to help the person to jump to the next level.

Mentoring for life

Beth wasn't making Sheri do drills or giving her feedback on her performance. Beth was simply there for Sheri, in any way to help her navigate her career as a goalkeeper. She did it in several ways:

- » Not judging or critiquing but supporting her

- » Listening and reassuring

- » Sharing her own experience

- » Offering wisdom she had learned

- » Being there over time

All of Beth's efforts were for Sheri. And that's one fundamental difference between coaching and mentoring. Coaching is typically focused on short-term results that benefit the team or company, whereas mentoring is for life. Mentors can help in many ways:

- » Providing advice from past experience

- » Sharing instructive stories

- » Inspiring with words of support

- » Acting as a sounding board for fears and concerns

- » Being an advocate to connect mentees with people and resources for career and life

Recognizing what coaching and mentoring share

The lines between a coach and a mentor aren't always clear. You can be a mentor one day to an employee and another day act as a coach. What they share is a similar overall goal: to help the employee grow to their fullest potential. Don't think of coaching versus mentoring. They're both needed to help people.

Coaching and mentoring share the end goal of teaching employees to be resourceful, show initiative, and learn by making mistakes. Both coaching and mentoring use questions to foster self-reflection and knowledge. Both Darrell and Beth knew that Sheri had to learn in her own way.

Putting the two together — A powerful combination

Coaching and mentoring together are a powerful combination. Having a coach who is observing how the employee works and a mentor who is present when an employee struggles or falls gives the employee a challenge and a safety net. Together, they give the employee the best chance for success.

If you're still not sold on being a mentor, consider why having a mentor matters:

>> Provides a psychologically safe place for employees to be honest and vulnerable

>> Teaches employees lessons from someone who isn't their boss

>> Gives people role models to follow and aspire to

>> Enriches the culture by creating important intergenerational relationships

>> Helps the mentor feel valuable and important by passing along stories and helping someone grow

>> Grows the organization often by sharing institutional knowledge with the next generation

What makes any successful pairing hinges on understanding the pitfalls of mentoring, which the following section discusses.

Avoiding the Pitfalls of Mentoring

Mentoring can be hit or miss, as you may have experienced. For all the talk from employees about wanting a mentor and the attempts that organizations put into mentorship programs, great mentorships are hard to find. Here are the most common reasons mentoring doesn't work and how to steer clear of these mistakes:

» **The employee isn't sold on the idea.** Mentorships that are arranged without the employee's buy-in are like an arranged marriage. The employee needs to see the mentor as someone who can help them, not someone assigned to help them. Employees need to identify what they need help with and why it's in their best interest to invest the time in the relationship.

» **The mentor isn't sold on the idea.** It's equally important that the mentor is interested and personally invested in wanting to be a mentor, not someone who is checking a box to appease their manager. The attitude that "no one helped me and everyone needs to go through struggles" isn't the foundation for a healthy, successful mentorship. Mentors need to want to help.

» **The mentor doesn't have an established relationship with the employee.** A *Harvard Business Review* study suggests that the most successful mentorships are ones where relationships are already established. If either the employee or the mentor doesn't respect or like the other person, the chances aren't good for success.

» **The mentorship isn't a priority.** Not all mentorships need to be formal. A mentor and mentee don't need to meet at a scheduled time. However, consistency in being in touch with each other on a regular basis is critical to having an impact. Many mentorships fizzle from a lack of follow-through and making meeting a priority.

» **The employee doesn't have any specific goals.** Employees should have a good idea of what kind of mentorship they need. They may need someone to help them navigate interpersonal challenges with colleagues or learn how to advocate for themselves. If you're both just showing up without specific goals, neither of you will get much out of the relationship.

» **The mentor offers too much advice.** Mentorships work best when both the employee and mentor are sharing, not just the mentor talking all the time. The goal is for the mentor to empower independent problem-solving, not to lecture or be superior. Use more questions and silence.

» **The mentor doesn't offer enough advice.** Employees hope to learn from their mentors, which means at some point, they want to hear your insights and wisdom, not just more questions. Offer your own experience and lessons learned rather than direct advice on their ideas.

>> **The mentor doesn't have the required patience.** I (Leo) get hired to teach delegation because I'm skilled at breaking it down and making the steps clear to someone new to it. Doers who are impatient with people learning a new skill undermine their effectiveness as mentors. They're so ingrained as a doer that they're not particularly tuned into beginner's mind (refer to Chapter 13).

>> **The roles conflict with each other.** It's sometimes difficult to be a coach and mentor. Instead of being supportive as a mentor, you can easily slip into giving too much specific feedback as a coach. That's why it's more common to have different people serve the different roles.

Coaching and mentoring can be challenging because people are diverse — in personality, needs, and style. Putting two people together successfully doesn't fit a step-by-step process. Let me repeat myself again: Relationships matter in mentorships. Strong relationships happen not from applying a one-size-fits-all template. In fact, that's why many mentorships fail.

Taking the Right Steps

Whether you want to mentor someone you manage or someone you don't, there are fundamental steps you can take to play an important role in a person's development. This section outlines what you can do to be an effective mentor.

Lead by example

If you want to encourage mentorship in your organization, lead by example and get a mentor yourself. You'll learn first-hand what makes a successful mentorship, what works, and what doesn't. Sharing your own experience with mentorship can be a great first step in engaging your employees.

By having your own mentor, you also show others that everyone needs help and looking for support in any form is okay. When you have the humility and wisdom to get support, you legitimize and normalize the concept of mentorship.

Revisit their mountains

Chapter 12 discusses the importance of promoting the concept that employees are responsible for their own careers. You can help them by working with them to develop their long-term goals, their *mountains*. Coach people so they understand their job performance is linked to moving closer to their mountain. Mentors are invaluable in helping employees reach their mountains by providing support and guidance along the way.

Ask your employee questions like the following:

>> What is your mountain or three-year vision?

>> In what ways has it changed or become clearer since we last talked?

>> What are areas where you could use support to get there?

>> What are your challenges?

>> What's missing in your experience?

>> Are there some people who could be mentors?

>> What ways can I support you?

>> What are your next steps?

You may have covered these areas in the employee's development plans. They may have given these questions a lot of thought, and they may be forthcoming with the answers. However, chances are you'll be introducing ideas that they may have not considered. You're kick-starting their thought process on questions that can affect their career and life.

REMEMBER

People are diverse: Some know they need help but aren't sure who to ask or how to get it; others could use help but don't know it or aren't comfortable admitting they need assistance. The fact is relationships at many levels are critical to being happy and productive at work. Cultivating mentors in and outside the organization who can help the employee get to where they want to go are indispensable. As a manager, you can aid in shaping your employee's thinking. If you have a mentor yourself, you're modeling that's it okay not to have all the answers (see Chapter 19 for a deeper dive into building a support team).

Do what you can

If your employee has identified a skill, experience, or some form of support, make a note in your meeting with them. Doing so not only shows your commitment but also reminds you what was said, so you can revisit it later. These types of discussions are important, but people often forget them in the rush to do work. Look for ways to help where you can, whether it's taking time for a mini-lesson, having them observe you in work, or connecting them with someone who has the right experience.

REMEMBER

If you're the employee's manager, you may not be the best mentor. That's a judgment call between the two of you. Some managers can coach and mentor their employees, but finding someone who isn't their boss to be their mentor may serve the employee better. Offer to make suggestions of people. As an executive coach for companies, I get to know the strengths and interests of the staff, and I often suggest the person I'm coaching to reach out to other people I've coached as mentors.

Prioritize it

If you've found someone who is agreeable to being mentored, talk to them about how they want the mentorship to look. Is it more organic, so that you'll keep them in mind as learning opportunities come up? Or is it more structured with goals and regular meetings? If your mentoring arrangement is structured with specific goals and timelines, make sure you keep your commitment to meeting appointments. Don't brush them off. Something will always come up to supersede it but keep the appointment. Be prepared and present. Look at your notes and give some thought to the meeting, as opposed to rushing into your meeting unprepared, fresh off another meeting. Show up, be engaged, listen, help where you can, follow up.

As a mentor, you can have a huge impact on people, sometimes without fully knowing it. Abraham Lincoln said, "I'm a success today because I had a friend who believed in me, and I didn't have the heart to let him down."

Using the Two Tools of Mentoring

Mentoring is a dynamic, organic interaction between two adults. It's not a piano lesson where the teacher gives strict instruction to the pupil and then critiques on the execution. The following sections examine the two tools of mentoring that will stimulate thinking and help guide employee development.

Sharing

Sharing — that is, passing on thoughts, insights, and words of wisdom — is central to mentoring and sets the stage for a meaningful exchange. Here are the key tools in this set.

Sharing knowledge and experience

When coaching your staff, if you have information to share, you pass it on. Let others learn from what you have learned from your successes and mistakes. Share your knowledge and experience strategically. No lecturing, patronizing, or talking down, "In my day . . ."

REMEMBER

Have a lighter touch, often by sprinkling it into casual conversations, adding "That's just something you may want to keep in mind." Sharing stories is an effective way of mentoring; sharing knowledge and experience through storytelling shifts the focus to the story, rather than you. You might start with:

>> "The first time I learned that lesson was very humbling."

>> "I went through a similar experience."

>> "I can share what I learned, if that would be helpful."

People enjoy listening to stories and are encouraged, in turn, to share their own stories. You might ask, "What similar experiences have you had in these kinds of situations?" You're encouraging sharing stories and information, rather than doing all the talking and teaching. They may come back later to tell stories about new experiences. Refer to the nearby sidebar for an example.

EXAMPLE

KEEPING IT CASUAL AND NOT DIRECTIVE

Ken, the president of a mechanical engineering firm, understood that he needed to spend more time with his employees. A colleague, another owner of a firm, told him that he spends at least two hours a week checking in with his employees. Ken was impressed and decided to follow his example.

One afternoon, Ken popped his head into the office of Janae, one of his senior project managers: "Hey, can you drop everything and go get coffee?" Janae considered it and wondered what was wrong. Ken saw her reaction and said, "Relax, you're not in trouble. It's just coffee." Janae laughed and joined Ken. The two didn't have a formal mentoring relationship, but they were relaxed and friendly with each other. Ken was a very grounded, accessible, and fair boss. The offer was out of character for Ken, but Janae wished he had made such an offer more often. Although she had a lot of respect for Ken, she just didn't know how to approach him.

When they sat down over coffee, Ken asked Janae how things were going. She said fine, but Ken could tell that Janae was overwhelmed and tired. Ken called her out in friendly way: "You look like you could use some sleep!"

Janae chuckled, "Busted. I'm not sure you handle it all, day in and day out." That was Ken's opening, "Well, I'll tell you how I used to do it and what I do now."

(continued)

(continued)

"I used to start my day by picking up my phone from my bed stand and answering emails and then responding to everything that came at me in the moment. I'd spend an hour in bed answering emails, and I wasn't even up yet. The pace of my day never stopped until it was time to go to bed. I was exhausted and worn out every day. One day as I was looking over mechanical drawings for a hospital, I had an insight from engineering that could help the way I approached my days. You know those soft start devices we install on electric motors of air-conditioning systems? Well, they make sure those motors start slowly to save on their wear and tear. I thought I could use a slow start on my own motor so I don't burn out!" Janae laughed and saw the connection right away. "So what did you do?" she asked.

Ken explained that his version of a soft start doesn't start by looking at his phone in bed. He begins the morning with coffee and quiet reflection on his back porch as the sun rises. He thinks about his day and his biggest priorities. He reviews his commitments in his calendar and looks at his to-do list from yesterday. He creates the day's to-do list of what he plans to do and when. He puts a star by the two 30,000-foot-level tasks that are essential to complete. He also makes sure to include getting back with people, even if he needs to move deliverable deadlines. Ken understands that his greatest impact and influence is focusing on people over projects. If he supports them, they'll do the work. "That's why I am able to have coffee with you, instead of stuck in email."

A week later, Ken popped his head into Janae's office to say hi. "Still haven't installed my soft start," Janae said. Ken laughed and went to his office. Two days later, Janae texted Ken, "Soft start installed." Ken texted back, "Nice, let me know how it goes!"

The following breaks down why this interaction worked:

- Ken and Janae already had a good relationship to build upon.

- Ken modeled asking for help by taking a lesson from Janae, a colleague.

- Ken was spontaneous and casual about it, which helped make the exchange more relaxed.

- Ken used his emotional intelligence skills to observe Janae's body language (when she got quiet and looked tired).

- Ken started with a question to find out where Janae needed help. Ken didn't go in with an agenda or lesson plan. He just let the conversation unfold.

- Ken didn't lecture Janae by saying do this or do that. Instead he shared a story that captured a similar challenge. He helped Janae feel like she wasn't alone.

- Janae was engaged enough to ask the question: What did you do?

- Ken used a story that had a metaphor that they could both relate to a mechanical device. He was talking engineer to engineer.

- Ken brought his story home by telling Janae that installing a soft start allowed him to have coffee with her. That's the bigger point — plan your day and be more intentional so you have time for important stuff, like mentoring.

- Ken planted a seed with Janae. He made his point, and it didn't take Janae long to act on it. Ken invited her to tell him how her soft start worked for her, which creates an opportunity to mentor her more by exchanging stories. Who knows? Janae might be able to teach Ken something as well.

Sharing observations

Sharing your observations is another way of mentoring. In this case, you pass on what you notice about the employee's behavior and work efforts. You want to share observations occasionally and in areas important and helpful to the individual's development — sometimes to point out their difficulties or challenges and sometimes to point out their successes.

You offer observations as insights and to spark discussion. For example, "I've noticed you becoming more irritable when you deal with Bob in Accounting. What's going on?" Or "I saw how you handled that difficult customer situation. You stayed calm and focused on the issue and got the situation resolved. In fact, tell me more specifically what you did that worked so well in this instance." Sharing observations invites self-reflection and the opportunity to learn lessons from past performance — both what to continue doing and what to do better the next time (see the nearby sidebar for an example).

EXAMPLE

BEING DIRECT WHEN OFFERING FEEDBACK

Sara was an engineer in a manufacturing plant. She managed three people, but even that was too much for her. Sara had a brash, unfiltered communication style and often berated people who didn't meet her expectations. She liked to call it as she saw it and had no patience for games. Her supervisor told her she needed to soften her approach or she'd have to look for another job. They already had two people leave and the job market was too tight to burn through employees. Sara had a good relationship with one of the people she managed and decided to take her out to lunch. Denise was well liked by everyone, and Sara thought she might be able to learn something from Denise.

(continued)

(continued)

"I know I'm not everyone's cup of tea, but I am really that bad?" Sara asked. Denise just looked at her and smiled. "Look, I need your help. I've got to get a handle on this or I'm out of here," Sara added. Denise said, "Okay, you want the truth? You're a bully, and people don't want to come to work. I know the other two are thinking of transferring to another team."

Denise's response was almost too much for Sara to take. She had asked for it and now it sunk in. To her credit, she couldn't only dish it out, but she could also take it. "Okay, things need to change," Sara said. "I need to change. I need your help. I'd like you to give me feedback when you see me say something stupid." Denise softened seeing how vulnerable Sara was being. "Sure."

Over the next few months, Sara improved dramatically, simply by being aware but also knowing she had a mentor in Denise, watching and observing her behavior. Sara would stop by after a team meeting and ask Denise, "How did I do?" Denise would be even-handed, "Better. You might work on letting people finish their sentences. You tend to cut off people." Sara was appreciative.

After a year, Sara actually had people wanting to come work for her team from other departments, and Sara and Denise became close friends outside of work.

Here's what made this interaction work:

- Sara identified the need and actively sought a mentor to help. The warning came from her supervisor, but seeking out Denise was all from Sara.

- Sara had the humility to ask for help from someone she managed — a bold and courageous move. Mentorships can work in many ways.

- Sara choose Denise because she respected and liked Denise. The relationship was there.

- Sara was specific on what kind of help she needed from Denise.

- Denise made good on her end by being honest with Sara.

- Denise was fair and shared observations that were both positive and constructive.

- Sara did the work to take Denise's observations and change her behavior.

- Denise grew in her own confidence and self-worth by helping her boss.

Providing suggestions and advice

You can use this sharing tool when an employee seeks your ideas or thoughts. In these cases, your advice is asked for, but the key is not to give it like a dictator — such as, "Here's how you handle that." When you suggest and advise, you want to ensure that you don't impose your decisions or solutions upon the employee.

TIP

When an employee asks for your advice, try responses such as the following:

>> "I can tell you what I did in a similar situation."

>> "Here's my take on it, for what it's worth."

>> "Here's something you might consider."

>> "If I were in your shoes, I might be inclined . . ." Here you're empathizing with the employee's predicament by offering advice. As you get to know your mentee and the relationship grows, your advice can be more candid. "From what you've told me, you've struggled with that before." "I know being organized is hard for you." "I know how you actively avoid hard conversations." Do this only after the relationship is strong enough to be direct and constructive.

Suggestions are just what the word says — they aren't the absolute answer. You give them to stimulate thought and encourage two-way conversations. As a result, the employee has the chance to disregard your suggestion or advice. And don't attack them if they do so because then you go from suggesting to making rules: "What do you mean telling me that you don't like my advice?"

REMEMBER

When advice hasn't been requested but you feel that it's needed, before giving the advice, say something like, "May I give you a suggestion about that?" Then when the employee says "Yes" or even "Okay," give away freely. One sign that managers are shifting from doers to coaches (see Chapter 2) is that they go from having many rules and few suggestions to having few rules and many suggestions.

Giving the big picture

When people understand the big picture of larger economic trends, industry developments, and organizational goals and changes, they can connect their personal goals to the realities around them. As a mentor, sharing your observations and experience about the bigger picture can be invaluable lessons for someone who's trying to figure it all out. Here are some examples:

>> Debbie is new to the consulting industry and is concerned when client demand for new projects suddenly dries up in October. Jake, the senior manager, offers up, "It's election time. Happens each time there's an election. People are uncertain and hold off making purchase decisions until they see who gets into office. It turns around after the first of the year."

>> Sanjay would love to move into international sales at his manufacturing company. His mentor Christie listens to him and then shares, "There's a strong chance that our company will acquire an international company in the next year rather than growing our own division. If they do, they'll probably also acquire the salespeople who have the connections already."

>> Roberto is passionate about sustainability but is frustrated that his company isn't as aligned with his own goals. Sophie, a friend of his, is head of a nonprofit organization promoting sustainability. She tells Roberto she'll watch for a potential new opportunity.

REMEMBER

Mentors are advocates first and foremost for the employee, not you, their manager, or the organization. They may share information in a big picture that causes the employee to leave or change direction.

Adopting the position of doing what's best for the employee may not be what's in the organization's best interest. However investing in people by providing coaching and mentoring that's in their best interest is a solid strategy of retaining happy people.

Mentoring by sharing messages

Messages to share with your staff are most often one-liners that your employees will remember and repeat. In fact, you know the messages sink in when you hear your staff repeat them to you and others. These messages also provide a sense of importance and are stated in positive terms. None start with "Don't do."

TIP

To use this mentoring-with-messages tool as a manager, you need to know first what messages you want to impart to your staff. Some may be ones that you've heard over the years that have stuck with you, like the following:

>> Underpromise and overdeliver.

>> If you have bad news, deliver it quickly.

>> When you emphasize what you can do versus can't do to help, you keep customers satisfied.

>> Fail forward. Learn from your mistakes.

>> Consistency, follow-up, and follow-through are keys to your success as a manager.

>> We're all in this together. It's not your problem. Ask for help.

>> Ask yourself what you would do if you were running the company.

>> Speak in terms that your audience understands in every presentation.

>> Taking initiative and attention to detail are two qualities that demonstrate success in this environment.

Mentoring with messages is sometimes a combination of company mission statements, acquired wisdom, and performance expectations. These messages give employees lessons to live by, as well as guidance and direction for their performance. The messages are often stated in conversations while setting assignments, giving constructive feedback, or working on solving problems.

Through mentoring with messages, you provide context and guidance of how the employee can be successful in your organization by:

>> Developing their technical abilities

>> Developing their business knowledge

>> Understanding the organizational culture

>> Developing personally and in their work habits

>> Developing management and communication skills

Target these five areas. Like rules, keep the key mentoring messages to a few and tailor them to what's important to helping your staff succeed and grow in their performance.

Challenging

The second set of mentoring skills is the *challenge-them-to-think for-themselves set*. It can often look like coaching, which is where the coaching and mentoring overlap. This set of tools is used in two-way conversations and in follow-up meetings (see Chapter 16), in which your employees share details of their projects and review their progress. (By following through with your employees, you encourage accountability while still showing interest and providing support.)

The following sections take a look at the four facets of the challenge-them-to-think mentoring and tutoring tools.

Using questions

You're often far more influential when you ask questions than when you give answers. As a tool, question-asking is powerful and sophisticated — powerful enough so that Chapter 11 is devoted to ways of doing it effectively.

Asking for plans

Asking for plans applies well to the meaty issues or problems that employees often raise. This strategy isn't a brush-them-off-with-a-busy-work-assignment strategy; it's a collaborative effort in which the employee takes the lead doing the research or other legwork, developing the ideas, and outlining a plan.

Your role is to give them direction, provide them with information and other resources they need, and conduct follow-up meetings to give feedback and mutually establish the next steps. With this kind of guidance and support from you, your employees come up with a plan of action. Refer to Chapter 13 for how a manager can mentor on delegation.

Depending on the scope of the issue, this effort may be done in a few sessions or in one or two meetings. After you and your staff members agree to a plan for addressing an issue, you can often expect the employees to take the lead in implementing the plan.

Asking for decisions and recommendations

This challenge-them-to-think tool shifts responsibility from you to your employees; however, the effort is a collaborative one. When asking for decisions and recommendations, you and your employees evaluate situations and explore options and consequences of actions together — a good give-and-take discussion. Together, you analyze a possible decision, looking at its pros and cons, its advantages and disadvantages, and its benefits and obstacles. If background work is needed, guess who does it? Not you.

You may want to use brainstorming as a way of generating as many ideas as possible. To make brainstorming work when the goal is to come up with potential decisions and recommendations, follow these tips:

>> You and your employee take turns offering ideas, one person and one idea at a time.

>> Don't evaluate the ideas until the brainstorming session is exhausted. Giving commentary as you go bogs down the brainstorming and often stifles creativity. Remember, there are no bad ideas when brainstorming.

>> Jointly decide which path makes the most sense.

>> Brainstorm on resources that could help address the issue, including online research, former projects or documents, other people in the office, people at other organizations, or educational programs.

>> Jointly decide on two or three ideas for the employee — not you — to pursue.

>> Together set timelines for delivering work for review.

When all is said and done, the employee tells you which recommendation they think will work best — and why. In many cases, you let the employee make the decision and run with it, making clear that they're accountable for the consequences of that decision — both positive and negative.

Giving challenging assignments

The idea here is to stretch your employees beyond what they think they're capable of doing. Often, the assignment is a little new and different for them, but not way above their realm of capability. Much of the support you provide is in terms of giving frequent constructive feedback along with much encouragement to plow ahead. Most importantly, you're seeking to challenge your staff to think and do for themselves and allowing them to experience success from it.

Studies have shown that stretch assignments do more to grow employees than another form of coaching or mentoring, mostly because they're taking full ownership of the project. It's a test to see how well they do. Your role is to assist and support where needed and to do the follow-ups — but also to let them carry out the challenging project, responsibility, or other assignment.

EXAMPLE

MENTORING IN ACTION — TOUGH DECISIONS

Here's a story about a manager, Dennis, who handled a potentially difficult situation by questioning and asking for decisions and recommendations. At the beginning of his shift one morning, without advance notice, Bridget, an employee, requested the afternoon off to go to a concert.

Dennis informed Bridget that all the other staff members weren't working that day, as scheduled, and that the two of them, the manager and employee, were booked in the afternoon with customer appointments. Dennis said that if Bridget left, he wouldn't be able to cover all the appointments. (He was sharing the big picture.)

Dennis asked her to evaluate what would happen if she left versus if she stayed. How would her leaving help her get to her mountain of having her own team to run and getting a significant raise? (He was coaching with questions.)

At this point, he let her do most of the talking as he evaluated the situation. He knew he couldn't get any coworkers to come in on the spur of the moment. However, even though he didn't have any good alternatives to offer, Bridget still asked to leave early.

Dennis asked "What would you do in my position?" (a shared message) and said that it was her decision to make. Bridget hated that question because it really just got to the heart of it. If she looked at it that way, it was no other response. Five minutes later, Bridget returned and said that she would work her entire shift. She learned two lessons that day: Not giving advance notice of a special schedule change isn't fair to the people left behind. It also doesn't help her reach her own goals. The long-term goal outweighs the short-term desire.

Building the Pillars of Commitment

When the mentoring tools are put into regular practice, they greatly impact the pillars of involvement and development, and positively influence the other three pillars (see Chapter 4 for further discussion of the five pillars of commitment). Here's a look at how each pillar is built with mentoring tools:

» **Involvement:** The mentoring aspects of coaching heavily involve two-way conversations, which push the employee to actively engage in developing ideas, shaping plans, solving problems, and helping make decisions.

» **Development:** Mentoring is about challenging employees to think and do for themselves and providing the support they need. They give employees opportunities to learn and grow through a variety of ways: solving problems, creating plans, taking on new responsibilities, gaining knowledge and wisdom, and feeling safe, included, and respected. The more these tools are put into practice, the more your employees increase their capabilities, confidence, and sense of belonging.

» **Focus:** Through mentoring, employees gain clarity on how to go forward and handle different situations. The observations and feedback you provide help focus your employees' attention on the areas they can work on for self-improvement. It can also help remove barriers to not feeling accepted or understood.

» **Accountability:** The emphasis of mentoring is to encourage employees to think and do for themselves. Instead of you doing for your staff, you're pushing them to take responsibility. In other words, they get to earn their paychecks, not just show up for them. With your ongoing dialog and follow-up efforts, you reinforce accountability. Plus, as employees grow and develop their skills and abilities because of your coaching efforts, they experience a sense of accomplishment — a critical aspect of driving quality results and instilling accountability.

» **Gratitude:** Those organizations that support a culture of strong mentorship are rewarded with employees who are grateful and loyal to caring for their people.

Chapter 19

Building a Support Team

Mentoring is sometimes defined as a formal one-on-one relationship between a senior leader and a junior employee. The idea behind many mentorships is that the junior person can learn valuable lessons and advice from someone who's more experienced.

Encouraging those one-on-one mentorships may be valuable; however, recognizing that people learn from a variety of people in the development of their careers is just as important. This chapter explores the many ways that your employees could use support and the many forms that support can take.

Encouraging Them to Look Elsewhere to Meet Their Needs

You may want to be your employee's primary mentor, the one who they go to for everything. However, you can't encourage them to expand their network and find answers for everything they need for the following reasons (and don't take it personally when they do seek guidance because you may not be the person to meet their needs):

>> **They don't feel comfortable asking you "dumb questions" they think they should know the answer to.** Even if you've tried to assure them to ask anything, your employee may not want to give you the impression they're incompetent or have problems understanding something you've tried to teach them.

>> **Your communication style may not be best for them.** I (Leo) have been surprised when someone else explains the same concept I've taught and people get more out of a different explanation. People have different styles of explaining things and different styles of learning. Some employees want to know a summary first and then the steps. Others want an example first to understand it. Some are storytellers. Some like to share every detail of a process. Some like to use questions to engage. Some like to use a step-by-step approach. There are different ways of mentoring and teaching; your employee may need to hear it by someone else who has a different style.

>> **You may not be available as a peer or other leader when the employee has a question.** People generally learn best by directly applying knowledge to a specific task in the moment. Let employees acquire what they need, when they need it.

>> **They can learn new things from different people's experiences.** People connect with each other's stories and perspectives. I (Leo) often hear from managers who hire me to teach their emerging leaders: "I've told them the same thing, but hearing it from you seems to sink in." I'm often sharing stories of other clients, which people enjoy hearing about.

>> **They may have different needs depending on where they are in their careers.** You may be a good mentor early on in an employee's career, but as they progress, they may need to tap the knowledge of someone else who has a specific kind of knowledge or experience.

>> **They may not feel comfortable confiding in you.** The fact that there's a power difference between you and the employee may not make you an effective mentor for all things. Maybe their issue is too personal. Maybe they don't trust or like you. Maybe they're still not over the last time you were impatient and barked at them.

People are complex and have a host of needs that you can't or shouldn't even try to address. The fact is relationships at many levels are critical to being happy and productive at work. Cultivating mentors in and out of the organization who can help the employee get to where they want to go is indispensable.

Identifying What Employees Need

Mentors can take many forms, depending on what kind of support an employee needs. It's common for people to have a combination of people help them depending on what they need, including any of the following:

» **Skills:** Mentors can be great teachers when they help employees fill in the gaps in your knowledge. A senior salesperson can advise how to overcome objections based on their experience. A colleague can share how to work with a municipality on a transportation project. A seasoned public speaker can give feedback on presentations. Mentors are typically more senior people, but employees can learn from anyone who has the knowledge — even younger people.

» **Career:** As the employees' manager, you're integral to their success in the career. You can help identify skills they need to develop, experiences they should seek, and people they should build relationships with. But it's not realistic that your employee would want to confide in you about larger career decisions, like if they should work elsewhere. A mentor, especially someone who the employee trusts, can help them answer questions like the following:

- Is this the right career for them?

- What are the downsides and upsides?

- What are different paths that might not be obvious?

- Is this a good company for their career?

- Are there other companies that might be a good fit?

- How do they move up at their current company?

- What are the right moves and what can someone tell them they wished they had done sooner?

- Are there good people they should connect with?

» **Psychological safety:** The workplace isn't always a friendly place for employees. The workforce will only get more diverse in gender, age, ethnicity, and race (Chapter 7 focuses on coaching for diversity). In a world that's increasingly tribal and polarized, it's all too common for people to be judged or perceive to be judged by attributes that have nothing to do with their ability to do the job. They often need someone safe they can share their frustrations, worries, and concerns who has gone through or is going through similar challenges. Even if you're the most empathetic, socially aware manager, the fact that you are who you are may not make you a good match for someone who's struggling. I once coached a team of emerging leaders and a woman from a different culture and race wanted to work with a female coach of color because she thought she'd relate better to her challenges. I respected that she had to work with someone she felt comfortable with.

>> **Aspirational:** Mentors can simply be those people who employees admire or want to aspire to be more like. They don't need to have a formal relationship with someone to learn from them. Encourage them to find someone who they admire and copy what they do. Want to know how to run a meeting, study the best meeting facilitator in the company. Want to know how to give feedback, carefully observe how the best people do it. Want to be taken seriously, find someone who is taken seriously and make note of what they do and say. This doesn't need to be a formal, sit-down-ask questions kind of mentor. Employees at any level, including you, need people to look to as models of what they want to become. These models may have demonstrated leadership in quantifiable ways, such as exceeding sales goals, publishing scientific papers, or being promoted to a position in the company. Employees can also find models that stand out in the way they motivate from personal influence (see Chapter 4) by developing and demonstrating strong interpersonal skills or emotional intelligence. These models inspire employees by showing others how to conduct themselves, communicate, listen, and interact with others (see Chapter 5).

>> **Community:** The work of developing yourself — even getting through the day — can be overwhelming and confusing. Finding community with anyone provides comfort and support. Mentors don't need to be in the form of teachers. They can be in the form of allies, often peers, who are facing similar challenges. Millennials and Gen Xers are more likely to seek advice and support from their peers, whether from social media or talking/texting one-on-one or in groups.

>> **Accountability:** Employees often seek mentors who can help them set goals and provide feedback. Having a mentor you regularly check in with can bolster your progress by increasing your accountability than if you didn't set specific goals. This mentor can be a senior leader, a peer, or even a friend/partner outside of work, but colleagues who can keep you focused and accountable to your goals play a special and important role in your development.

As you coach and develop your employees, keep in mind they may need different things at different times from different people. You can encourage them to find other mentors, but it's not your job to provide them.

Differentiating between Allies, Advocates, and Optimists

Every employee needs someone they can lean on. As your employees make their way through their career, they'll need not just mentors they can learn from, but also other kinds of support. These next sections define the different kinds of support roles that can help your employee stay positive, engaged, and motivated at work.

Understanding what you're going through — Allies

Allies are people who understand what you're going through, often because they're going through the same challenges. Peers inside and outside your company can be great allies.

EXAMPLE

Here's an example of an ally: Crystal worked hard to become a manager for her team, but she noticed that her team treated her differently now. It was if things changed overnight. She was no longer just another member of the team. She was the boss. Team members who invited her out for a drink yesterday secretly excluded her from happy hour today. Crystal reached out to Amy, another new manager at the firm, to go out for drinks. They could talk openly about the challenges of managing people. Crystal and Amy were allies in a common challenge. As a result, they both felt less stress and more energized and helped each other problem-solve on how to build their teams. When one person found a helpful LinkedIn post or webinar, they shared it with the other person.

Allies don't need to be peers. You can have direct reports who understand and support you. Crystal built allies among key employees who shared her vision for what she wanted to do. Those allies also became strong advocates for Crystal.

To help you understand the importance of allies in the workplace, ask yourself these questions:

>> Who is an ally for you?

>> How can you develop stronger allies?

>> How can you be a stronger ally for someone else?

As the workforce continues to be more diverse, finding allies who share common bonds can help promote a sense of safety and belonging.

REMEMBER

Having your back — Advocates

An *advocate* is anyone who actively promotes you. Inside a company, an advocate can be a manager (you), colleagues, or other senior leaders who speak on your (or the employee's) behalf — whether it's to advance you or defend you.

EXAMPLE

Here's an example of an advocate: Dan was a mid-level manager at a national financial services firm. His goal was to run his division, a team of 12 people located in a branch office. Dan enjoyed the support of management at the corporate office, but when his primary advocate and mentor retired, there was a shift in the organization. New people were more in charge of his future. Not only did he not have the relationships with these new leaders, but he also didn't work in the same office, so they couldn't see him work or even really know what he did. When he had his first review under new management, he knew he needed a new advocate at the corporate office who could be at the table speaking on his behalf. Dan reached out to Janet, someone he trusted at corporate. He arranged to spend time with Janet, reviewing his plans and progress. He asked about the personalities of the new people in charge and what their goals were. Janet assured Dan that he didn't have anything to be concerned about. Dan was highly valued, and management wanted him to be happy. Janet offered to share Dan's plans and progress with management. Janet and Dan continued to stay in touch regularly. Dan even heard from someone else how Janet had been praising Dan's work at corporate headquarters. Three months later, Dan was invited to make a presentation to management about what he was doing. Soon afterward, he was told that he gained new advocates. Six months later, Dan was appointed new branch manager. This is what it looks like to be an advocate.

REMEMBER

As a coach manager, you can score big points with your employees anytime you advocate for them, either with management or with clients.

In my coaching business, advocates are colleagues and past clients who refer me to potential clients and are ready to help lend a hand in promoting my services. Develop advocates in many areas of your life and career. The nearby sidebar is an example of how you can be an advocate for your employees.

To help you understand the importance of advocates in the workplace, ask yourself these questions:

>> Who advocates for you?

>> How can you develop stronger advocates?

>> How can you be a stronger advocate for your employees?

BEING THERE WHEN YOUR EMPLOYEES NEED YOU

EXAMPLE

Brian, a project architect for a 200-member firm, learned the power of making strategic deposits with staff. He was working on a major hotel project, and a developer was his client. In private- sector construction projects, time is money. The sooner a developer can deliver a functional building, the quicker the hotel can start taking reservations. Everyone gets paid when revenue is generated, but up to that point, everything is an expense. Consequently, there's a constant push to make the architect and contractor do more in less time. Work overtime. Double up efforts. Finish quicker.

Brian was well liked by the hotel developer for his can-do attitude and ability to deliver on projects. Mild-mannered by nature, Brian always came through and did whatever the client wanted. But saying yes all the time to the client meant more work on his already overwhelmed staff. Deposit for client. Withdrawal for staff. Full bank account for client. Dangerously low account for staff members who were drained from the stress of too much work and unreasonable deadlines.

One day, the developer phoned Brian and said they needed to finish the lobby design a week earlier than scheduled. The developer expected a yes, but this time, Brian pushed back, politely. "I'm sorry," he explained, "I know you want this done sooner, but we can't work any faster than we are." The developer surprised Brian by backing off on their demands. Brian had always assumed that he could never say no to the client, but he learned that with enough equity in his account, a small, reasonable debit doesn't adversely affect the relationship.

What Brian hadn't calculated was how the small withdrawal with the client was seen as a big deposit by his staff. When he told his team they didn't have to work the weekend to meet the new schedule, they were so happy and relieved that they could have hoisted him up like the conquering hero and paraded him down the hallway. In the scheme of things, it wasn't a huge deposit, but it was symbolic because Brian was saying, "I understand and appreciate how hard you work. I have your back." That small but significant gesture wasn't soon forgotten, even when Monday rolled around with new demands to speed up the schedule. Advocates are in your corner when you need them.

Cheering you on — Optimists

Optimists know how to lift you up when you get down or tired. They're your friends cheering you on as you struggle to finish a marathon. They're your parent who always believes in you and can't see how you can't do anything but succeed. They're your colleague who helps you shake off losing a big pursuit: "You did the best you could. You'll have another chance soon enough. Let's go get a beer!" An optimist is like a dog in the park — nothing gets them down and every day is a gift. Don't you love those people?

REMEMBER

Optimists are important to have on your team because they're in short supply. Finding people who complain and see only what's wrong is more common. They can bring you down rather than up. Surround yourself, instead, with people who set goals, get things done, and see an open road rather than barricades. You draft on their success. They draft on your success. And together, you're better and continue with more energy and resolve.

TIP

If you want more optimism, be more optimistic in your outlook and share your optimism with everyone around you. Be known as that person who inspires and motivates others. As a coach, I try to fill that role as optimist. I'm always looking for any signs of progress, even if it's incremental. Because I'm not immersed in working with people all the time, I have the vantage point of gauging progress periodically: "I remember when we started working together and look how far you've come. Just keep it up. Imagine where you'll be at this rate in another six months!"

To help you understand the importance of optimists in the workplace, ask yourself these questions:

» Who makes you feel better?

» How could you be more of an optimist?

Finding Support

Support in the form of mentors, allies, advocates, and optimists can come from a variety of sources:

» Peers at your company and in other organizations

» Your manager

» Senior leader in another department

» Retired leader from your organization

» Leader at another organization

» Former colleague at your current or past organization

» Trade associations

» Break-out sessions from trainings

» Special interest groups

» Community and online groups

As a manager, you can help brainstorm potential sources of support for your employees. Keep in mind that some people are more inclined to seek community with colleagues and some are less inclined. You can at least make suggestions. Understanding how to manage work and life is difficult, and advocating for your employees is a good practice. When you seek support, you also model that building a network isn't a sign of weakness. The best and most effective leaders know how to surround themselves with helping people.

EXPERT ADVICE ON MENTORSHIP

Carl Sergio is a mid-career architect who has learned how to provide mentorship for younger architects. While running three separate mentorship programs concurrently, he observes that a lot of people don't think of themselves as mentors or don't know how to find a mentor. Almost anyone and everyone can and should be a mentor. His advice for those looking for mentors is to just get out there, network, and keep having accidental collisions until you find someone who you really connect with or reach out to someone you want to meet! You aren't looking for a lifelong mentor. Mentorship isn't a marriage — you can and should have more than one mentor.

You often just need to get through this season of life or this bump in the road. It's easy to put a lot of pressure on the situation thinking you have to find the perfect mentor — you find that person you're just dying to talk to and ask, "Will you be my mentor?" But you don't really have to have that conversation. It can be as simple as saying, "Hey, I really love what you're doing, or I'm interested in your point of view or career experience. I'd love to buy you coffee or lunch." And just go from there. Few people will say no to that proposition. And people want to help, especially if you can identify what it is you need, that they can relate to.

Carl shares a story:

> We had a mentoring relationship between a young African American woman and an older white guy who, outwardly, seemed as stuffy as you can imagine — and he was also new to the program. We were shocked that both were very interested in being paired together! At the end of the mentorship program, she told me how wonderful he was as a mentor and what a great relationship they had. It was really eye-opening to see how much they both got out of that relationship. It gave me a new perspective that anyone can be a good mentor even though they're not on the same path, even if they don't look like you, or even if they don't have the same set of shared experiences. It just puts a new light on who your potential mentors can be.

Identifying Keys to Successful Mentoring

Here are some tips for supporting mentorship and other forms of support for your employees:

>> **Model that seeking a mentor, ally, advocate, or optimist is beneficial.**
Too often, emerging leaders think the right path to promotion is doing it all themselves and not asking for help. When you take action to cultivate your own mentors, allies, advocates, and optimists, it sends a powerful message to

your employees that it's not only okay to seek support, but you also personally endorse the idea.

>> **Take advantage of opportunities to spontaneously share what you're working on or ask someone's input.** The foundation of coaching is fostering collaboration among all staff. Just because you're in a senior position doesn't mean you can't be open to feedback and critique on your work from peers of junior people. You may be surprised that you can get just as much out of the experience of learning from others as you do from being a mentor.

>> **Let it happen organically.** Successful mentorships are based on relationships. People need to connect, like, and respect each other for it to work. You can't arrange and force mentorships successfully.

>> **Let people learn in their own way.** Post Boomer generations of employees have been raised by using social media, group texts, podcasts, and YouTube for educating themselves. When my daughter was 16, I offered to buy her ukulele lessons with an instructor. She laughed and said, "C'mon Dad, you know I don't learn that way." She then sat down with a YouTube tutorial on how to play ukulele and within 20 minutes had her first song down.

>> **Regularly engage your employees in conversations about how they're doing and what kind of support they could use.** When you encourage your employees to make connections with people other than you, you're making them more independent and freeing up your time, as well.

>> **Suggest to your employees that they'd be very good mentors to younger staff.** Suggest to younger employees to reach out to employees who like and encourage others to come to them.

>> **Find someone who has different strengths than you.** The Clifton StrengthFinder assessment (www.gallup.com/cliftonstrengths) is one tool that can help your employees discover what they naturally do best, how to develop their greatest talents into strengths, and how teams can work more successfully when each member understands and counts on the different strengths of others.

Employees have a lot on their minds. Learning to navigate life and career is only getting more complicated. They need the support of other people in their lives to make better decisions, reduce stress, and be more productive and happier overall. Employees can't do it alone. They need help — at different times and from different people for different things.

6

The Part of Tens

Discover short tips and insights that can help you grow as a leader.

Surprise yourself by what you might discover by investing in becoming a coach.

Dispel common myths about coaching.

Avoid pitfalls and traps that prevent you from being an effective coach and mentor.

Chapter **20**

Ten (or So) Surprises for You

Coaching and mentoring rely on life skills. Technical or hard skills are relatively easy to measure and develop: your ability to draft a building plan so a contractor can build it is straight-forward. It works or doesn't. It has errors or missing information or it's complete.

Life skills aren't always as easy to measure or predict. How much have you increased your listening skills over the last year? How much do people trust you more or less than they did six months ago? Are your employees more engaged and productive now that you've read this book and used the strategies?

Even though there's not often a straight line between effort and result, this chapter shares some of the insights I've gleaned over the years of coaching.

Change in Behavior Takes Time

I (Leo) once mentored a third-grade girl in reading. I worked with her every week for three months without seeing any progress. School ended for summer vacation and on opening day of the next school year, I ran into the girl's mother in the hall.

She greeted me with a big smile, "Joni jumped two reading levels over the summer!" she exclaimed. You could have knocked me down with a feather. It was an important lesson for me that change in behavior takes time and has its own course. As a coach, you can only plant the seed and water it. Be patient.

You'll Grow as a Coach over Time

No matter how clueless or incompetent you may judge yourself to be, you're infinitely wiser and better than you were when you started. People ask me how I developed my skills: by doing it a lot! Each coaching session is a lesson for me. I'm still growing as a coach. Take comfort in knowing that every minute you spend investing in trying to be a better delegator, communicator, and listener, you're growing as a coach.

You Can Do Only So Much

There are limits to how much you can change behavior through coaching and mentoring. I like to think I'm a good coach who can adapt to just about any personality, but my personality and style don't work for everyone (despite my desire to help everyone). Before you start beating yourself up (trust me I've done this too), consider any number of reasons why coaching may not stick:

>> People aren't interested or motivated to change.

>> They're overwhelmed by work and responsibilities to focus on making the effort.

>> They get enough value from their current operating mode to want to change.

>> They have personal or health issues that interfere with investing in their professional development.

>> They're doers and learn best by trying things. Conversations and self-reflection don't work for them.

>> Their strengths lie in other areas and trying to coach them to be different than who they are is too much of a stretch.

>> Peer pressure to not change is too strong.

>> They haven't made the connection between taking time to work differently and getting a different, better outcome.

You May Like It

In my experience, managers are either enthusiastic about learning how to be a coach or are resistant. Those who are enthusiastic are generally good with people already and have high emotional intelligence skills. They want to build on what skills they have to be more effective. Those who are resistant haven't spent a lot of time on their soft skills. They're often confused, overwhelmed, and intimidated by having coaching conversations, reading people, listening, and letting go of tasks to focus on people. One of my biggest sources of fulfillment is when I see people like coaching more than they thought they would — when a resistant manager gets excited about letting go of controlling a project and allowing someone else take over or when an enthusiastic manager becomes a model employee and advances in their career sooner than they imagined.

Your Friends and Partners Will Appreciate You More

Chapter 5 mentions how developing emotional intelligence pays dividends in all your relationships. When you find out how to tune into people, listen, empathize, and not jump in and solve issues, you develop a skill that your friends and partners appreciate as well.

REMEMBER

Building your competency as a coach and mentor others also helps you be happier and more at ease with yourself. As you work to being more self-aware and manage your emotions to be a better coach, you're investing in your personal growth. You discover more about what's important to you, how to acknowledge your emotions, how to manage your ups and downs, and, in doing so, find more balance and satisfaction.

Your Employees Become Coaches

When you delegate effectively, you're teaching an employee the value of delegation and how to do it. Giving timely feedback helps employees learn how to give timely feedback. When you openly question your own bias toward people and are vulnerable, you're inspiring your employees to do the same. Coaching and mentoring is teaching all the time.

REMEMBER

Think of the impact on your organization over time as your behavior teaches and inspires emerging leaders. Not only do they become coaches and mentors, but also the people they coach and mentor learn and get inspired. Your actions are passed down, multiplying over generations.

You'll Discover Something New

Developing yourself as a coach and mentor helps you on the path of learning something new every day. The power of questioning, listening, and staying open is powerful. That's particularly true when you challenge your assumptions and unconscious bias you may have. If you've never worked with someone from a different culture, you may have certain preconceived perceptions until you spend time to get to know that person. When you take the time to learn the stories that shape who people are, you learn that everyone is unique and the same, too. People everywhere want to be respected and valued for who they are.

Everything Changes

Chapter 6 sets the stage that change is the only constant you can count on. Just as the weather changes, so do people's moods. Just as night turns into day, so does what work you do each day. Just as we all get older by the second, so does each conversation we have differ in what we say and how others react. There's no coaching template that works each time. What works for one person won't work for someone else. And what works today, may not work tomorrow. Seeing and accepting that everything changes will help free you from trying to predict and count on things. It's better to go with the flow.

You May Find a Second Career

These days it seems like everyone wants to either be a consultant or a coach. I don't know if it's part of the Great Resignation and shake-up the economy has gone through, but helping people grow in their careers and lives draws many people into considering making coaching a second career. My own business has grown to include coaching more people to be coaches. Go for it. The world needs more coaches and mentors!

Chapter **21**

Ten (or So) Coaching Myths Debunked

A big factor that holds some managers back from learning to function as a coach is they are stuck on certain misconceptions or myths about coaching. These myths tend to fuel insecurities and reluctance to gain new skills, let alone put them into practice. This chapter contains nine such misconceptions.

You Can't Afford the Time to Coach

Of course coaching takes time. Everything you do as a manager involves the use of your time. The question to ask is: Who *can't* afford to put time into coaching?

When you function as a doer (see Chapter 2), and then attempt to shift to managing as a coach, the way you use time needs to change as well. Time becomes something you budget and balance. You use it more to help others be more effective instead of spending it primarily on your own activities. Coaching thrives on the use of quality time; that is, spending time with your employees that helps them go back to their jobs to perform effectively and self-sufficiently. That's time well spent.

Coaching Is Only about Being Nice to Employees

Although coaching certainly isn't about being mean to your staff, coaching also isn't about being nice. Coaching doesn't focus on your personality; it focuses on your personal influence. What behaviors do you display that can have a positive influence on employee performance? Those behaviors go far beyond whether you are nice or mean.

REMEMBER

Some managers are too nice and, as a result, aren't able to be direct and firm with their employees when they need to be. Other managers don't do the nicest thing you can do as a manager, which is to honestly communicate with your employees and give them constructive feedback that lets them know the pluses and minuses of their performance. Be assertive rather than nice and you'll make coaching work.

Everyone Needs to Support Coaching

Coaching isn't dependent on what your boss or other managers do. It's dependent on your own behavior and the tools you apply with it to stimulate employee performance.

Even though having your own mentors and role models certainly helps, not working to develop yourself to function as a coach because you don't have one can be an excuse to hide behind. You want your employees to take responsibility for their own actions, so do the same and take responsibility to give them the best coaching and leadership efforts you can.

Coaching Means Seeking Consensus on Every Decision You Make

This myth often comes out of the collaborative nature that coaching requires. Collaboration means working with your employees — it doesn't mean making all decisions by consensus.

You and your employees have different levels of responsibility. In some cases, you make decisions for which no input or discussion is needed from your staff, and that's the best way to handle the situation. In fact, they want you to make decisions; that's why you're in charge of the group. In other cases, because the responsibility for action rests with the employee, you have that employee make the decision. That's building accountability, and now you're coaching.

If You Hire Good People, Coaching Isn't Really Necessary

Hiring good people certainly helps and is a good practice. But it's after you bring someone on board that your real work as a manager begins!

Even good employees need direction, goals, feedback, training, and challenging work — all efforts that involve coaching. Management by this sort of osmosis approach — hiring good people and letting them be — is a hands-off approach that doesn't provide the guidance and support employees need to maximize their capabilities. And maximizing capabilities is the emphasis of coaching.

Employees Have to Ask for Coaching in Order to Be Receptive to It

At the core of this myth is the thinking that people have to want to be coached for you to coach them. Managing as a coach and applying coaching tools to your management practices are not based on who you think is coachable or who is asking for coaching. It's based on providing leadership and getting the best out of people's performance — efforts that make a business succeed.

Coaching doesn't require invitations from your employees. Your role as a manager requires you to work with your staff to deliver quality performance to meet the needs of the business. Coaching is an effective way to make that happen.

Coaching Collaboratively Doesn't Work When You Have a Disagreement

When you have a difference of opinion, working through it collaboratively is the best way to handle the situation. That means you recognize that you and the employee aren't going to see eye-to-eye on every issue, but that you're willing to listen to the other person's viewpoint and expect the same in return. It means you maintain respect for the other person.

REMEMBER

Collaboration doesn't mean that you agree to something you find unacceptable or that you push your authority and browbeat the employee because of a disagreement. It means you are firm as necessary, but positive and willing to explore ideas with the employee. This dynamic is the key to resolving conflicts, and the involvement of others in developing mutually beneficial solutions is one of the reasons that coaching is successful.

Coaching Involves Being Direct — People Don't Like That

Some managers have a hard time being direct with their employees. They worry they'll hurt their staff members' feelings, especially with sensitive issues. As a result, they give indirect or mixed messages or say nothing — all of which complicate the situations further.

Direct and blunt aren't the same thing. Blunt means being harsh and slamming the point so the other person takes it personally. Direct is getting to the point and doing so with tact. It is being sincere and honest with all the messages you express, from the positive to the negative. If you think your employees don't like this, consider this: Who doesn't like when someone is honest, clear, constructive, and to the point in communications?

REMEMBER

In general, you'll find that people want you to be straight with them. Coaching employees is about working with adults, and most adults want to be treated like adults.

You Have to Be a Psychologist to Coach Employees

If this were the case, organizations would only hire psychologists to be managers — and businesses would likely fail because no one would have the expertise in the various functions of the business to help run it effectively.

Besides having technical expertise in the area you manage, no other background or education makes someone more or less suitable to coach employees. The aptitude to work with your employees and to want to understand them as people is what is needed first. From there, you can learn the tools that help you get the best out of their performance and stimulate their commitment.

Index

delegating and, 246

development and improvement plans, 318

emotional intelligence and, 89

mentoring and, 318

overview, 63

performance plans and, 278

performance reviews and, 292

personal influence and, 50

strategies for motivation and, 173

using questions, 196

IQ (intelligence quotient), 66–67

isolated managers, 30

J

job hopping, 51, 203

job rotation, 300

job-related behaviors, focusing on, 119–122

judgements, avoiding, 106–107

K

keeping your word, 214

King, Martin Luther, Jr., 117

knowledge, sharing, 328–329

knowledge, skills, and abilities (KSAs), 270, 277

Kolbe, 75

L

leadership, attributes of, 24, 26

leading by example, 53, 122, 326

learning from experiences, questions for, 181–182

letting go, cost of, 25–26

letting people down, as challenge to coaches, 25

life skills. *See* emotional intelligence

Lincoln, Abraham, 328

listening

active, 81–82

body language, 82–83

employee resistance to delegating, handling, 245–246

facilitating discussions, 188

with heart, 83–85

passive, 81

responses to questions, 191, 195

understanding of delegated assignment, checking, 239–240

logical flow in discussions, 187–188, 195

low expectations, assumption of, 115

low interest in delegated assignments, 244–245

lunch and learns, 151

M

management by walking around (MBWA), 42

management-by-osmosis path, 18

manager-employee mentoring discussions, 300–301

manner, describing expectations for, 236

manner of feedback, 250–252

mastery of skills, as motivator, 149–151

materials for delegated assignments, 238

MBTI (Meyers-Briggs Type Indicator), 74

measurable goals, 271

measuring progress in development, 305–306

mentoring

asking for feedback, 77

for career self-reliance, 199, 217–219

challenge-them-to-think for-themselves set, 335–337

coaching versus, 11–12, 322–323

combining coaching and, 324

common pitfalls of, 325–326

decisions and recommendations, asking for, 336–337

doer versus coach approaches, 15, 20

doing what you can, 327–328

employee skills, developing, 222

expert advice on, 347

help with spotting biased behavior, 122

insights on, 351–354

keys to successful, 347–348

leading by example, 326

manager-employee discussions, 300–301

mastery of skills, as motivator, 151

overview, 321

pillars of commitment and, 338

plans, asking for, 335–336

prioritizing, 328

on professionalism, 211

questions, asking, 335

revisiting mountains, 326–327

sharing tools

casual approach, 329–330

direct feedback, 330–331

giving the big picture, 333–334

knowledge and experience, 328–329

messages, 334–335

observations, 330

overview, 328

providing suggestions and advice, 332–333

stretch assignments, 337

examples of, 40–42

mixing live and remote meetings, 44–45

mutually setting goals, 274–276

organizing, 38–40

overview, 37

postmortem meeting, 289–292

status-review meetings, 283–286

one-size-fits-all management style, 115–117

open floor plan, 99

open personality trait, 168–169

open-ended questions, 184–187, 195, 239

opportunities within organization, identifying, 217–218

optimists, 345–346

output, 119

outside coaches, 301, 306

outside exposure, 300

outsourcing, 198

ownership, employee, 50

P

parameters for delegated task, defining, 237

passive listening, 81

passive management style, 59

past successes, drawing on, 189–190

pay as motivator, 143–147

people issues, balancing task issues and, 23–24

people management, assessment of, 68

performance

asking questions about, 178–179

coaching versus mentoring for, 322

doer versus coach approaches for dealing with issues, 15, 18–19

emphasizing, 118–119

strategies for motivation

encouraging initiative, 165–166

focusing on performance, 159–161

individual needs of employees, 166–173

matching business needs to employee needs, 161–166

motivation plan, 163–165

motivation questionnaire, 162–163

overview, 157

pillars of commitment and, 173–174

Platinum Rule, 167–171

rewarding behaviors, 159–161

performance bias, 109

performance feedback

constructive feedback versus praise and criticism, 248–249

content, 250

defensive reactions, dealing with, 258–261

doer versus coach approaches, 15, 17–18

focusing on discussion after giving, 256–261

frequency, 254–255

manner, 250–252

overview, 247

pillars of commitment and, 261–262

positive and negative feedback scenario, 253–254

positive outcomes in discussions, facilitating, 257–258

significant-events list, 255–256

timing, 252, 254

performance goals

best goals, 267–268

checkup meetings, 286–289

example of, 269–270

overview, 267

performance review process, 280–281

performance plan

development goals, 270

importance of, 264–265

keys to success, 276–277

mutually setting goals, 274–276

overview, 263

performance goals, 267–270

pillars of commitment and, 277–278

SMART goals, 271–274

strategic goals, 266–267

performance reviews

anxiety about, reducing, 280–283

checkup meetings, 286–289

development plans versus, 294–295

overview, 279–280

pillars of commitment and, 292

postmortem meeting, 289–292

process of, 280–281

status-review meetings, 283–286

personal accomplishment, desire for, 153–154

personal background, 114, 120

personal influence, 48–50, 55, 63

personal problems affecting work, dealing with, 316–317

personality

assessments of, 74–75

Platinum Rule, 167–171

person-to-person feedback, 252

physical attributes, stereotyping, 114

piggy bank analogy, 138–139

pillars of commitment. *See* five pillars for building commitment

Pink, Daniel, 147

pitfalls of delegating, 227–231

planning

  coaching with questions, 182–183

  doer versus coach approaches, 15–16

  mentoring and, 335–336

Platinum Assessment, 75

Platinum Rule, 167–171

portfolio, building, 218

positional influence, 48–49

positive feedback

  defining, 248–249

  expressing appreciation, 251

  positive and negative feedback scenario, 253–254

  timing for, 252

positive outcomes in discussions, facilitating, 186–187, 194, 257–258, 260

positive reinforcement for delegated tasks, 241–242

postmortem meeting, 289–292

praise, constructive feedback versus, 248–249

Predictive Index, 74

priming effect, 110

prioritizing mentoring, 328

problem solving

  as challenge to coaches, 25

  questions for, 180

  sign of professionalism, 213

profanity, addressing, 121

professional development, assessment of skills for, 69

professionalism

assessment comparison, 215

mentoring on, 211

professional behaviors, spotting, 211–215

project teams, in development plan, 300

Promoter personality, 170–173

promotions, 21, 306–308

proposals, offering, 218

psychological safety, 341

punctuality, 118

purpose in work, as motivator, 147–148, 151–152

purpose of delegated assignment, explaining, 236

Q

quality of work, 119, 236

quality relationships, desire for, 153–155

quality time, investing in, 31–33

quarterly checkup review, 210, 277

questions

  adapting to different generations, 132–133

  for analyzing and problem-solving, 180

  better coaching with, 190

  case study, 192–195

  challenges when using, 188–192

  challenge-them-to-think for-themselves mentoring tool, 335

  close-ended versus open-ended, 184–186

  for developing plans, 182–183

  drawbacks of not using, 177

  for evaluating options and decision-making, 180–181

  facilitating discussions, 186–188

  I-don't-know responses, dealing with, 189–190

for learning from mistakes, 181–182

overview, 175

pillars of commitment and, 196

power of, 176–177

relationship management and, 85

responses you do not agree with, managing, 190–192

space and tone, 186

understanding of delegated assignment, checking, 239–240

when not to use, 178–179

when to use, 180–183

quiet quitting, 51

R

readings, 300

recency bias, 110

recommendations, asking for, 336–337

reflection time, scheduling, 35

reflective listening, 81

Relater personality, 169–173

relationship management

  case study, 87–88

  coaching and, 85

  interactions, setting example in, 86–87

  overview, 85

relevant goals, 272

reliable producers, 213

Remember icon, 3

remote work

  advantages and disadvantages of, 42–43

  coaching remotely, tips for, 43–44

  mixing live and remote meetings, 44–45

  office design, 99

  staying in touch, 45

reports on progress, 305

reptilian brain, 76

resistance from employees, handling

to career self-reliance, 203–207

to delegation, 243–246

resources, providing for delegated tasks, 237–238

responses to questions, dealing with difficult, 189–192

responsive listening, 81–82

restructuring, 198

retaining employees, 51–52, 204, 264–265

reviews, performance. *See* performance reviews

rewards as motivation, 141–142, 159–161

ridicule, addressing, 121

rightsizing, planning for, 198

role models, doers as, 21–22

S

sabotage, addressing, 121

salary as motivator, 143–147

schedule, 34–37

scheming, encouraging, 150

Schultz, Howard, 35

self-assessment

of motivation, 153–156

of tone setting, 54

values assessment, 71–73

self-awareness

coaching and, 69–70

generational differences, 131–132

overview, 69

personality assessment, 74–75

self-reflection questions, 70–71

values assessment, 71–73

self-care, 80

self-enhancement bias, 18

self-management, 77–80

self-reflection questions, 70–71

self-report, 305

service-oriented employees, 214

70-20-10 Model of Learning, 221

shared values, 266–267

sharing tools

casual approach, 329–330

direct feedback, 330–331

giving the big picture, 333–334

knowledge and experience, 328–329

messages, 334–335

observations, 330

overview, 328

providing suggestions and advice, 332–333

shrinking to what works, 34

Shultz, George, 35

significant-events list, 255–256

simplifying questions, 189

sincerity of feedback, 251, 259

Sinek, Simon, 26

skills

coaching development of, 219–222

development goals, 270

encouraging progress, 304–305

EQ, assessment of, 67–69

measuring progress, 305–306

mentoring for development of, 341

overview, 10–11

targeting in development plan, 295, 297

training for delegated assignments, 238

slurs, addressing, 121

SMART goals, 271–274

social network, expanding, 107, 122

social values, 98

social-awareness

active listening, 81–82

body language, 82–83

coaching and, 80–81

listening with heart, 83–85

overview, 80

Socializer personality, 170–173

soft skills. *See* emotional intelligence

sources of support and mentors, 346–347

space, in questions, 186

specific goals, 271

sports analogy, 322

staff for delegated assignments, 238

stakeholder coaching, 305–306

status-review meetings

benefits of, 284–285

checkpoint meetings for delegated assignments, 240–241

overview, 283

running, 283–285

tracking sheet for, 283–284

staying connected. *See* connecting with employees

stereotype threat, 110

stereotyping, 114–115, 121

strategic goals, 266–267

StrengthsFinder test, 74

stress, 54–55

stretch assignments, 221, 337

style, 120

success, measures of, 266

such-is-life approach, 245

suggestions, mentoring with, 332–333

About the Author

Leo MacLeod is an author, coach, trainer, and speaker on leadership. He's the author of *From the Ground Up: Stories and Lessons from Architects and Engineers Who Learned to Be Leaders* (Piehouse Publishing). As founder of Training. Coaching. Pie., Leo helps firms with leadership development, transition, and emotional intelligence and why baking pie is a great way to develop soft skills.

With a BA in English with honors from Portland State University, he has had a successful career as a freelance writer, fundraiser, and advertising executive and marketing consultant. For many years, Leo has written columns for *Zweig Letter, Daily Journal of Commerce,* and the *Business Journal.* He helped develop a successful leadership program for the Oregon chapter of the American Council for Engineering Companies (ACEC). Leo is a sought-out speaker on leadership development, known for his humor and storytelling.

He lives in Portland, Oregon, with his wife, Lisa, and enjoys gardening, writing songs on his ukulele, and cooking with his son Alex and daughter Maddie.

Dedication

To Lisa for her encouragement, support, and love.

Author Acknowledgements

First, I want to acknowledge the great work of my co-author, Marty Brounstein, for writing the first edition of this book. So much of the original manuscript was as relevant and useful as it was when it was published 20 years ago. I wish we had an opportunity to work together, but your work lives on!

Thanks to everyone at the Dummies editorial team. Your guidance and support helped keep me focused and productive. A huge thanks to Julie Lamothe Jensen for reading the whole book and offering your insights and feedback as the technical editor. I'm also grateful for the following people who offered suggestions, including Dan MacLeod, Alan Bahm, Josh McDowell, Tonya Finley, Amy Perenchio, Carl Sergio, Tim Ganey, and Eliza MacLeod. I wouldn't have had the opportunity to write this book if it hadn't been for Vanessa Campos and Jen Dorsey from Broad Book Group recommending me to the editorial team at Wiley.

Writing a book that will stand the test of time is difficult when the world seems to change overnight. Thanks to the authors of two other Dummies books, *Diversity, Equity, & Inclusion For Dummies* by Dr. Shirley Davis and *Managing Millennials For Dummies* by Hannah L. Ubl, Lisa X. Walden, and Debra Arbit, who are also dedicated to helping people navigate and capitalize on change.

Publisher's Acknowledgments

Senior Acquisitions Editor: Tracy Boggier

Project and Development Editor: Chad R. Sievers

Managing Editor: Sofia Malik

Technical Editor: Julie Lamothe Jensen

Proofreader: Debbye Butler

Production Editor: Tamilmani Varadharaj

Cover Image: © Jorg Greuel/Getty Images